FOCUS

Marc Hijink

FOCUS

The ASML Way

INSIDE THE POWER
STRUGGLE OVER THE
MOST COMPLEX
MACHINE ON EARTH

Uitgeverij Balans

For Dad. Whatever he could think of, he could create.

This book has been made possible in part by
het Fonds Bijzondere Journalistieke Projecten (fondsbjp.nl).

First Published in the Netherlands by Uitgeverij Balans, 2023
Original title *Focus. De wereld van ASML*
Copyright © 2023 Marc Hijink/Uitgeverij Balans, Amsterdam

Copyright translation © 2024 Mark Whittle, Marc Hijink,
Dorien Muijzer/Uitgeverij Balans, Amsterdam

Photograph credits:
Author photograph Bob Bronshoff
Infographics Roel Venderbosch
Images book block ANP, ASML, Intel, Philips, Samsung,
TSMC, Trumpf, Zeiss, private collections Frits van Hout,
Frits Klostermann and Marc Hijink.

Cover design Bas Smidt
Typography and typesetting Bas Smidt
Printed by Wilco

www.uitgeverijbalans.nl
x.com/balansboeken
instagram.com/uitgeverijbalans
uitgeverijbalans.nl/nieuwsbrief

www.focus-theasmlway.nl

CONTENTS

CONTENTS

PROLOGUE:
A STARRY SKY

The band signals to dim the lights. The most magical moment of the evening is about to begin.

"Can you shine your lights?"

Of course. In the blink of an eye, phones light up in every corner of the room, waving back and forth in a sea of invisible hands. It's one big starry sky.

Imagine how enchanting it would be if the band got all the smartphones in the world to light up at the same time. That's almost seven billion phones – 85 percent of the world's population has one. This gives you an idea of the scope of the company this book is about.

Now, whatever you had in mind, think bigger. An even vaster starry sky is possible. Imagine the band gets every chip, in every device in the world, to light up.

Everybody, shine your lights!

They glow: every chip in every laptop, every Wi-Fi router, and every cell phone tower. The chips in every car, traffic light, washing machine and smartwatch, every pair of headphones, coffee machine, camera and TV monitor in the world. The chips in all the data centers, factories, hospitals, control towers, planes, trains, power plants and windmills. The chips in the cruise missile searching for its target and in the radar trying to intercept it. The chips in the supercomputers deciphering a new infectious virus and in the servers of the data center creating a vaccine to fight it.

All the chips that track your online behavior, carry out your search queries, file your tax returns and play your favorite music and videos. The chips that predict the weather and tell you how many steps you've taken, how many messages you've missed, where your daughter is hanging out this time.

And finally, the memory chips light up. An infinite digital memory, home to all your emails, apps, photos and videos from the past ten or twenty years. Kilobytes became megabytes, megabytes became gigabytes, gigabytes became terabytes. An explosion of data.

Deleting photos or cleaning up your mailbox doesn't make a difference – the world has enough chips to store all your data. Right?

Every year, manufacturers such as Intel, TSMC and Samsung produce billions of chips, each of which consists of billions of switches. These are semiconductors, miniature constructions built on a silicon disc or wafer. You wouldn't give at silicon in its raw sand-like state a second glance. However, once processed, it has the capacity to alter conductive properties, which means you can use it to turn electric currents on or off – in other words, to transform a '0' into a '1'. Silicon Valley, the birthplace of the chip industry, owes its name and fame to this unique material.

Nowadays, the vast majority of these chips are made using the machines of one company: ASML. But don't let that fool you: four decades ago, this Dutch enterprise was nothing more than forty employees, an experimental device and a hopeless business plan. They had no idea their invention would play a key role in an industry now worth over 600 billion dollars a year.

And demand keeps growing. In 2030, the turnover of the chip industry is expected to be more than one trillion dollars. By that time, ASML's yearly revenue will have also doubled from 27 billion euros in 2023 to 40, 50 or – according to the most optimistic forecasts – 60 billion.

As of 2023, this makes ASML Europe's most valuable high-tech company. It has 42,500 employees across over 60 locations in 16 different countries, a global operation with only one goal in mind: to maintain total dominance of the lithography machinemarket. These machines are the hypercomplex devices chip manufacturers use to produce their chips, and ASML is not only responsible for over 90 percent of the supply, but also has a monopoly on the most cutting-edge technology. It is better to think of these machines as 'systems': to give you an idea of scale, it takes seven Boeing 747s to transport ASML's most advanced tool to a chip factory. The units may be large, but they are extremely fragile. The separated parts of the machine need specifically designed metal incubators to keep the sensitive equipment at exactly the right temperature during its travels.

But what is this machine, and how does it work? In short, a lithography machine prints intricate patterns onto a photosensitive silicon wafer. It is basically a super-precise projector which casts the same image onto the same wafer hundreds of thousands of times at lightning speed until, step by step, photo by photo, a wafer full of chips starts to form. By the end, each of these chips will house billions of tiny integrated circuits. This painstaking process can take months, with each chip consisting of potentially hundreds of different layers that all need to be perfectly aligned, one on top of the other. The slightest deviation is enough to ruin a whole production line of chips. Hundreds of thousands of dollars can turn into a lump of worthless silicon, all in the blink of an eye, or the flash of a machine.

The more fine-grained the light such a machine can project, the more transistors – miniature electrical switches in a chip – will fit onto the same surface. And the more transistors, the faster, more efficient and more powerful the chip. Back in the '60s Gordon Moore, co-founder of the chip manufacturer Intel, was paying close attention to this process. He noticed a recurring pattern: approximately every two years, the number of transistors that could fit on a chip doubled. Moore adjusted his prediction over the years, but there was no going back. His observation had ignited the imagination of scientists and engineers the world over and became known as Moore's Law. Computing power and digital storage continued to become cheaper and more energy-efficient, and with it the number of applications for chips grew: from computers and servers to phones and wireless gadgets, to sensors for just about every conceivable device. Whether natural law, self-fulfilling prophecy, or fiction, the result is just the same.

If you look closely, you can still see it at play today: the phone in your pocket costs a few hundred dollars, but has more processing power than all the computers used by NASA for the first moon landing combined. In 2013, Apple's fastest laptop had a central processing unit with just over one billion transistors. By the end of 2023, that number was 92 billion. Gordon Moore may have passed away, but his law is still holding up.

As the circuits on the chips shrink, the machine that produces them grows. A modern lithography machine is comprised of over 100,000 components, all working together in a tightly coordinated dance. As the *New York Times* wrote in 2021, 'ASML's machine is the most complicated machine in the world,' and the size of a city bus.

That was then. The latest series of ASML machines are even more impressive: they're the size of a steam locomotive and capable of aiming one tiny beam of invisible light with an accuracy of 1 nanometer, or one millionth of a millimeter. This latest version isn't quite finished yet, but the first machines have already been sold. The price: almost 400 million euros. But for all the specifications and descriptions in the world, nothing can prepare you for entering one of ASML's dust-free cleanrooms and seeing one of these things up close. The sheer size of the separate modules is enough to take your breath away. Meters-high metal frames, shiny tubes and pipes, fist-thick cables, heavy magnets and intricate mechatronics. It feels like you're walking on the set of a science fiction movie, but with one difference: this machine really exists.

Despite the best efforts of competitors such as Nikon and Canon, no one has been able to keep up with the technological advances made in Veldhoven, the small Dutch town that is home to ASML. This has left the chip industry heavily dependent on the Dutch company. The lithography machine is the most important piece of equipment in any chip factory, and without doubt the biggest investment in a facility that can set you back 15 billion dollars to build. It is easy to see why working at ASML is known to come with a little pressure.

As the world continues to digitize – for the energy transition, a less polluting industry, better medical care or more powerful weapons – the demand for chips is exploding. And ASML has to grow at the same pace, just as explosively. It is a constant drive to attract and house new staff, integrate hundreds of new employees each month, and manage the ever-expanding logistics as well as a network of hundreds of suppliers who have to deliver more for increasingly complicated devices. ASML has now itself become a hypercomplex machine, difficult to manage and in need of constant maintenance. A reminder that even the most complicated technology still relies on people.

For a long time, ASML was able to operate in the shadows: it was just some obscure high-tech company busy developing incomprehensible machines that balanced on the edge of the impossible. Every conceivable scientific discipline was needed to harness the natural forces released in the lithography machine. Optics, mechatronics, physics, chemistry – and all with the aid of complex algorithms which themselves require enormous computing power. Fodder for nerds and scientists, but not something for the front pages. Until the politicians got involved.

The strategic interest in the chip industry is hard to exaggerate. Sixty years after the invention of the microprocessor, the entire world runs on chips. They are an indispensable resource for all aspects of modern society. And thanks to the pandemic, international superpowers such as the United States, China and the EU are now keenly aware how dependent they are on chips for their prosperity and security. The moment they're gone, you notice.

The computers in Microsoft's Dutch data center sing in perfect unison. Their eerie hum fills the Middenmeer polder, reverberating from the racks full of servers blasting their warm air into your face. As you step closer, the note becomes clear. It's a pitch-perfect high B.

'You're hearing the GPUs,' says a maintenance worker. 'Those are the graphics chips that run the artificial intelligence software.'

The tone drops in the next hall, filled with data servers. Here, the buzz is closer to a low E. It's a chorus of computers, as far as the eye can see.

In this data center alone, Microsoft replaces 3,000 servers with new equipment every month. A costly but necessary precaution: if these servers go down, so does the cloud. The service relies on users being able to trust that this global network of the largest data centers, known as hyperscalers, is fully functioning twenty-four hours a day, seven days a week. They cannot be allowed to falter.

Despite the name, the cloud is closer to the ground than you might think. As a user, you only see the little magic icon on your screen that you tap to start your game, download your apps or bombard your colleagues with emails. Not many imagine that it is actually tucked away in a drab Dutch polder landscape. But for the longest time, no one had to think about the reality of what these services rely on. It was just business as usual. Until an invisible virus shut down the world.

At the beginning of 2020, the coronavirus pandemic spread across the planet. Lockdowns or not, there was no stopping it. Borders closed, and shops and companies had to shut down. Wearing facemasks and keeping your distance were the only remedies while the wait for a vaccine continued.

As public life ground to a halt, the digital world kept running. However, it faced a whole new set of hurdles. Everyone was suddenly working from home and wanted to video conference at the same time, which left the Microsoft cloud constantly battling malfunctions. Relatively unknown apps like Zoom and Teams were thrust into the spotlight as their usage exploded. The amount of data the world produced shot up exponentially, forcing Microsoft's data center in Middenmeer to bring in trucks filled with racks of thousands of extra servers. It was the only way to keep the Teams sessions running. With all the extra computing power, extra memory and extra GPUs, the high B was reaching a crescendo.

The sudden increase in demand for chips sparked a series of unforeseen consequences. It hit more than just servers for data centers; laptops, screens, game consoles and Wi-Fi routers started flying off the shelves at a rate far quicker than they could be restocked. Billions of schoolchildren and employees were forced to work from home and depended on their online connection, whether they liked it or not. Lockdowns kept the world glued to the couch, sending Netflix usage through the roof and keeping game servers working overtime. All services reliant on cloud computing.

Shortages arose in other sectors requiring processors, sensors and memory chips, with the car industry hit the hardest. Car manufacturers scaled back their orders to chip factories in early 2020, expecting the coronavirus crisis to dampen demand for cars. But this turned out to be a huge mistake. As soon as the market recovered, the automotive industry found it was actually in need of more chips to keep up with the transition from combustion engines to electric vehicles. Every new car has more than a hundred processors and thousands of separate chips, the electronics alone make up a staggering 40 percent of the production costs for each vehicle. It was the wrong time to hit the brakes.

With the chip factories running at full capacity due to the pandemic, new orders from the car manufacturers ended up at the back of the queue. The pinch of the chip shortage was starting to be felt. By the end of 2020 there were no longer enough chips for digital dashboards, driving assistants or airbag sensors, and the first production lines came to a standstill. Toyota, vw, Nissan, Renault, GM: everyone had to put part of their production on pause.

Anyone who ordered a new car had to wait for more than a year. Or settle for a model with an old fashioned handle to crank down the windows rather than a button. Muscle power instead of chips, just like the olden days.

Back in the south of the Netherlands, ASML was on the receiving end of a flurry of anxious calls. It was the end of 2020, and in his office on the twentieth floor Martin van den Brink had just finished a Teams

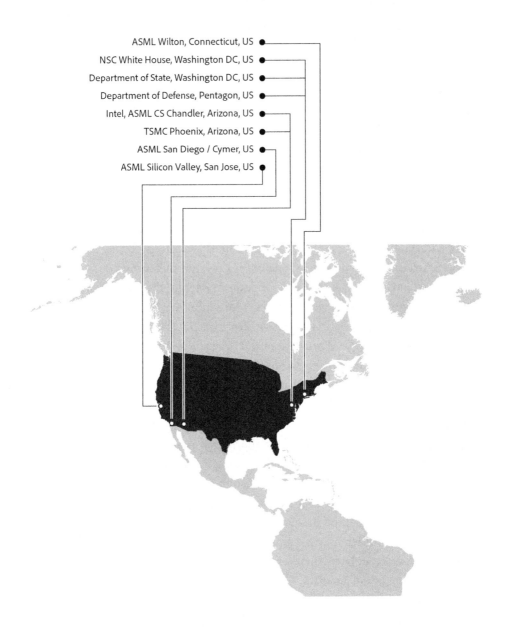

ASML Wilton, Connecticut, US

NSC White House, Washington DC, US

Department of State, Washington DC, US

Department of Defense, Pentagon, US

Intel, ASML CS Chandler, Arizona, US

TSMC Phoenix, Arizona, US

ASML San Diego / Cymer, US

ASML Silicon Valley, San Jose, US

This map highlights the locations visited in this book.

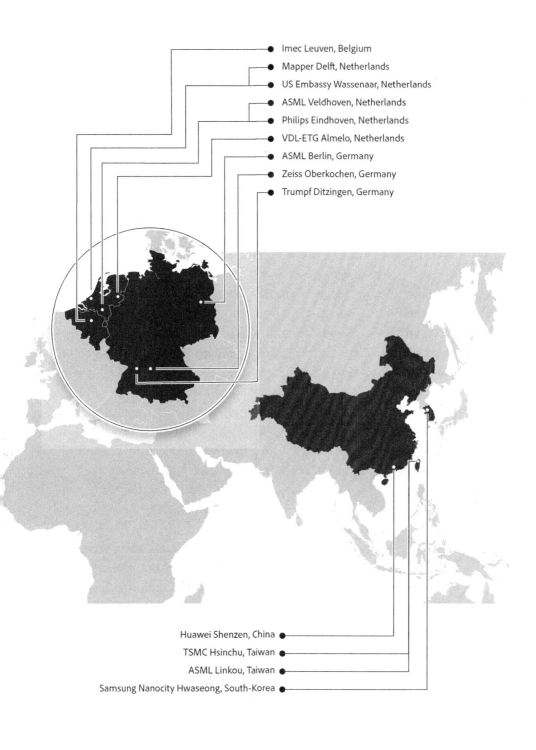

Imec Leuven, Belgium

Mapper Delft, Netherlands

US Embassy Wassenaar, Netherlands

ASML Veldhoven, Netherlands

Philips Eindhoven, Netherlands

VDL-ETG Almelo, Netherlands

ASML Berlin, Germany

Zeiss Oberkochen, Germany

Trumpf Ditzingen, Germany

Huawei Shenzen, China

TSMC Hsinchu, Taiwan

ASML Linkou, Taiwan

Samsung Nanocity Hwaseong, South-Korea

conversation with his biggest customer, the Taiwanese chip manufacturer TSMC. The message was clear: TSMC was angry.

Van den Brink has been ASML's technical director and an employee from day one. As Veldhoven's chief strategist and technical conscience, he has spent the last forty years charting the path for the company to follow. And when the shit really threatened to hit the fan, he was the one you would turn to: the highest and most feared rung in ASML's ladder of escalation.

The person on the other end of the line was Wei-Jen Lo, senior vice president of research and development at TSMC. The pandemic had presented him with an impossible task: his company was responsible for supplying half of the world's processors, and around 90 percent of the fastest ones. Everyone was aware of their dependence on Taiwanese chip production, and in this time of scarcity it was beginning to cause friction.

TSMC had the world breathing down its neck. Angry politicians wanted their car industries up and running: Germany's Chancellor Merkel had called to ask for chips to be delivered more quickly to the German car industry, while US President Joe Biden was demanding that TSMC give priority to American car factories. And on their end, the Taiwanese company was pressuring ASML to help expand their plant's capacity, and quickly. 'We need more productivity, Martin. More machines and higher output. Otherwise, we're finished.'

Angry chip manufacturers were a dime a dozen in the life of Van den Brink. By this point he had experienced so many crises in the chip industry there was not much left that could faze him. But this was different. The pandemic threw production chains into chaos. Even the chips that ASML and its suppliers needed to produce the machines that could make the chips were no longer available. The chip shortage was biting itself in the tail.

ASML had also been forced to switch to remote working. At the beginning of the coronavirus crisis the Dutch high-tech company ordered 20,000 extra Teams licenses from Microsoft, allowing it to support the global network of ASML technicians with their onerous task of keeping

5,000 lithography systems running. The world had realized just how much it relied on the chips these machines produce. Everyone needed them to keep stamping chips.

Van den Brink still harbors a deep hatred for remote meetings. 'I need to know how you're feeling, how you're holding yourself, how you look and what you're looking at. I want to read people.'

Peter Wennink's office is right across the hall from Martin's. Peter became CEO in 2013 after fourteen years as financial director, and is also co-chair of ASML's board of directors together with Van den Brink. Two opposing personalities, united in joint leadership. 'They're like yin and yang,' according to a supervisory board member. 'They complement each other perfectly.'

For a long time, the company only had the laws of nature to reckon with. But since 2018, it has found itself subject to a new realm: the unpredictable machinations of geopolitical forces. And this is where Wennink shines. Peter is ASML's face for the outside world: if you're a shareholder or politician, the first thing you'll remember about Veldhoven will be his welcoming yet firm handshake. And it's on him to keep the ship steady and guide ASML through this geopolitical storm. It is an endless task: lobbying in Washington, strategic planning in The Hague, shaking hands in Brussels, giving guided tour after guided tour of Veldhoven. After all, ASML is no longer some 'relatively obscure' company (in the words of a BBC journalist) – it is global front-page news.

China is on the heels of the Western world. The US wants to keep them at bay technologically by preventing them from setting up independent chip production using ASML's machines. The Americans see this as a direct threat to their national security: as far as they're concerned, every chip produced by China could be used for military aims. In the face of this existential threat, the US has become deeply committed to maintaining its lead in the fields of artificial intelligence and complex weapon systems, giving the semiconductor industry little choice but to go along with this.

The Trump administration may have set up the play, but President Biden pulled the trigger when he brought in tighter export regulations to freeze the Chinese technological advance. However, the US knows this is not enough. It needs its allies to go along with these export restrictions, in particular the Netherlands – and that means ASML.

The chip machine manufacturer may have grown up in an era of globalization, but that time has long passed. The fault lines of the world are clear, and ASML has no choice but to consider where it stands. When it comes to strategic readjustments like these, there's no manual or playbook to fall back on. The choices you make are your own.

The pandemic laid bare the vulnerability of the supply chains of the West. Attention has shifted to Taiwan, the island just off mainland China where TSMC operates its factories. Dependence on TSMC is the Achilles' heel of the worldwide tech sector, and the US and EU are deeply anxious about it. Both have thrown billions into developing chip factories on home soil in recent years in an attempt to reduce this dependency.

Peter Wennink knows ASML is the beating heart of this strategy. In 2023 alone, chip manufacturers planned more than 300 billion dollars worth of new factories. The company helped shape the European Chips Act, and Wennink was the guest of honor with a front row seat at the opening of TSMC's new factory in Phoenix, Arizona. As the first chip machine was hoisted inside in December 2022, even this mammoth device was dwarfed by the 'Made in America' flag flying from the façade.

Yet, he downplays his role on the world stage juggling two rival superpowers: 'No one is really important. At most, there are just positions with a lot of responsibility.'

When Wennink shook hands with President Joe Biden and Apple CEO Tim Cook, the largest purchaser of TSMC's chips, in the Arizona desert, he was indifferent about the fact that it said "Wennick" on the name tag dangling from his neck. 'Wennick, Winnick ... I've seen all the variations.'

The American media and politicians do not seem to be bothered by it either, but for a different reason. They have no idea who he is to begin with. Everyone is perplexed by the mysterious tall man shaking the hand of the president. 'ASML? What kind of company is that?'

This book is the story of ASML. It is the tale of the two top executives who, over the course of several decades, led their company to unimaginable heights. On the one hand you have Martin van den Brink: the brilliant technician who designs the most precise machines on earth, with a confrontational style of management that lies somewhere between cross-examination and shock therapy.

'Martin puts the fear of God in you,' says Wennink. It even took him a couple of years to get used to it.

And on the other hand, you have Peter Wennink: 'Peter loves to cut a ribbon,' teases Van den Brink, as his fellow CEO hosts yet another group of politicians at the ASML headquarters. He grins – he's not cut out for such formalities. He's too direct for diplomacy.

Peter is a non-engineer leading a high-tech company, a people person. He manages to keep a handle on ASML's nonconformist high-tech culture and hold together the crucial network of suppliers. He is at the center of every web, and it's the reason his word carries the power to move the share price of one of the world's most valuable tech companies. He is also the person who came up with the plan to finance ASML's biggest technological leap – the EUV machine – jointly with the chip manufacturers. It is thanks to this advance that Moore's Law will continue to apply for years to come.

In the span of forty years, ASML has grown into a dominant market leader, an industrial powerhouse expanding so fast the humble Dutch province it still calls home can barely keep up. But it is not planning on moving – it is on everyone else to keep up with the marching pace of the high-tech giant living in their backyard. ASML doesn't often hear no, let alone accept it.

At the turn of 2024, ASML is preparing to enter a new phase. Wennink's and Van den Brink's contracts will run out, and the two

67-year-olds on the same salary (5.94 million euros in 2023) will step back when they do. Although ASML has been working on their succession behind the scenes for years, theirs will be a hard act to follow.

Martin and Peter may be nothing alike in character. At all. But over the course of endless meetings, negotiations, trips and walks in the Kampina nature reserve by Veldhoven, they came to understand each other. They developed a mutual respect for what made them different, and once they combined their formidable skillsets, they became unstoppable.

Together, they helped build a company that overcame crisis after crisis by never losing sight of one key thing: focus.

Because in the world of ASML, focus is everything. And it has been from the very beginning.

PART I

GOOD IDEA, BAD PLAN

Flashing lights fill Pennsylvania Avenue. Nestled between six police motorbikes, eight black cars, an ambulance and a bus filled with armed officers, the 46th president of the United States Joe Biden collects his thoughts. It's just before 8.30 PM on February 7 2023, and the heavily secured convoy is escorting Biden to the Capitol to deliver his State of the Union address. A cold air whips through the fleet as it draws to a halt. It's time.

To everyone's surprise, Biden quickly starts talking about the chip shortage that hit the American economy during the pandemic. 'Cars got more expensive, refrigerators and phones got more expensive,' he hammers, both index fingers tapping along on the paper in front of him. The implication is clear: keep your hands off American cars and refrigerators, and definitely don't touch our iPhones.

'That should never happen again. We invented the chip. In recent decades, we have lost our edge. Once we made 40 percent of chips, now only 10 percent. We are going to make sure the supply chain starts again in America.'

He looks up: 'The supply chain starts in America.'

At the Dutch embassy in Washington, analysts follow the address keenly. America is in uproar over a Chinese spy balloon shot down over US territory, yet Biden chooses to first raise the state of the American chip industry. With The Hague eagerly awaiting their briefing that same evening, the analysts take note: 10 minutes and 15 seconds. This is all it took for the president to start talking about the American chip sector and its troubles. In other words, this has just been declared a top priority.

The standing ovation from both Republicans and Democrats lasted exactly 13.5 seconds. Biden knows his history; after all, America was the birthplace of this technology. The transistor was invented in Bell Labs in 1947, and by the late '50s Jack Kilby and Robert Noyce had soldered the first of their pioneering integrated circuits. These were the glory days of a US chip industry built exclusively on all-American lithography technology. But it was not to last. With the help of one particular company that came to dominate the lithography market, competitors in the east soon caught up with Silicon Valley. The company was ASML.

Or, as they call it in the corridors of Capitol Hill: *that company*.

However, forty years ago *that company* was not yet a reality. What existed was nothing more than a good idea with bad prospects.

1

THE REPEATER

It feels like the millionth time he's written this down. With a sigh, Steef Wittekoek puts the finishing touches to his article. 'Optical aspects of the Silicon Repeater' would go on to appear in the September 1983 edition of the *Philips Technological Review*. Established in 1936, this was the place to read about the latest inventions from Philips' Physical Laboratory (NatLab) in the words of the scientists themselves.

With the Silicon Repeater, writes Wittekoek, you can produce chips with far more precision and efficiency than would ever be possible with conventional lithography machines. Essentially, it's a big photocopier that repeats itself over and over, step by step. First, it projects an image field through a highly specialized lens onto a silicon disc, topped with a light-sensitive layer. This circular disc – also referred to as a *wafer* – then moves around as fast as possible, from one exposure step to the next. This carries on until the entire disc takes on the image: in this case, a pattern of miniature transistors. The adjustment and focusing of the Repeater was also completely automatic, making the machine faster and more efficient than its competitors. Ultimately, his point was simple; if the chip industry wants to take its next leap forwards, this is the tool it needs. When Wittekoek, one of NatLab's top scientists, reread his praise of the Repeater's 'excellent specifications', he couldn't help but feel a kinship with the machine. Philips had been trying to turn this idea into a good product for more than ten years. The first versions of the Repeater dated back to 1973, and even these were based on breakthroughs made by NatLab researchers Herman van Heek and Gijs Bouwhuis two years prior. But so far, it had been met with silence.

Gijs Bouwhuis was a talented optical scientist with an impressive list of patents to his name, responsible for devising the technology underlying the CD player and the lesser-known Videodisc player. Having grown up during World War II in the far north of the Netherlands, he was able to pursue his studies when his assistance was no longer needed on the family farm. As his daughter Pien recalled: 'My father was a modest man – working at the NatLab was a hobby to him. He would always be puffing away on his pipe when he was thinking, much to my mother's irritation.' Shortly before his death in 2016, Bouwhuis and his former NatLab colleagues were given a tour of ASML to see the fruits of their old hobbies one last time.

The CD was a commercial hit for Philips, finding its way into living rooms for years to come. But a lithography machine is a different beast. A product far more complex than a CD player and of no interest to the mass consumer market, it was by all measures a deeply unsuitable investment for an electronics giant in danger of decline.

In the early '70s, Philips had over 400,000 employees, approximately 90,000 of them working in the Netherlands. As an old-fashioned conglomerate everything was designed and made in-house, ranging from TVs, radios, medical equipment and household appliances to lighting. This included the industrial machines needed to produce these electronics, as well as the integrated circuits to control them. At the time, this made it the second-largest manufacturer of semiconductors in the world. But their chip factories had grown tired of the existing machines. They were far too slow and produced too many unusable chips. So, at their request, the NatLab set to work developing what would become the Silicon Repeater.

Philips' NatLab was a sanctuary for free-thinking scientists and inventors, and attracted a great degree of technical expertise. It quickly established itself as a breeding ground for pioneering innovations, comparable to the famous Bell Labs of the American telecom giant AT&T. But while the NatLab was constantly brimming with new ideas and patents, the wider organization may as well have carried the patent on bureaucracy. Doing something new in Philips required an unthinkable amount of consulting and political strategizing, a style of business totally unsuited to the high-paced innovation that drove the chip industry. Speed was everything – and Philips did not stand a chance of keeping up.

2

THE GO-GETTER

Steef Wittekoek felt like a lone voice crying out in the wilderness. He knew that the Repeater (later renamed the 'Wafer Stepper') was a step above its American competitors. But back in Eindhoven, Philips had other concerns. Their turnover had relied heavily on consumer electronics, and the rise of Japanese companies like Sony, JVC and Toshiba had forced the Dutch multinational into a difficult position. While Sony was preparing to take the world by storm with the Walkman, Philips was busy taking a knife to the organization. The strategy: to spin off costly parts of the company via joint ventures, before gradually selling their stakes in the part.

Eyes soon fell on the lithography machines. In early 1978, Philips had the idea to set up an independent branch for the technology, a move that would also allow for the sale of the devices to external customers. But enthusiasm among the management was thin on the ground – there was a vague idea, but no real plan. Only Wim Troost, deputy director of the Science and Industry division, raised his hand. Already dealing with products for industrial applications, he glimpsed the potential of the technology and fancied the challenge. As far as the other division heads were concerned, the technology was a total dead end and a complete waste of time.

'Wim, stop throwing away money,' he would frequently hear. But it was of no use. He had made up his mind.

Upon meeting Wim Troost, you immediately sense that you are standing face to face with someone from another era. Born in the mid-1920s, Troost was raised in a time when the first radio sets were released, the stock market stood on the cusp of the crash of 1929, and World War I was still called The Great War.

Cut to the early 1980s, and just as he was about to retire, Troost found himself playing a decisive role in launching the chip-machine manufacturer that would come to be called ASML. If it were not for Troost, Philips would have written off the wafer stepper entirely. As it was, the budget allocated for the responsibility hardly gave him a chance to begin with. He still pronounces 'budget' with a hard Dutch *g* in the middle: an echo from a long distant past.

When Troost opens his front door in the summer of 2022, he is almost 97. Tucked away in the garden of his converted farmhouse, he recalls how he would drive back and forth to the Philips plant from this same house every day, his journey cast under the smoke of neighboring Eindhoven. Despite being frailer than he once was, his memories remain razor-sharp in his mind. Just as clear are his hand-written notes, covering the events of these years in painstaking detail.

Troost recounts the visit of PerkinElmer, a leading US lithography systems manufacturer that developed their own machine to great commercial success in the '70s. Now the early '80s, the company was intrigued by reports of the NatLab's inventions. A delegation of ten Americans was dispatched to the Netherlands. Stunned by what they found, PerkinElmer decided they wanted to work with Philips. However, they heard nothing back. Philips never even responded to them, a short-sightedness that still annoys Troost some forty years later. 'The management had absolutely no forward vision, no idea of what was possible,' he bemoans.

Troost knew it would simply never be profitable to only produce chip machines for Philips' own factories. With this in mind, he travelled to Asia and the US in an attempt to garner interest in the PAS 2000, or the Philips Automated Stepper, the first commercial version of the wafer stepper. The number 2000 was popular at the time in Philips, with the twenty or so years to go before the turn of the millennium lending the number a distinct air of futurism they hoped would rub off on any product it graced. Who wouldn't want a P2000 home computer, or a Video 2000 system? However, the reality never caught up with the branding, and none of these Philips products were successful enough to make it to the year of their namesake.

The PAS 2000 was no different – though in this case, it was clear why. This version of the stepper had an 'oil table', hydraulic motors that moved the surface on which the silicon disc lay. But oil fumes are lethal to the highly controlled environments in which these chips are produced. Cleanrooms have to be clean; if they reek of a garage, you can forget about it. The machine was unsellable.

Something needed to change, so the NatLab set to work on a variant of the stepper with electric motors. They were soon successful, creating what would be known as linear motors due to their back-and-forth motion. However, the cost to complete the development of these motors was skyrocketing. The Ministry of Economic Affairs, which was heavily subsidizing the development of Philips' lithography technology, had reached their limit and threatened to pull support unless the company focused more time and effort into seeing it through. The walls were closing in, and Troost was short of options. In the end the Ministry itself came up with a solution – why not team up with successful Dutch entrepreneur Arthur del Prado? His company ASM International was also working on chip machines and had just completed a successful initial public offering (IPO) on the NASDAQ, the American stock exchange. They were the perfect candidates to get Philips over the line.

Arthur del Prado was the pioneer of the Dutch chip industry and a trader of heroic stature. Born in Batavia (modern-day Jakarta), Del Prado was interned and forced to endure a Japanese prisoner of war camp as an adolescent. He survived, and made his way to the Netherlands to study chemistry and economics. He then travelled through Silicon Valley in the '50s, becoming the go-to European distributor for US semiconductor technology. By the '70s, what was now ASM International began building vertical furnaces. These machines apply the thin layers to the wafers that are later exposed in the lithography machine. Once the chip pattern is developed on this layer, an etching machine uses gases and chemicals to remove the excess material. The wafer is then sent on a new round through the chip factory until, layer by layer, a chip with transistors and connections grows.

When Del Prado was crowned the 1983 Dutch Entrepreneur of the Year in The Hague, the ministry made sure Troost was invited along. A charming man with an exceptional eye for business, Troost concluded, but he had his concerns. ASM International was still primarily a trading house, and Del Prado simply did not have the right connections at a board level. Buying a lithography machine, the heart of chip production, is the single most important strategic decision that a chip manufacturer has to make. Reassurance has to come from the very top; questions need to be run by the board, not discussed with the purchasing department. Especially when taking a chance on new technology.

Philips rebuffed the deal, but Del Prado and the Ministry were insistent. Del Prado had clocked the potential of NatLab's wafer stepper and wanted in. The jewel in Philips' crown would take him one step closer to his dream of supplying a complete production line to chip manufacturers – all the tools needed to turn a disc of silicon into a stack of working chips, the power to turn sand into gold. That dream would never fully come true. However, Del Prado's desire to start a joint venture with Philips would soon be fulfilled.

No other options arose for Philips to divest the wafer stepper, and it became clear that a deal with ASM International was the only way forward. And so it was that Troost, together with his boss at the time George de Kruiff, found himself knocking at Del Prado's door. The deal for the joint venture was concluded in less than an hour, with both companies putting in 7.5 million guilders (roughly half of the equivalent number in euros) for a 50 percent stake in their joint subsidiary: Advanced Semiconductor Materials Lithography, or ASM Lithography for short.

In these early months the company presented itself as ALS, until it dawned on them that this was also the name of a serious motor neuron disease. After a quick rebrand as 'ASM Lithography', in 1996 the company officially changed its name to ASML – a name that has come to be used the world over, and which will be used for the remainder of this book.

The contract was signed in Eindhoven in March 1984. But there was no time to celebrate – there was work to be done. Troost marked forty people from the Philips team that worked on the wafer stepper for immediate transfer. Whether they liked it or not, they would be joining the joint venture. For many, this move struck a bad chord.

The engineers at Philips had been graced with exceptional employee benefits, including a full pension at sixty and access to a fund that helped pay for their children's education. But now, they found themselves part of an unnegotiable transfer to a breakaway company they all feared was destined for bankruptcy. Even Steef Wittekoek was hesitant. He would only transfer over if the NatLab gave him a two-year return guarantee. The clause was agreed, but he never had to use it.

In a makeshift building between the Philips factories in Eindhoven, the administrative department of ASML started to settle in. Meanwhile, the technical work pushed on in the draughty hall of a nearby factory. Amongst the workers were two young engineers who would determine the future of ASML: Martin van den Brink and Frits van Hout. *The boys*, as they were called, spent little time worrying about their sulking colleagues. Like the other newcomers, they embraced the challenge and threw themselves headfirst into the new technology.

Frits was the first new employee to be brought in under the banner of ASML. Martin was a different story: he was still technically listed as applying for a job at Philips in late 1983, and it would be more than a decade before he got an official contract with ASML. By then, it was merely a formality – he was already the rock on which the company stood.

The two young hires appeared to be an odd couple: Martin was a physicist specializing in district heating, while Frits graduated in low-temperature physics. Nevertheless, according to Wittekoek the two youngsters were a good combination. 'Martin was incredibly gifted technically, and while Frits understood the technology, he was more of a people person. He knew how to handle connections the right way.'

Troost retired with the start of the company, so the role of CEO was taken up by Gjalt Smit, a former colleague from his days at Philips. Smit had completed a PhD in Astronomy before working for both NASA and the European Space Agency, ultimately ending up as the director of the Dutch branch of telecom company ITT. When he quit his steady job for the risky research project, his colleagues assumed he had lost the plot. Looking back at the start of his tenure, Smit can see why. 'ASML was a problem child from day one. In all honesty, it seemed doomed from the start.'

Smit nurtured a long-lasting love-hate relationship with Philips. While grateful for what he had learned at the Dutch electronics company, as well as from their 'finger-licking good' technology, he always felt the management to be 'terribly politicized'. Gjalt could never get along with this – he wanted to do things differently.

Gjalt himself is different.

Chip production

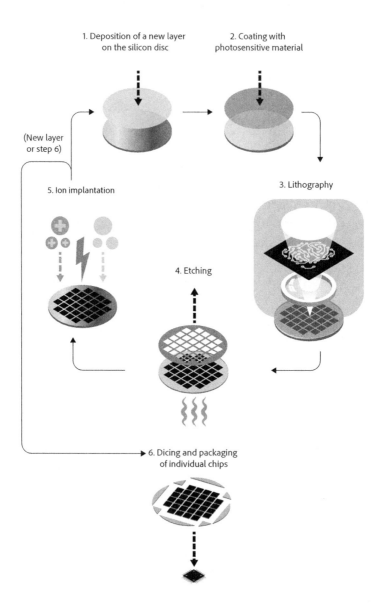

1. Deposition of a new layer on the silicon disc

2. Coating with photosensitive material

(New layer or step 6)

5. Ion implantation

3. Lithography

4. Etching

6. Dicing and packaging of individual chips

3

THE HIGH-FLYER

'How old do you think this coat is?'

It's early 2023, and Gjalt Smit is walking along the promenade in Montreux, not far from his home in the Swiss mountains. Smit likes to step out in style – this time it's a dark hat and striking Italian leather coat that reaches almost to his ankles. 'I bought it in Vienna in 1986,' he answers with a smirk. 'The secretary at ASML was shocked when I walked into the office with it.' It was as if the secret police had come to Veldhoven.

Smit had always been frank about his dislike for the way Philips worked, something that landed him in good favor with Arthur del Prado when they met in 1983. Del Prado was also not enamored by the corporation, as Philips had shunned ASM International when they had previously needed to purchase chip machines. A bond was made, and things clicked between the two men. While this relationship would later sour, culminating in Smit's departure four years after this meeting, in this short time he managed to establish a winner's mentality at ASML that would define the company for years to come.

When discussing his hobbies, another dimension of his business acumen becomes clear. Smit is a glider pilot. Successfully piloting these aircraft requires a high level of oversight, as well as responsiveness to unexpected turbulence – just like running a business does. In his words, 'when you are in a glider, you need to know where you are going.' The same could be said for the young ASML, and it was up to Smit to figure this out.

For the first few months, Smit took stock, holding talks in and outside Philips to gauge the lay of the land. As he found out, no-one believed the company had a snowball's chance in hell – even the employees were not hopeful. Making it in Silicon Valley as a lithography manufacturer required both a decisive organization and machines that were virtually faultless in their reliability. Getting such a company off the ground would take time and money, both of which were in short supply.

But as he also found out, the industry standard machines had hit their limit. A leap in the available technology was now needed to produce chips with smaller resolutions; chips with not just thousands, but hundreds of thousands of transistors, allowing them to perform far more complex tasks. The only problem: a lithography machine capable of producing such a chip would have to be able to project lines approaching one micron (one thousandth of a millimeter) in width. No established lithography manufacturers had the technology for this – but Philips did. They were clueless about the high standards chip manufacturers demanded of their suppliers, however.

At the end of May 1984, Smit flew to the SEMICON trade fair in San Mateo, the heart of Silicon Valley. This was the annual convention for chip manufacturers, like Intel and Texas Instruments, to meet with suppliers of lithographic machines, such as PerkinElmer, Nikon and GCA. But none of the manufacturers had any interest in Gjalt. As far as they were concerned, there was no need for yet another bidder on the scene, and they weren't interested in hearing what ASML could offer them in the future. Smit was promptly dismissed. The message: 'Come back when you've sold fifty machines.'

Smit was taken aback. He took a plane to the US office of ASM International in Arizona, supposedly responsible for selling his machines on the US market. However, it was increasingly obvious that ASM International wasn't aware of the latest developments in lithography techniques, leaving Smit with a growing skepticism about the partnership. To Smit's surprise, the management of ASM were also uneasy. They feared ASML was naïve and would make rookie mistakes.

The memo was clear; with around ten companies still viably competing, the market was crammed enough. ASML appeared to be redundant from the outset. Disillusioned, Smit trudged onto the plane back to Amsterdam. As he slumped in his seat, he considered throwing in the towel. No-one wants to lead a company destined for failure. With a bottle of red wine in hand he drifted off, leaving his ideas to hazily float around his head while he slept. After a while, they began to form a picture.

Smit jolted awake – 'Bingo,' he whispered to himself. The flight path was clear. Given the scale of investment that had already gone into their machines, the established players would always first defend their existing positions. If ASML could come along with a machine with a far more accurate alignment system, electric motors and precise lenses, they could stun the market and set a standard no company would be able to rise to before it was too late. The leap in technology ASML held the key to would create the opening they needed. But time was not on their side – such a device would need to be ready to go to market, and quick.

A shake out was in the air. Smit returned to ASM and Philips, asking for an investment of 200 million guilders. This was far more than those in the joint venture had envisioned, but the figure was not plucked from thin air. Philips had previously requested this amount in support from the Dutch Ministry of Economic Affairs. They never received that money, but Smit had done enough to win over the supervisory board. They were convinced: ASML was going for gold.

The pilot in Smit had noticed parallels between the chip machine industry and the aircraft industry. Both utilized a diverse range of scientific expertise, converging in the development of one device. But in order to concentrate their efforts on the complex overall industrial designs of their machines, aircraft makers like Boeing and Airbus sourced most of the parts involved. ASML quickly embraced this as their modus operandi. Just like aircraft, lithography machines are built in small series and intended to stay in commission for years, with minimal setbacks and optimally utilized capacity. This requires constant maintenance. Marketing also needs to work hand in hand with engineering, as they know exactly how customers can extract the most value from the machine they supply.

This strategy flipped Philips' approach on its head. For ASML, it was now about getting close to customers and outsourcing as much production as possible to suppliers. With the plan rubber-stamped, Smit hired a management consultancy, Hay, to set up the organization. He also brought in employees from America to Veldhoven to help the small Dutch company appear 'Silicon Valley–friendly'.

Smit fostered a culture of freedom at ASML, guaranteeing engineers the space to figure out their own solutions to technical problems. He often compared his approach to the 'total football' of the Dutch national soccer team in the 1970s, a tactic in which every player could be utilized for both attack and defense. The goal was clear: no matter what you do or how you do it, the most important thing is to win.

The number of ASML employees grew rapidly. Job listings for new engineers started to appear in trade magazines. A telephone line was set up in Veldhoven for applicants to speak to former Philips specialists, each of whom would personally try to convince the caller to move to the fledgling start-up. The drive worked, and specialists were brought in from fields such as optics, mechatronics, control engineering and software. They used newspapers to hunt for business economists and people to help test the machines, otherwise known as 'troubleshooters'. Unable to resist the pull of 'an ultra-high-tech company with ambitions to be a world-leader', people flocked to the calls. Fortunately for ASML, projecting self-confidence was never an issue.

Sights were set first and foremost on customers in the US. During the 1980s Japan was successfully chipping away market shares from American semiconductor companies, and there was no point in trying to pry Japanese chip manufacturers away from Canon and Nikon. So ASML geared itself to become an American-style company, bolstered by a comprehensive and readily available service department. The promise of a strong maintenance crew that could keep the machines running in the factories was essential; after all, every idle second is money lost.

Smit's optimism was contagious. Although the designers had to work to tight deadlines, hierarchies were kept to a minimum and the employees bought in. The project managers – the ones responsible for actually realizing the machines – found themselves largely in charge. They were told not to worry about the money: all that mattered was that the machines were finished on time, whatever the cost.

Richard George, one of the pioneering engineers of the wafer stepper in the Philips era, recalls this moment as one of relief. ASML had been inundated with enthusiastic newcomers, and Smit was already sending out growth forecasts that were just as positive. Suddenly, George found himself with 250 more people on his team, and one man in particular stood out to him: Martin van den Brink. 'Martin was brilliant from the start,' he recalled, 'it took him less than two months before he improved the alignment system of the wafer stepper with his own nifty invention. All I could say was, "Damn, that's a good idea."'

The machine aligned itself to each wafer one at a time based on two small grid patterns already engraved in the disc. These profiles, or marks, need to remain visible when you apply new layers to the chip to prevent deviations. Van den Brink came up with an improved system that could measure both alignment patterns. The machine worked faster than the competitors with far fewer deviations and his idea was immediately worth a patent. This was huge for the company. In the words of Smit, 'ASML started out of nothing, like the Big Bang. But the arrival of Martin was an *act of God*.'

4

THE LEAKY HAT

Now partly seceded from Philips, in 1985 ASML started the construction of its own head office. The new building rose beside the highway in Veldhoven in less than a year, complete with the dust-free cleanrooms needed to manufacture their machines. The municipality had been quick to say yes to the high-tech player, eager for the additional employment it brought to the area. However, the neighboring municipalities of Eindhoven and Son were less pleased. Veldhoven hadn't acquired the necessary permits, and they lodged a complaint with the courts. But ASML couldn't afford to wait, and they pushed ahead with construction.

The first headquarters exuded Gjalt Smit's ambition. Inspired by the futurism of Silicon Valley to help their American customers feel at home, the 30-million-guilder statement boasted of a budget that far outweighed the age of the company. Although employees did not yet have to wear face masks, there was mandatory special clothing to keep the workspaces clean. An easy way to display their seriousness; during the early years at Philips, you could still enter in your own dust coat.

ASML'ers, as they tend to be called, are not ones for fuss. The first building was simply named 'Building 1', and 'Building 2' followed soon after. It isn't hard to guess what they called the third. Everything was clearly numbered, like a takeout menu from an Asian restaurant. There was also no logo on the façade, at the request of architect Rob van Aken. His design said it all; you knew you were about to enter the headquarters of ASML.

Building 1 has since been demolished, but back in 1985 it was an unusual sight. It looked like a portal to the digital age, stuck in the middle of bucolic Brabant. The sloping white walls, shrouded in blue mirrored glass, gave its pyramid form an air of mystery. At night, local children imagined the building was a UFO, its strange lights emanating from tech-heads burning the midnight oil. Van Aken used to imagine the triangular shape as a big hat falling over the production areas and offices, symbolically embracing all the departments. However, despite the display of futuristic engineering, a construction fault caused the hat to leak. Sometimes the best tech isn't necessarily high-tech: when it rained, you would still see a bucket or two in the lobby.

ASML immediately wanted to play at the highest level and compete alongside the USA's GCA and Japan's Nikon, the big hitters of the moment. In the press, Smit exuded self-confidence. 'In this industry, only one business strategy is conceivable: focus on first place. You have to want to get the gold. If you decide you'll be satisfied with bronze before you start, you'll probably end up sixth. Then you're done for.' This was May 1985, in conversation with the Dutch national newspaper NRC Handelsblad. The director of technology Nico Hermans concurred: 'It may sound arrogant, but we are miles ahead of the competition. We're simply a class above.'

With the infamous 'We hear you, Jerry' ad running in several electronics magazines, the US campaign got off to a flying start. This was a cheeky reference to Jerry Sanders, the boss of chip manufacturer AMD, who had recently publicly called out the unreliability of US lithography machines and threatened to switch to Japanese equipment.

But for all the bravado, these campaigns from ASML were effectively bluffs. Their only machine was the PAS 2400, a device hastily assembled to show the chip world they had something better than the oil-driven machines. It wasn't as accurate as hoped, but the PAS 2400 still spat out as many as ninety exposed wafers per hour – a record at the time, according to the ad.

The bold approach worked, and with the help of Steef Wittekoek's technological expertise, Smit managed to get a foot in the door at AMD.

The reward for their endeavors: a chance for the Dutch to compete with four other suppliers in a test of their capability, a lithographical beauty contest in which the most promising machine gets the contract.

The week of the competition, a lone ASML technician was already on-site. He decided to fire up the machine, just to check everything was in order before the AMD experts set about their tests. To his horror, he discovered an embarrassing fault. The electric motors were warped, and the test machine was projecting deviant chip patterns. The machine did not stand a chance.

Without telling AMD, the teams in Veldhoven set to work. Tension was high: they had only thirty-six hours to come up with a solution. The next day, an ASML engineer flew to Silicon Valley with a modified version of the motor parts in his suitcase. With a 'borrowed' access pass in hand, the crew snuck into the chip factory in the middle of the night to screw in the motors. The wily scheme paid off. The machine worked and ASML eventually won the contract, promising the delivery of twenty-five machines by 1987.

ASML proceeded to set its sights on the chip companies just below the top end of the market. These were the manufacturers in a position to compete, yet looking to find ways to expand their production at lower costs. ASML figured they would be more willing to take a risk on the Dutch newcomer that promised more 'value of ownership'. Players like Intel or IBM would not want to risk their market position, so would be difficult to lure away from the tried and tested lithography machines from Nikon and Canon. After all, the Japanese chip companies had enjoyed great success with these machines.

Famed for their optical technology and high-quality cameras, Nikon and Canon had the means to develop their own specialized lenses in-house. ASML was not so fortunate; it had to look elsewhere to source the optical system, the heart of the lithography machine. The German lens specialist Zeiss had by far the best technology ASML could find, but the company was reluctant to supply to an unknown start-up. Not only that, but Zeiss itself would need to make extra investments to actually produce the highly specialized lenses ASML required. The Germans didn't dare; they only wanted to sell non-custom-made items.

In a demonstration of confidence in the nascent machine, Philips placed an order. The deadline was tight, but in 1986 the electronics company received the first truly competitive wafer stepper: the PAS 2500, equipped with a standard lens from Zeiss. The beginning was here.

Meanwhile ASM International were unable to keep up with the capital injections demanded by ASML. Del Prado was particularly annoyed by Smit's ability to casually burn through huge sums of money. On one of his returns from Taiwan, Steef Wittekoek needed to travel to New York to talk with IBM. Smit told him to 'just take the Concorde', a supersonic plane that commanded equally impressive costs to fly.

For his part, Smit was also annoyed with Del Prado. In his eyes, the chip pioneer of the Netherlands had failed to grasp that lithography was a business in its own right. And ASML needed to take the market by storm: they had no hope of success if they indulged the Dutchman's penny-pinching. Smit made an inquiry to Philips about whether it was possible to buy out Del Prado. The response: don't even think about it.

This was a step too far for Del Prado. He vowed to take Smit to task, and an upcoming trade fair provided the opportunity. ASM international and ASML were due to share a stand at the event, held at a race track in San Mateo. Here, between the cowboys of the chip industry and surrounded by the smell of horses, beer and hotdogs, the two collided. As soon as Del Prado asked, 'Can we talk?' Smit knew what was coming. A colleague had even just whispered, 'Arthur hates you,' but he hardly needed the warning. Smit's time was up. In 1987, after taking up an offer from a German company, he left ASML.

Del Prado quickly conjured up a new chief executive, a British man named Clive Segal. However, on his first day, Segal failed to show up. A second day passed – still no Segal. The ASML managers took it in turns waiting for him by the entrance, but no one knew who he was or had any way of contacting him. As it turned out, Segal was also none the wiser. He didn't realize he had said yes to Del Prado, and was waiting to sell his own company before making any sort of move. But ASML was in no position to wait. Thankfully Wim Troost, a retired chief executive, agreed to take the reins until the ship was steadied.

One year later, and against his will, Del Prado was out. By this point ASM International did not have the capital to fund the upcoming rounds of investment ASML needed, leaving them no choice but to withdraw from the joint venture. In 1988 Philips took over Del Prado's share, which ironically gifted the company full ownership of the wafer stepper they had so desperately wanted rid of.

But things were slightly different this time round, at least on paper. By cleverly depositing ASM International's stake with the NMB bank, Philips made sure ASML's government subsidies would continue to flow in. With the stage set, ASML could finally begin to make good on their word. The bluff was no longer a bluff.

And with that, Arthur del Prado bid farewell to ASML. The narrative since has emphasized Philips' involvement in the early years of the company, and the role of the other founder has largely been ignored. 'Art', as he was known to the Americans, never found peace with this. The lack of recognition for his contribution would weigh heavily on him until his death in 2016.

5

THE MEGA LEGACY

Despite the collapse of the joint venture with ASM International, ASML lived on through a combination of fortuitous circumstances. First was the timing; in 1985 there was a dip in the chip industry, hitting established chip machine manufacturers hard. However, the young company had little to lose and powered on with production. They trusted the market would pick up, and wanted to be two steps ahead of the rest when it did.

In addition, they emerged well from the first venture with ASM International. Del Prado's inexperience with lithography came at the cost of his relationship to Smit and his share in the company. But for ASML, it proved an advantage. They were not forced to mold themselves on already successful companies, leaving the young start-up with space to develop their own culture and strategy in these formative years. An American lithography company would never have tolerated that amount of freedom.

The partnership with Philips also came to their rescue. During the chip market's heaviest downturn, the electronic group's financial muscle was able to keep ASML afloat, ordering new lithography systems and even opening doors to new customers in Taiwan. They also got help from another player – the Dutch government. The founding of ASML coincided with a reassessment of government policy when it came to their relationship with industry. The success of Japanese chip manufacturers had hit the US and European sectors hard in the early '80s, and a large part of the reason companies like NEC, Hitachi and

Toshiba were able to take such a lead was due to the scale of the investment by the Japanese government in their research projects. Other countries took note, and ASML found themselves on the crest of a new wave of strategic public investment.

The Dutch Ministry of Economic Affairs was tired of keeping languishing industries afloat. The struggling shipyards were dropped, and they turned their focus to supporting innovation. It was clear microchips were the future, and with NatLab's wafer stepper they had been gifted the key. They needed it to succeed, so the ministry invested over 100 million guilders for research and development. Steef Wittekoek and Frits van Hout pushed for more, working around the clock to bring in new subsidies. In these initial years, about half of ASML's money for research came from The Hague or Brussels.

This was not the only large government project that played into ASML's hands. In 1984, Philips teamed up with a German partner Siemens in an effort to make the next leap in chip technology. With a name that seemed like it could be lifted straight from an old monster movie, the 'Mega' Project aimed to take on the Japanese by entering right at the top of the market for memory chips. The plan gained support from the highest levels, with the European technology project ESPRIT and both the Dutch and German governments contributing vast amounts of money. In today's terms, the latter two put forward roughly half a billion euros combined. With this, Philips plunged into the production of static random-access memory (SRAM) chips. These could store data without the need for their own power source, and with the help of ASML Philips built an entire test line for these chips. But the initial production was a loss; there was not enough demand for the chips and Siemens walked away from the project, opting instead for an already established Japanese chip technology. This spelled the end of the monstrous Mega Project, and with it the dreams of a European technological resurgence.

Despite racking up a tab of hundreds of millions of guilders, the Mega Project turned out not to be a waste of money for Philips. In 1987, the company was contacted by Morris Chang, former technical director of the US company Texas Instruments. Raised in China and educated in America, Chang was an expert in increasing the yield, the percentage of faultless chips on a wafer. The Taiwanese government noticed and tapped him to be the lead in establishing a national chip industry, promising to cover any and all costs. This marked the start of the Taiwanese Semiconductor Manufacturing Company, or as it is widely known today, TSMC. Chang sought another large, experienced investor from the sector. But the Japanese were not interested, plus talks with Intel and Texas Instruments fell through. So he turned to Philips, in his eyes the cream of the second-rate chipmakers. Hardly a compliment, but what mattered was getting the collaboration – and Philips was the next best thing.

Philips happily agreed, taking a 28 percent stake in TSMC and sharing the expertise cultivated from the Mega Project. But the partnership also opened the door for ASML to get their machines onto TSMC's factory floors. Chang held fire. He needed to be convinced of the quality of the equipment. While on holiday with his wife in Bali, Wim Troost received a polite tap on his shoulder. 'Mr. Troost, a call for you.' He wormed out of his cross-legged position in the middle of a dance performance and snuck out of the audience to take the call. It was Veldhoven: the deal with TSMC had come through. It turned out there was a way to win Chang over. Troost had given away the first machine to TSMC for free on a no cure, no pay basis. The highly demanding Taiwanese were convinced.

With the partnership between TSMC and ASML in full swing, the Taiwanese chip industry proceeded to boom. The two companies turned out to be surprisingly likeminded. Both functioned in an equally speedy and chaotic manner, with each totally dependent on the other to churn out endless piles of wafers every hour, free of faulty chips. 'We have their backs and they have ours,' was the mantra of the ASML'ers. This one sentence became the formula for dominating the chip market.

All the while, Philips was slowly reducing its stake in TSMC, earning billions in the process. In 2006 it pulled out of the semiconductor market altogether, divesting its chip division NXP. Now left to its own devices, NXP went on to become a major supplier to the automotive industry. How valuable the now-decimated Philips could have been if it had held on to these shares, or to ASML, is a question that still haunts the Dutch to this day. In truth, Philips likely would have collapsed at an early stage.

Philips laid the technical foundation for TSMC, and it was thanks to orders from Taiwan that kept ASML afloat in the early days. 'Without them,' says Frits van Hout, 'we would have certainly gone under.' Their luck was further bolstered in 1988 when the initial order from TSMC received an unexpected sequel. A fire had torn through the Taiwanese chip factory, causing serious damage to dozens of machines. The news reached ASML: they were to deliver another shipment immediately, all at the expense of the insurance company.

In the years that followed under Morris Chang's leadership, TSMC would grow into the world's most advanced chip manufacturer. TSMC was a foundry, focused on producing designs from other tech companies instead of their own. The model proved a success. As the whole process of chip production was growing increasingly complex and costly, the process of making these wafers was being outsourced by more and more chipmakers. The chips hit the market quicker, and at a far lower price than it would be if production was kept in-house. In the end, most let go of their own factories and became 'fabless'. These changes played straight into TSMC's hands. Through their close collaboration with ASML, they then were able to push through new technology at breakneck speed, expanding their capacity and turning Taiwan into the world's supplier of advanced computing power.

Intel could only watch from the sidelines, having let slip the chance to team up with Morris Chang in 1987. Thirty years on, Intel could not keep up the pace with TSMC anymore. As Joe Biden would later declare in his State of the Union address, America had lost its edge.

6

THE 4022 NETWORK

In 1990, Willem Maris took the reins as ASML's new chief executive officer. The mechanical engineer transferred from a management role in Philips' chip division to find himself at the helm of an unstable company. ASML barely made it through the early '90s, relying heavily on the acquisition of government subsidies and a rare act of generosity from the head of Philips, Jan Timmer. In 1992, Timmer initiated a harsh restructuring plan, named Operation Centurion, with devastating effect. He cut fifty thousand jobs from Philips' three hundred thousand-strong workforce, hitting Eindhoven and the surrounding Brabant area particularly hard. The mass lay-offs left scars in the families of many Brabanders, and the abandoned Philips buildings turned the city of Eindhoven into a desolate place. It was the worst moment for ASML to find itself on the brink of collapse and desperately in need of a 36-million-guilder loan.

Miraculously, fellow board member Henk Bodt managed to sway Timmer, or as he was now called, 'the Butcher'. The chip industry was facing a lull; if ASML went to market with an improved machine, they could take it by storm. It was now or never. To everyone's surprise, the Butcher agreed and granted the loan. According to ASML's former financial director Gerard Verdonschot, this was a well-calculated risk. Disbanding ASML at that moment would have come at a far greater cost for the parent company than this final bet on success. The only condition was that ASML had to repay the loan extremely quickly; sure enough, nine months later Verdonschot and Maris triumphantly presented the check. The pace was beginning to pick up.

As Philips downsized and the region of Eindhoven plunged into an economic crisis, ASML continued to grow. Philips' machine factory Acht kept up the supply of parts to ASML, and the NatLab continued to tinker with the lithography technology. But more was still needed. As per the business model, ASML only dealt with the development and assembly of the machines, buying up around 90 percent of the parts. Luckily, there were plenty of manufacturing companies around the corner in Eindhoven already supplying to Philips. New specialist companies were frequently opening up, often founded by former Philips employees jumping the sinking ship. And so a network of manufacturers took root in the region that knew each other intimately and spoke the same technical language. Quite literally: every component for ASML has a 12-digit code, based on the 12nc system that Philips used for decades in its own factories.

Forty years after its founding, the code of all ASML components still starts with '4022'. That number can be found everywhere, from the warehouses in Veldhoven to the many suppliers and chip factories the world over. You can even use it to identify the second-hand components up for grabs on Ebay. It is the key to a system that holds together a complex global chain of production, a code that unmistakably bears the DNA of Philips.

VHE, the family business of Harry van Hout (no relation to Frits), was one such regional supply company. They produced the cables and power supply boxes for the first lithography machines. ASML decided what is needed, and VHE would oblige. However, cooperation with Veldhoven in the early days was chaotic. VHE found themselves beholden to a volatile market and to a company that did not hesitate to react accordingly. Orders were halved or doubled at the drop of a hat, leaving some companies hesitant to pin too much of their sales on such a fluid base. Especially given how loose and informal the contracts were: most only needed a single sheet of paper, a few verbal agreements and a handshake – that's how they got things done in Brabant.

'If there was a problem, there was always someone who would lend an ear,' recalled Harry van Hout. 'During one of the first dips in the chip market, I was suddenly told they didn't need my deliveries for a month. I'd already ordered materials worth hundreds of thousands of guilders, so this was a serious problem.' One phone call to financial director Verdonschot sufficed and 750,000 guilders were transferred that same day. As long as everything kept working, ASML knew the money would find its way back.

In those early days, ASML had only two requirements for its suppliers: the work had to be good, and it needed to be fast. Gerard van der Leegte's tool shop was one of the first ASML partners, providing precision parts meticulously cut, ground or drilled to exacting specifications for their lithography machines. However, unlike the standards it required of others, ASML itself was not that precise. As Van der Leegte recalled, 'You were given a pile of drawings and could just figure out on your own which parts you wanted to supply.' The purchasing department were not tech-savvy and didn't really pay attention to prices, so were prone to taking offers at face value. Of course, some suppliers abused that trust and submitted highly inflated bills. If it was supplied to Veldhoven, you could get away with asking the higher price.

Orders from ASML soon accounted for half the revenue of Van der Leegte's business. This made him quite happy to be at the beck and call of ASML's chaotic schedule. Gerard didn't mind answering calls for a new order at ten o'clock in the evening or well into the weekend. But he refused to sign a contract that would commit him to grow at ASML's pace. That astute decision spared him from misery in the years when the chip market dipped. By the year 2000, when Gerard gave his toolmaking shop a more international-sounding name, GL Precision, he noticed the relationship with ASML had soured. 'It became far less friendly than it once was,' he recalled. It signaled the beginning of a much tighter procurement regime from the company.

The supply network was key in keeping Veldhoven competitive, fast and flexible. It was too important to be managed by the purchasing department alone. Each board member was assigned responsibility for several of the companies, needing to provide presentations on financial projections and explaining plans for the next generation of machines so manufacturers could sign up to supply parts. They also regularly put on get-togethers and networking events for the entrepreneurs to encourage a feeling of comradery. Rounds of golf racked up, an activity chosen for its easy pace, always topped off with drinks and dinner. Martin van den Brink, an early riser from the pool of engineers and already the bearer of ASML's technical conscience, usually only showed up towards the end of the day. Golf was never his thing.

The partner network grew, reaching some seven hundred companies in size. The majority were based in Brabant, but not far south in the Belgian city of Leuven sat one of the most important players: imec. Founded in 1984, just like ASML, this research institute spanned across several Flemish universities and afforded chip manufacturers and their suppliers the chance to work together on 'precompetitive' research. No one building a chip factory or fab wanted to run the risk of investing in the wrong technology – the costs in this industry are too unforgiving for that. All the steps needed to produce a working chip are intertwined, and even the smallest change can have a huge impact on the process as a whole. So imec established itself as a high-tech garage, a place for the entire industry to come and figure out its future.

Imec housed equipment from all the major suppliers. Everything from machines for measuring to etching and deposition – the application of new layers to the wafer – could be found in their cleanrooms. Initially these consisted of US-made lithography machines, but with European government support imec installed the first DUV systems from ASML in the early '90s. These used lasers to produce a deep ultraviolet light; compared to the standard mercury lamps, the light those generated had a far smaller wavelength, allowing for the imaging of smaller structures and far more complex chips.

From that moment on, all the major players in the semiconductor industry would stop by the high-tech lab in Leuven to experiment with the tool from Veldhoven. As ASML grew in importance, imec was better able to map out the road ahead and judge what innovations the coming years might bring.

At the end of the 1980s, imec's chief executive, Luc Van den hove was traveling around the world trying to decide between Japanese and American lithography machines. Never did he expect to find what he was looking for in Veldhoven, only a hundred kilometers away from where he started. According to Van den hove ASML's technology had clearly already been pioneering in those early years. But what stood out was the driven corporate culture, an ethos of total commitment, whipped up by none other than Martin van den Brink.

7

THE SPOUSE FROM
THE SOUTH

A visit to ASML's main supplier requires traveling further afield: six hundred kilometers to the southeast of Veldhoven to be precise. There, in the German state of Baden-Württemberg, lies the village of Oberkochen, home to the headquarters of German lens manufacturer Carl Zeiss.

When the shuttle from Aalen to Ulm stops at Oberkochen station in the evening, it doesn't take much to imagine that you're on vacation. The timber homes, the fresh mountain air: you could easily imagine settling into a German spa, drifting away in seclusion from the bustle of the world. Time seems to stand still in Oberkochen, but make no mistake – a leaflet in the station carries a clue from the Mayor, 'Wir machen Zukunft': Here, we make the future. This is all because of Zeiss. Known for its microscopes, glasses and camera lenses, the company usually supplies advanced optical equipment to hospitals and universities. But it also makes lens systems for lithography machines. To project the minute pattern of circuits onto the light-sensitive silicon disc, you need a lens that is beyond razor-sharp.

Oberkochen already had a strong tradition of metalworking and mechanical engineering before Zeiss came to town. Extensive mining meant German regions like Bavaria and Baden-Württemberg grew into heavily industrial areas. And as former Zeiss chief Hermann Gerlinger put it, people in these regions don't get itchy feet. They want to settle into the one company and 'focus'. This led to a boom in expertise and craftsmanship that stayed local, passed down and built on through the generations that lived and worked in these towns.

Around 150 years prior to this, researcher Carl Zeiss marketed his first microscope from his workshop in the German town of Jena. After the Second World War the city fell under the control of the Russians, however, and would later be demarcated as part of East Germany. Through Zeiss' supply of lenses to the German army, the Allies had become keenly aware of the company's strategic importance. US troops occupied the Zeiss factory in April 1945 and spent the following three months seizing its patents and tools. By 1946, the Americans had deported over 70 researchers and craftsmen from Zeiss to Heidenheim, then part of the Allied zone. It was from here that they went to work in nearby Oberkochen. The Russians then moved in; just as aware as the Americans of the importance of good lenses and mirrors for their weapons and spy systems, they looted what remained of the Zeiss plant in Jena. Ever since the invention of the binoculars, the optical sector has found itself embroiled in geopolitical maneuvering. Throughout history, any tool that can reveal what the enemy is up to has held immense strategic value.

It didn't take long in Oberkochen for Zeiss to re-establish itself as a renowned lens factory. In the early 1980s, they landed in the sights of the newcomer ASML as it sought the best glass for its machines. Zeiss SMT, the semiconductor division of the group, would go on to essentially merge with ASML in all but name.

But as Steef Wittekoek recalls, it was hardly love at first sight. In 1984, ASML's chief researcher was tasked with persuading Zeiss to make a highly specialized lens with the specifications ASML needed. The scientist responsible for the development of the wafer stepper had to convince the reluctant Germans that ASML was no novice. He's still not sure which was more challenging.

Exchanges were sharp and laced with skepticism. 'Are you *really* going to get the lenses for dozens of steppers from us?' Wittekoek countered: 'Is your glass supplier *really* good enough?' The Dutch also needed to see the exact designs of the lenses so they could calibrate the machines to get the best possible image from the glass. Wittekoek put in a request, but the Germans refused. 'That's our secret.' Trust was in short supply, and the two companies needed time to feel the other out.

With the success of ASML in the years that followed, the mutual dependency between the two companies grew. But the relationship was still fraught with tension. Zeiss' modus operandi was at complete odds with the volatile behavior of the chip market. Lens production involves months of cycles of measuring, polishing and remeasuring by hand. It asks for time and endless patience, something the engineers in Brabant clearly lacked.

The early days were marked by continuous negotiations, calls and late-night trips between Veldhoven and Oberkochen. Fortunately, there was a good hotel. ASML'ers took fondly to Das Goldene Lamm, nestled in nearby Unterkochen. The old brewery from four centuries ago became the place to meet for a beer or bite to eat with their colleagues from Zeiss. Little by little, they learned more about what made their counterparts tick.

However, there was a limit to the differences a few beers could absolve. The German tendency for properness and penchant for hierarchy could not be assailed with Dutch directness, and Zeiss' measured pace of production was completely out of sync with the dynamic nature of the semiconductor industry. Add to this Martin van den Brink's heated temperament, and it quickly became a recipe for disaster.

At the first meetings in Oberkochen, Steef Wittekoek served as a vital intermediary for the 'hard and volatile' Van den Brink, who had left the quiet lens experts stunned. 'For the Germans, it was good that I was there – I was more diplomatic. Seeing there were at least some respectable people at ASML made it easier to accept Martin's abrasive behavior. It was *Herr van den Brink* and *Herr Doktor Wittekoek*. In the end, I was like a guardian angel to him.'

PART II

THE BIG BOYS

A face full of fresh sea air can do wonders for new ideas.

It is springtime 1989, the year in which the Iron Curtain will fall, and the leadership of ASML is spending a weekend sailing on the Wadden Sea. As soon as the boat clears Harlingen harbor in the north of the Netherlands, a punishing headwind blows the entire management to the first buoy, sending them straight back to square one. They try not to read into it.

Reconvening under the hold to wait out the weather, they discuss ASML's fragile position. ASML wants to get ahead of the Japanese, but something needs to change if they are to take the wind out of market leader Nikon's sails. Until now, the Dutch have only supplied chip manufacturers just below the top of the market like Micron, AMD and TSMC, and sales are still small enough that any crisis could be the last. The big players like Motorola, Intel or IBM (the inventor of the personal computer) will need to see something truly special if they are to be won over, and the technology ASML has in-house is not enough to catch the interest of these chipmakers. Sales director Dick Aurelio knows this, and so, huddled in the belly of the boat, the question is put to leadership: 'Is there *anything* we can do to stand out and beat the Japanese?'

They may not know it yet, but the winds have already changed – a young engineer and project leader by the name of Martin van den Brink has been working on something new.

Coming up with memorable product names has never been ASML's strong suit. To outsiders, they read as nothing more than a random assortment of numbers and letters. But if the name of any device deserves to be remembered, then it is this one: the PAS 5500. This lithography machine turned out to be ASML's salvation, a lifeline for a company in danger of going under. And to this day the machine seems unstoppable; even thirty years later, the PAS 5500's are still stamping chips.

These machines were the first in the industry to utilize modular design. Broken down into roughly ten components, each of these parts are independently manufactured until, like pieces of a puzzle, they are clicked together in the factory to form a single working system. The lens, the wafer-table, the frame for the mask, the light source, the robot that picks the wafers: these are the Lego blocks that, when you bring them together, form a lithography system.

The individual modules are produced in series, making it easier to upgrade individual designs and swap out components at will. This way the machine you buy is never the final product: every part of the machine can be continually improved upon. Just like ratcheting in a new, more powerful engine for your car instead of forking out for a new one.

ASML set about building a prototype of the PAS 5500 in the spring of 1991. All the while, IBM kept a watchful eye on them. The big player from the US didn't dare blindly trust the unknown Dutch company, sending instead a bimonthly delegation to Veldhoven to inspect the progress. As February rolled around, Martin van den Brink, the architect of this machine, called his team together. IBM were about to do their last round of inspections. The plan: ten project leaders would present their module, after which a team would take these units and assemble the machine on the spot. Et voilà – a PAS 5500, ready to start spitting out wafers.

But three days before they were due to arrive, a call from IBM came through. A war in Iraq was looming, and with the announcement of Operation Desert Storm, American companies were banning their employees from flying internationally. Van den Brink could see where this was going. IBM would play it safe, staying with their Japanese competitor and leaving his project in the dust.

He refused to let that happen. That same weekend he recorded videos of Veldhoven's work and took the whole team to IBM's factory in Fishkill, New York, in a last-ditch attempt to salvage a deal. If they could not come to him, he would bring it to them – after all, the Dutch were not affected by the American flight ban. The stunt was a success; the video was enough to win over 'Big Blue'. The first big player was in.

However, 1991 and 1992 proved to be a financial disaster for ASML. The company sold only 36 lithography machines, nowhere near enough to offset the spiraling development costs of the PAS 5500. The project teams, spurred on by Van den Brink, were burning through far more money than ASML could afford. And by this time, he had already built a reputation as someone who not only refused to shy away from confrontation, but actively sought it out. It was his way of keeping people on their toes. As his former colleague Nico Hermans put it, 'Martin is quite unique, if a little autistic at times. But if you gain his trust, he will accomplish remarkable things.'

8

MOVING THE MOUNTAIN

Martin van den Brink snatches the microphone from the hands of the guide. 'I got a little emotional,' he later admitted – after all, he knew the place intimately, and there were stories he felt needed to be told. It is 2021, and along with a group of managers, Martin is taking a tour of the former Philips site in Eindhoven. Grasping the mic, he proceeds to tell the onlookers his own story. Gesturing towards a bench, he recounts sitting there in November 1983 after having applied for a role in the company. 'Philips used to let applicants drive up to the entrance in a taxi, just so you felt that little bit more important,' he recalled. 'But I hated it. So I told them, "You enjoy yourselves, I'm gonna go do something else." It was then that Wim Troost pulled out this leaflet for me to look at. "We're going to start a new company. It will involve lithography and it won't be called Philips anymore." I took one look at the leaflet and knew immediately: that's it. That's what we're gonna do. Just like that. Boom.'

That one impulse pulled the trigger for a long career at ASML. A talented engineer and influential project manager, Van den Brink quickly climbed to vice-president of technology in 1995. In 1999 he joined the board of directors while also heading the marketing department, and fourteen years later, he officially became president and chief technical officer. From then on, he wielded the final word on anything and everything ASML conjured up or brought to market.

Born in 1957, Martin van den Brink grew up in Bennekom, a small village in the province of Gelderland. His family had strong ties to the area: his parents were raised around the nearby Veenendaal, born into families of farmers from the Veluwe region. It's a beautiful area, dotted with cows, pigs and an impressive number of churches, where schisms fracture the religious landscape. Bennekom itself lies at the heart of the Dutch Bible Belt, a stretch of largely conservative Christian communities that runs across the heart of the Netherlands. If visiting on a Sunday, you would be hard pressed to find a shop open in these parts.

His father died young, suffering a heart attack when Martin was only nine years old. His mother raised the family as reformed Christians, and Martin, his sister and two brothers were told by the preacher from a young age that salvation was reserved only for God's chosen few. But Martin was of a different persuasion: he saw the burden and sorrow that such ideas could lead to. 'I hate it,' ten-year-old Martin told a shocked group of elders during a house call, 'and I can't stand the long hours in church.'

Instead, he sought his comfort in technology. Even in his early childhood, Van den Brink was curious about how things worked. He would buy his mum an assortment of devices for Mother's Day, gifting clocks or electronic lighters – just what every mother wants. And as soon as she was out of the house, the tools appeared. The devices would be splayed out across the table, awaiting Martin's fateful hand and probing screwdriver. And why not, he would think to himself as he resolutely drove the tool in. He just wanted to know how things were put together. After all, he had paid for it with his own savings.

School was difficult for the curious boy. Dyslexic in a time of little support for special needs, Van den Brink carved his own path via three levels of engineering school. It was a long route, and every step took him further from home. First came a technical secondary school in the town of Ede. He then studied electronics at a technical college in Apeldoorn. Finally, young Martin found himself studying engineering and technology at a higher level in Arnhem. Here he specialized in power electronics, qualifying him to control industrial motors and systems. He cut his teeth on a hefty graduation assignment, writing optimization software for a project so complex his teacher had been unable to finish it himself. The extreme level of abstraction had him hooked. Far more so than studying physics, although he would later receive a degree in that subject from the University of Twente.

As a student he was fascinated by energy transfer to an almost obsessive degree. This led him to specialize in district heating, a sector seemingly far removed from the world of lithography. But when Wim Troost showed him the brand-new brochure of the PAS 2000, his curiosity was piqued. The drive he had known from a young age struck him once more – this was a machine he wanted to get to the bottom of.

When he left for the south of the Netherlands to work at ASML, his mother asked one final time if he really needed to go. For her, leaving the region and going south of the rivers that divide the country was like moving a world away. But Martin was determined. The light of the machines in Veldhoven had lit a new path for the young man.

The second Martin stepped foot in the factory, Steef Wittekoek knew he had something special. Standing before him was an energetic and enthusiastic 27-year-old physicist, already an expert in electronics and mathematics. What more could he ask for? But as Wittekoek quickly found out, Martin was not one for restraint. The young ASML'er could erupt at any moment if he felt someone was talking nonsense or beating around the bush. You never had to wait long to know exactly what Martin thought.

As far as Martin was concerned, engineering consisted of solving problems, not avoiding them. Doing the job properly meant seeking them out so they could be dealt with now rather than left to cause problems later. To this extent, he really was suited to be a physicist. For both physics and engineering the overriding priority is to find out why something does or does not work, even if it means asking difficult questions or breaking with accepted norms. Nothing is off limits: why is a certain number that number? Why not double or half?

During technical discussions, Martin would probe the weak spots of every argument. He also had an uncanny sense for when someone was deflecting, never hesitating to confront them and pry them open, regardless of whether this was in front of colleagues, customers or suppliers. And if anyone thought they had a better idea – bring it on. You just had to be prepared for how it would be received if Martin thought otherwise. His second nature was to challenge the world around him, and this brazen and ruthless attitude would become one of the pillars of ASML.

Wittekoek took the unbridled young man under his wing, beginning a friendship that would at times resemble a father-son relationship. Steef could see that the loss of Martin's father had made the boy self-reliant from an early age. He was an independent spirit – sometimes to his own detriment. Together they regularly attended the Society of Photographic Instrumentation Engineers (or SPIE) conference in California; the meeting place for lithographers and companies from around the world to showcase their latest developments. The Dutch were fond of being recognizable at the conference, often donning colorful suits to stand out in the sea of gray and blue jackets. Martin was no different, never shying away from a pair of orange pants or a bright green tie with a suit to match. Initially Wittekoek led the presentations, until one year he let Martin take the lead. Unphased by the room full of potential clients, Martin did as Martin does: he provided brutally direct and honest replies to any questions that came his way.

ASML's commercial boss was fuming. 'That guy should never hold a presentation again, all he did was insult our customers.' Martin, on the other hand, was annoyed at being regarded as just 'some young boy'. They didn't take the Dutch rookie seriously.

Over time, Wittekoek helped polish the young man, taking care to show Van den Brink that there was more to life than technology. You were allowed to enjoy the moments in between all the work: the social side of touring conferences, the dinners, a glass or two of wine after a long day. 'He got to see that I had a life outside of my work, with my own family, and he noticed how much joy I got from that. For Martin at this time, that was an eye-opener.'

In the week following these SPIE conferences, the pair would often visit US chip manufacturers, leaving the weekend free to go skiing in Idaho or Lake Tahoe. Standing at the top of a Black Diamond run, they always wondered if they would dare, or if they would even survive, before taking the plunge down the icy slopes.

Both Martin and ASML were well suited for taking risks, Wittekoek believes. 'We had our backs against the wall in our early days. It was all or nothing for ASML. And in those moments – this is something I did learn from Martin – sometimes you have to be hard on people to get results.'

Wittekoek saw the same drive and determination in Martin's skiing. While Steef would gracefully carve his way round the slopes, respecting the path nature had offered, his young colleague would barrel over the mounds of snow with full force. When Martin saw the path he wanted to take, not even a mountain could stand in his way.

This sheer determination also came with its quirks. With his head in the clouds, he would often lose his boarding passes or leave his passport behind during trips. Martin didn't seem to think much of these things. His mind was on more important matters. No trip was complete without someone running after him, delivering forgotten documents.

One such time, as Wittekoek and Van den Brink arrived at their hotel near Lake Tahoe, they hopped out of their rental car to quickly check in. The doors slammed shut, locking the car with the engine still running and the key in the ignition. Like good physicists, they were intrigued by the question of how long a stationary car could keep turning, after which they went to have a bite to eat and retired to their rooms. Only the next morning, when the engine appeared to still be running, did they call the rental company to ask if someone could come and open the car.

Martin frequently appeared to be in his own world. But what looked like absentmindedness from the outside was actually a remarkable ability to zero in and maintain focus on intractable technical problems, whether it be for hours, days, or even years.

9

THE MONEY PRINTER

Sometimes history gets in the way.

The PAS 5500 was a hit, but deliveries were slow. Zeiss was failing to keep up with the demand for lenses, creating a bottleneck in Oberkochen and leaving a growing number of machines stranded in Veldhoven awaiting their optical systems. However, this time the fault didn't lie with the arduous production process, but the historical upheaval in Germany. Following the fall of the Iron Curtain, Zeiss reunited with its sister plant in the now former East German city of Jena and sunk into debt. With money cautiously starting to trickle into Veldhoven, ASML was just about able to scrape together a loan to rescue its top supplier. With the blockage resolved, the machines started to move out and the money started to flow in. In 1993, the company made a profit for the first time, and in 1994 more than a hundred lithography machines were sold. Two years later, this figure would double.

Meanwhile, another major player was starting to eye up ASML's machines. The South Korean manufacturer Samsung had become interested in using ASML's devices for producing memory chips. Standards had slipped with their current Japanese supplier Nikon, who had been delivering devices with faulty lenses and refusing to follow up on the Koreans' complaints. This deeply angered Samsung, and created just the opportunity ASML was looking for. However, convincing the Koreans to change supplier was another story. Aware they held the upper hand, Samsung plied ASML with requests for highly specialized devices in line with exhaustive lists of standards. Yet ASML could only supply its factory-issued machines. There was little capacity for customization, let alone to the degree Samsung were asking.

Tempers ran high during discussions in Seoul. The Korean company was marked by an uncompromising ruthlessness – given the exceptionally tight margins of the memory chip game, everything was about efficiency. Best of luck to anyone responsible for a delay, as might happen if a lithography machine jammed. The ensuing meetings were more like interrogations. Passports were taken upon landing in South Korea, after which the ASML'ers were whisked away for 'negotiations'. In between the yelling, everything from chalk markers, plates, ashtrays and coffee cups flew through the air. Anything within reach was permissible.

Nevertheless, in 1995 an agreement was reached, much to the delight of Veldhoven and anyone who had to frequent these meetings. ASML now had to expand to cope with the sudden increase in demand, but there was no building space around the main property. However, Chris van Kasteren, a former milkman with remarkable financial foresight, had a solution. The A67 highway south of Veldhoven was lined with grasslands owned by local farmers. Using his connections in the community, Van Kasteren managed to procure large swathes of these meadows. With the land he made available, ASML had enough room to expand – for the time being.

Architect Rob van Aken was tasked with keeping the designs mostly functional. The most important requirement was for the buildings to be separable so they could be sold off should ASML almost inevitably fall into trouble. One thing is for sure: no one else would ever be able to make full use of the constructional extravaganza in Veldhoven; thick vibration-dampening floors, suspended foundations and state-of-the-art clean rooms – all without a speck of dust.

By this point, ASML had outgrown the graceful pyramid that once enveloped it. The number of engineers and system architects was rapidly increasing, and more office space was needed around the cleanrooms to house the now bulging development departments. These were the driving force of the company, its beating heart with only one goal: to develop new technology faster than the Japanese competition, and with it, to poach the big players from their grasp. And step by step, their plan was beginning to work. Their strategy was focused on 'adding value' for the chipmakers, offering tools that could expose as many wafers per hour with as few defects as possible. Lithography technology is essentially a printing press, and the standards that make for a desirable machine are no different. Only rather than books, papers or dollar bills, these machines print semiconductors. And with these, you can make billions of dollars.

Chief executive Willem Maris had a fondness for self-deprecation. He was frequently seen roaming from meeting to meeting, exclaiming what a sight it would be if real management got hold of the company. Business operations at ASML hardly exemplified the efficiency they promised of their machines, but so long as they kept the money flowing in no one really cared. Maris, who transferred from the Philips factory, was himself a former top tennis player. As an 18-year-old mechanical engineering student he became the Dutch singles champion, much to his and everyone's surprise. But, as Maris told newspaper De Telegraaf in 1958, he didn't see a sporting career on the horizon. Now that he was champion he would always be expected to win, something that 'tends to suck all the joy out of playing.' If there's no fun in doing it, forget about it.

In Maris, ASML had found an accessible leader. He tucked his office in an inconspicuous corner of the building, preferring to be nestled amongst the rest of his workers rather than isolated on the highest floor. From here, he would often wander through the halls of the company, always keen for a chat. With his neatly slicked-back hair and approachable demeanor, Maris struck the figure of a natural salesman. He was also not one for confrontations, preferring to let people have their say before calmly presenting his thoughts and leaning on his fellow board members to cast the opinion in more difficult situations.

It was an approach that suited ASML's horizontal structure. Maris fostered a feeling of togetherness, even among suppliers who were being asked to take risks and grow in line with ASML's expansion. For the partnership with Zeiss, an essential supplier, he came up with the slogan *Two companies, one business.* For all the ups and downs and contractions in the market, he made sure there was never any doubt about their position: there was a common goal, and so the best way to reach it was by working together.

Maris was also the one who managed to retain Martin van den Brink when he was on the cusp of jumping ship. The design of the recent 5500 model had eaten up too much of the budget, and Martin was not granted permission to develop a new machine. The blueprints began to gather dust in a bottom drawer. Frustrated, he considered leaving for Varian, an American supplier in the industry who offered him a position as chief technology officer. Without the freedom and resources to keep innovating, he saw no future for himself and ASML. 'And so I thought: time to move on.'

As he was finishing packing his bags for Silicon Valley, he decided to visit his former colleague Frits van Hout. Despite having left for a leadership position at a Swiss company in the crisis of 1992, Van Hout encouraged Martin to rethink his decision: would he really feel at home in an American organization, let alone at a company where he would need to prove himself all over again?

News of Van den Brink's impending departure reverberated throughout the chip industry. The word travelled to Maris via AMD, who asked the CEO if he was aware that his most important technician wanted to leave. The startled Maris took heed of the warning and promptly gave in to Van den Brink's demands. The latter found himself at the helm of the research and development department in Veldhoven, and, at his insistence, ASML began building 'scanners'. The machines were quickly named the 'Step & Scan', a variant of a technology developed by the American competitor PerkinElmer. The scanner operates with a beam of light, similar to a photocopier, which glides across the mask while the wafer moves in the opposite direction, resulting in an increased sharpness of the lines exposed on the chip. Imagine an Olympic runner that, with a pen in one hand and paper in the other, could start sprinting and still manage to produce a highly precise drawing. This gives you an idea of the kind of tightly orchestrated high-tech dance these machines are designed to perform. The 5500 also received a new light source, utilizing for the first time deep ultraviolet light, or DUV for short. Wittekoek and Van den Brink had to persuade Zeiss to adapt their lens design, and went as far as providing the specifications for doing so. This rubbed the Germans the wrong way: these belligerent Dutch know-it-alls thought they were better than their own experts.

With DUV and the scanner now under their belt, the team from Veldhoven finally had the tools to give Canon and Nikon a run for their money. The American competitors had already fallen behind, but more capital was still needed to make the leap to first place. Henk Bodt, advising from Philips, deemed going public would be ASML's best bet. External financiers had so far proven difficult to bring in; according to Bodt, 'they were only interested in your business if you were nearly belly-up.'

In 1995 ASML entered the American stock market NASDAQ along with the AEX in Amsterdam. To ensure they retained their pool of talent, a group of forty workers deemed the most valuable were offered share packages, but only on the condition that they couldn't sell their stake until four years after the company was listed. Thirty technicians and ten managers made the cut. Yet the company's works council was deeply outraged when it turned out that it was mostly high-ranking managers that were receiving the shares. The Council felt ASML's success should benefit everyone, not enrich a select group. As a result, those who didn't receive the package were instead offered an alternative stock option plan.

The timing was unfortunate for Frits van Hout, who had been long considering a return to Veldhoven. He entered into talks with the company in 1995 but found himself just too late to reap the benefits of this deal. It wasn't until 2001 that, at Martin's request, he would take the leap and go back to ASML. As he put it, 'In my heart, I never left.'

The IPO took place in March of that year to great success but muted celebrations. The champagne corks would only fly a few years later when the stocks freed up and Veldhoven suddenly found itself home to forty new millionaires. While much of the newfound wealth found its way to beautiful homes and new cars for the whole family, none of the spending was outrageous. At ASML, it is considered bad manners to flaunt your wealth. It can only distract from what really matters.

If you invested one dollar in ASML in 1995 and held onto it until 2024, you would be looking at a share worth more than six hundred times that (including dividends). The success on the market spelled a variety of fortunes for those involved. Philips reduced its stake in ASML after 1995 to 23 percent, and from 2001 would start to decrease that minority interest further. Richard George, ASML's project leader from the very beginning, sold his shares as quickly as possible. Too quickly, as he admitted with a laugh: 'If I had kept hold of them, I would have been close to 100 million better off. Can you imagine!' There was no bitterness, but only pride that his work contributed to the financial success of the company.

Some missed the golden ticket altogether. Joop van Kessel, the chief operating officer who set up the ASML organization in 1984, had perhaps the most cause for remorse. He deliberately declined the option plan, later calculating with his wife that he missed out on around 10 million euros. 'Quite a lot of money,' as he acknowledges now. But at that moment he couldn't stand the thought of taking a up a new role in Korea, where ASML still had to accommodate the extremely demanding memory chip manufacturers and provide them with flawless machines. 'That was a job for someone in their forties, not someone in their sixties.' A hefty price, but one he never regretted paying.

All this time, a young accountant from Deloitte had been assisting ASML with the preparation of their IPO. His name was Peter Wennink, and years later he would find himself at the helm of ASML, shaking hands with President Joe Biden.

10

THE QUICK LEARNER

'Do you want me to take over from you?'

It was 1997, and Peter Wennink was standing on the golf course with ASML's financial director Gerard Verdonschot. The released ASML shares had soared in value, meaning the money was no longer some distant promise. With these newfound riches in the palm of his hand, Verdonschot was considering his options carefully.

Wennink, the chartered accountant from Deloitte, could well see himself as financial director in Veldhoven. He was taken by the rawness of the culture at ASML: the experience for him was like night and day when compared to the world of accounting and consulting. There, everyone's only concern was how their own business was doing, and they kept an envious eye on their associates' turnover. He grew tired of the fragile egos, of being surrounded by smiles from people you knew would gladly take a knife to your back the second it was turned. Make no mistake: at ASML, you could easily find the wind knocked out of you, but it would be to your face in the middle of the day at a boardroom meeting. And it was never personal – everyone knew where they stood, precisely because ASML was never about individuals or about status, but about fulfilling a shared mission.

This was a place where Wennink felt at home. Although hardly tech-savvy, he was at least a quick learner.

Born in 1957, Peter Wennink was raised in the small town of Huizen, set on the shores of the Gooimeer. From its harbor you can easily catch sight of the dikes that line the other side of the lake. These mark the shores of Flevoland – the twelfth province of the Netherlands, wrought from the sea by the Dutch in the '60s.

Raised in a large Catholic family as one of six children, the path to studying was not a given for Wennink. His father drew electronic circuit diagrams for the Philips branch in Huizen, but his passion was always to work with the land. He instead married a farmer's daughter, and compensated by spending as much time as possible tending to his garden. He could never quite wrap his head around the world his son moved within or what it meant to be in the upper echelons of corporate life. 'My friends say that you're doing something important,' he would tell his son.

Wennink was taught from an early age to 'know your place'. 'Born a dime, never a quarter,' as his grandmother would say: a Dutch proverb meaning once poor, always poor. The world was divided; it was a simple fact that some were more important than others, and he should be mindful to respect those above him. Aspire beyond your level, and you would only find disappointment. This belief caused great difficulties for the young Wennink, instilling a nervousness that manifested itself in a stammer. As he put it, 'I had the feeling there was something out there for me, the desire to go be part of something – but also always felt that no matter what I did, I would never truly belong.'

At his high school in Bussum, the young Peter received lessons on arithmetic and accounting from a substitute teacher by the name of Rob Boelen. A partner at the accountancy firm Deloitte, he had only taken up the position at the school as a way of avoiding military service, but he immediately recognized the numerical talent of the young student from Huizen. 'I can still picture him, standing in his shorts in front of the blackboard,' reflected Boelen. 'Although he came from a humble background, he was an exceptionally quick learner.' He asked Peter to join Deloitte once his final exams were over; first as an assistant, but later as a partner.

Peter had his heart set on student life, but a lack of money proved insurmountable. He ended up taking evening classes to become a chartered accountant, before beginning his military service in 1977.

Surrounded by soldiers from all walks of life, his eyes were opened to a world beyond the close confines of the Gooi region. As a numbers man, Wennink was given the responsibility of managing the payroll of a company of two hundred soldiers. 'I always held this sense of responsibility,' he later reflected. 'That's the story of my life.' Even back home, everyone assumed he was the eldest, despite being the second child. Stepping up to a position of accountability came naturally to him, and he extended his military service by three months.

At Deloitte, he was exposed to an entirely new environment – this was the world of international business. Together with Boelen, Wennink embarked on trips to Arizona and New York to audit ASM International's US reports. In this life of chartered accountants, evenings were for fine dining and lofty conversations with clients. Peter had no trouble adapting to this, with the pleasure-seeker in him quickly taking to the newfound freedom. He lived for good food and drink, learning to cook with great flair. He also had an affinity for fine wine, a hobby he took to the moment he first tasted wine at his high school graduation party (from a box, admittedly, but still from a good year). The first check he ever wrote from his Deloitte salary went to a restaurant, and the second to a liquor store.

Boelen taught Wennink the ins and outs of good leadership. Essential to making your life easier was to delegate, to surround yourself with people that would become better at what they did than you ever could. Yet Boelen also learned from his apprentice, who had a gift in dealing with people. 'Peter knows how to listen: it was entirely from him that I picked up the art of having patience with people. I was always taught to be strict, but he was more empathetic, more light-hearted.'

However, despite standing at 1.96 meters tall, Wennink still acted with his colleagues at Deloitte as if it was he who needed to look up to them. Whether this was a hangover from his upbringing or due to the stammer that plagued him, the hierarchical nature of the company only exacerbated this feeling. This didn't go unnoticed by Rob Boelen. 'He would insist on calling me "Mr. Boelen", and I would always tell him, "Peter, please, stop calling me that."'

In late 1994, Wennink heard that ASML wanted to go public. ASML was wholly owned by Philips, so it seemed certain the latter's accountant KPMG would be the one to lead the IPO. But Wennink sensed an opportunity. Seizing the moment, he bluffed his way through the selection committee with a hastily prepared presentation and a fictional team of employees, and landed the assignment for Deloitte. He had never done an IPO before, and lacked the papers to arrange a NASDAQ listing. But with months of hard work, and a hefty dose of luck, in 1995 the IPO was successful. That one bluff, the one moment he believed in himself the same way that he looked at others, determined the rest of his career. Proof that a dime can become a quarter after all.

Rob Boelen set about preparing his apprentice to become chairman of the partnership, the highest position at Deloitte Netherlands. But midway through an assessment review, Wennink dropped the news: he would be joining ASML. Boelen tried to talk him out of it, but it was a lost cause. The decision was made. 'He got the bug. I had to let him go.'

Henk Bodt, chairman of the supervisory board at ASML, noticed that he didn't just have a new numbers man in Wennink, but also someone who could quickly build relationships and was talented in communicating with customers. The new 'relationship man' Wennink was immediately put to work; talking to the CEOs of chip manufacturers along with Martin van den Brink and ASML's new British chief executive Doug Dunn. Getting things done requires making acquaintances, listening, gaining trust. This is how deals are closed – and these were all qualities that came natural to him. Dunn, the successor to Willem Maris, could also see his talent. 'Peter is a creative businessman. I always knew he would eventually lead ASML.'

Wennink felt liberated by the culture at ASML. No one set themselves above another, and everyone, including the leaders, were held accountable. He even stopped stuttering. 'Within ASML, it's all about humility. It's not about you, but the bigger goal we all want to achieve together.'

Nonetheless, for the first year he still steered well clear of Van den Brink, who didn't spare anyone from his painfully aggressive outbursts. All Wennink could say was: 'He scares the freaking hell out of you.'

11

DOUG'S IRON FIST

At the end of the '90s, ASML underwent a changing of the old guard. CEO Maris departed in 1999, leaving only three months to show his successor the ropes. Maris' replacement was the former head of Philips' semiconductor division and British national Doug Dunn, who was brought in to whip ASML into shape. It was now a publicly listed company, and shareholders had started to keep a keener eye on their wallets. They demanded tangible results. Dunn's mission was clear: ASML needed to work more efficiently, or they would not stand a chance of keeping up their pace of growth. And so, together with the bright-eyed Peter Wennink, he set out to instill greater discipline within the organization.

Producing over 200 lithography machines annually (and, in 2000 the number was to surge to 368) required constant tight-knit coordination between the designers, the factory, the procurement department, and the customer service division. However, ASML was not a well-oiled machine. Kinks in the process were still being worked out, and ASML's project leaders showed little concern for controlling costs. They were wholly focused on getting the scanners built and sent to the manufacturers as quickly as possible. Simultaneously keeping a lid on spending was never on the cards.

So Dunns first task was to bring the tech-heads back to earth and introduce them to the reality of financial responsibilities. However, he soon found that attention at ASML would quickly fade at the mention of stringent supplier regulations and inventory management. Eyes would roll and bodies would slump back: they had better things to think about.

Although such disinterest is common among engineers, the reason so many felt at home in Veldhoven was precisely because of the harmony between their values and the culture of the company. ASML had its roots firmly in the Rhenish model, in which money isn't the sole benchmark of success and profit is only really visible over the long term. In the economies of Rhenish countries, such as Switzerland, Germany, and France, solidarity and craftmanship are traditionally deemed far more important than a polished set of quarterly figures. This is why ASML sought its suppliers for their most essential components in these regions: they value what matters the most in high-tech manufacturing. However, as the company and its worth grew, a style of management started to seep in from a world that revolves around short-term profit and the satisfaction of shareholders: the Anglo-Saxon style.

Few things are more Anglo-Saxon than a British CEO, apart from a British CEO with a Scottish right-hand man. For ASML this was Stuart McIntosh, a former chief operating officer at Philips with an accent so strong it took many in Veldhoven more than a second to realize he was speaking English. McIntosh quickly took the lead on overseeing the day-to-day affairs, allowing Dunn to step back and maintain a more remote and supervisory presence.

Veldhoven now had no choice but to become familiar with the Anglo-Saxon way of working. Under Willem Maris you could feel comfortable expressing disagreement or questioning your superiors. Now ASML had become a place where one had to be far more mindful of their words. This did not sit well with the employees. Not only that, but as Steef Wittekoek observed, Doug tended to 'shoot from the hip', expressing himself in a hard and rude manner without nuance or consideration for who might get caught on the other end.

The duo further failed to win over hearts with their double act during meetings. For example: one time, while an employee was struggling to address a difficult question, Stuart leaned over to Doug and asked – audible to all – 'What do you think, want to hear the rest or shall we call it quits here?' He then sharply turned to the worker. 'If that's all you have to offer... then hopefully your successor can do a little better.'

Despite this, chairman of the board Henk Bodt was pleased with the rigidity of Dunn's command. So long as the Brit had a grip on the finances and Martin van den Brink still felt free to do what he needed to do, the company stood a chance of continuing its growth. Dunn himself actually enjoyed his time at ASML, though admitted he was 'not the easiest to work with' while in Veldhoven. It would take some time before he mellowed out.

Those who worked with Dunn state that not much was needed to bring out the jerk in him. And even with that attitude, he was still unable to prevent his company sleepwalking into a crisis. By January 2001, not much seemed to be wrong. Although signs indicated there would be a mild downturn, the annual report was still optimistic. Official plans estimated that 500 lithography systems would need to be produced to meet demand. But internally, ASML estimated they could sell seven to eight hundred, nearly twice the amount as the previous year.

All of a sudden, the market crashed. The dot-com bubble had already burst in March 2000, but now the internet companies were starting to drag the tech sector into the downturn. This then spread to chip manufacturers and their suppliers, and to the suppliers who provided the suppliers and so on. The whole production chain had ground to a halt.

Instead of 700 machines, ASML sold a measly 197. Hundreds of millions of euros worth of surplus inventory filled the books, and cancellations from chip manufacturers poured in daily. On paper, the company was bankrupt. Radical cost-cutting measures would be needed. Around this time, Dunn confided to an analyst, 'We're in free fall, and to be frank, I can't see the bottom.'

The Anglo-Saxon spirit stirred. Dunn dug in, making short work of his purchasing obligations, a regulation that allowed suppliers to limit their risk in the event that ASML reduced orders. The state of affairs was rammed home to suppliers: 'This is how the industry works – get used to it. There will be a downturn every five years. Everyone knows this. You need to be as flexible as ASML. One year orders could double, the next they could half. Either get with the program, or get lost.'

'Banging your fist on the table' was his name for this approach. The only problem was Dunn had a knack for punching it through.

Harry van Hout, who had been supplying ASML through his company VHE since 1984, ran into trouble when his turnover dramatically dropped from 30 to 12 million euros. The bank was breathing down his neck: he had already laid off 100 people and was losing millions on inventory. The family business was on the verge of collapse. Van Hout strode into the office of the procurement department at ASML, tossed their agreement on the desk and gave an ultimatum. Supply needed to continue and he needed to be paid according to the contract: a deal is a deal. The purchaser took one look and swept the contract off the table. Their response: either ASML goes bankrupt, or the suppliers do.

VHE ended up drawing the short straw. Fortunately, Van Hout had a plan. Bankruptcy was declared Wednesday afternoon, and by Friday he was already back to supplying ASML.

The relationship with Zeiss also soured over ASML's abrupt reduction of orders. But as far as Dunn was concerned, it was up to the Germans to suck it up. 'In this world, you need to have your eye on the ball. It's pointless producing so much in advance. By the time you're done chip manufacturers will want something else anyway.'

True to their word, ASML followed up the spat by asking Zeiss to prepare for the next technological leap, which involved bringing in new materials, taking on additional staff and expanding capacity. But the Germans were reluctant to risk more money on behalf of such an unpredictable and rude client.

COO McIntosh pulled no punches with Zeiss' management. Following an extensive VIP tour of Zeiss' new factory and cleanrooms, the otherwise incomprehensible Scot left nothing on the table before leaving for his taxi. 'This all looks nice – you must be very proud. But in the end, you're a shitty supplier that doesn't deliver what we need.'

In Oberkochen, after another meeting, Dunn and Martin left the building and began the long journey back to Veldhoven. Even Martin, the loudest voice in most rooms, thought his CEO had crossed the line.

'Doug, you're pushing them too hard. We need Zeiss, and they're doing their best.'

II – THE BIG BOYS

He knew the relationship with Zeiss was essential for ASML's future, something Doug quietly recognized. 'Martin was already sorting out the inefficiencies at Zeiss, and then I started amplifying the problems.' Some things never change: Doug would always be ready to jump in guns blazing.

As soon as they hit the autobahn, they put the pedal to the metal. It was going to be a long five hours back to Brabant.

12

THE COMPASSION OF
GEORGE W. BUSH

On Tuesday, October 16, 2001, one month after the attack on the Twin Towers in New York City, ASML declared a state of emergency. The press release got straight to the point: 'As a result of the ongoing crisis in the semiconductor industry, ASML Holding NV announces that it will cut 23 percent of its global workforce, amounting to 2000 workers in total.'

The timing was poor, but they had their reasons. Doug Dunn had just acquired an American competitor, Silicon Valley Group (SVG). With SVG on board, ASML's workforce doubled overnight to around eight thousand employees. But almost a quarter of these workers needed to go. Dunn had set his sights on attracting Intel, the last remaining large client of SVG. He saw the move as ASML's quickest way to market leadership, provided the American president was on board. For the first time, Veldhoven was about to be subject to the whims of world politics.

Dunn had met Intel CEO Craig Barrett at a fundraiser in 2000 for then American presidential candidate George W. Bush. While Bush was busy preaching his 'conservatism with compassion' to the voters, Barrett disclosed to Dunn that Intel was facing a problem. The chip manufacturer was being supplied by both Nikon and SVG and was using machines from both lithography companies in their factories. Yet the success of Taiwanese chip manufacturer TSMC with ASML's equipment had not passed him by. With promising new technology from SVG failing to get off the ground, Barrett had made up his mind. He wanted to try out the Dutch machines.

However, Intel was under pressure to keep SVG alive. Their collapse would cause an acute problem for Intel's factories, which actively ran about two hundred of their machines. Furthermore, this would mean the end of the last remnant of American-owned lithography technology, already a sensitive matter in Washington. The superpower would not want to relinquish the ability to produce chips on home soil with homegrown equipment.

Barrett saw the solution standing in front him: Doug Dunn. He knew ASML was already in talks with SVG, so the Intel CEO encouraged Dunn to buy the company. American lithography technology would at least remain in Western hands, and Intel could make use of ASML's machines while also guaranteeing the continuity of the existing machines. In turn, the Dutch company would finally achieve its dream and leap to market leader. It was a win-win-win situation.

In October 2000, ASML announced the takeover of the Silicon Valley Group to the tune of 1.6 billion dollars, paid with stock. However, the deal could only proceed if the Committee on Foreign Investment in the United States (CFIUS) granted approval. This was the body responsible for assessing the threat foreign companies posed if they acquired crucial American technology. And so ASML came head-to-head with the policymakers in Washington, the city where economic logic competes with national security. It's hard to call the winner in matchups like this. As Doug Dunn puts it: 'There's reality, and there's politics.'

Relaxing in his vacation home in Spain towards the end of 2000, Dunn heard the phone ring. He had been summoned. That Monday he would need to be at the Pentagon, where CFIUS would be holding a meeting at the US Department of Defense in a small room on the second floor. Dunn just about made it, immediately apologizing to the committee members as he walked in the door. He had come directly from his flight, and with no time to change he was still dressed in his vacation outfit.

The discussions with CFIUS were conducted together with Peter Wennink. Given the political reactions unleashed by the SVG acquisition, the committee at the Pentagon pulled the ASML representatives through the wringer and back. It was now Dunn's turn to be on the other side of the table.

SVG was comprised of multiple companies, each requiring their own in-depth assessment and posing potential challenges. A stumbling block proved to be Tinsley Laboratories, an operation that polished lenses for military applications and espionage satellites. And there was another challenge; SVG held the license for a relatively undeveloped lithography technique, utilizing light with a much tighter wavelength – known as extreme ultraviolet light, or EUV for short.

Having caught wind of proceedings, a group of lobbyists converged to urge the government agencies that it was a matter of national security to keep SVG American. Opposing them was the lobby from Intel and the semi-conductor industry association SIA. They claimed that the acquisition was necessary to advance lithography technology, which was squarely in America's interest.

The CFIUS case ended up lasting months, with opponents of the deal going to great lengths to discredit ASML. No secrets were safe: any skeletons tucked away were prized out and thrust into the spotlight. Chairman of the supervisory board Henk Bodt found himself in a tough spot. He also served as a board member of Delft Instruments, a company that had supplied banned night vision equipment to Iraq during the first Gulf War. However, he came through unscathed: this was some years before Bodt actually joined Delft Instruments.

One of the parties opposing the acquisition was Ultratech, a competitor embroiled in a patent dispute with ASML. But by far the most outspoken opponent was a man by the name of Edward Dohring, the former CEO of SVG. He feared that America was losing essential lithography technology, and that countries hostile to the States would be able to build significantly faster chips if they gained access to it. In April of 2001, with YouTube still a distant dream, US congress members got a videotape in their mailboxes. The title left little room for interpretation: 'Why the Sale of SVG Co. is bad for the United States.' Six hundred and fifty copies of the tape found their way to the Pentagon and the Department of Commerce. Even George W. Bush, freshly inaugurated as the 43rd president of the United States, received a copy. After all, he carried the final word on the SVG acquisition. Bush demanded an extra two weeks. This would take some consideration.

Meanwhile The Hague was growing impatient. With the Cold War over and globalization firmly on the rise, they were at a loss as to why the US was causing such a great fuss over what was in their eyes a simple acquisition. Exasperated, Minister of Economic Affairs Annemarie Jorritsma cornered the US ambassador, insisting on a swift resolution. 'She firmly stated her annoyance,' was the report from her spokesperson in the national newspaper NRC.

Looking back, Doug Dunn can only scoff: 'No one puts pressure on the US. As soon as they say it's a matter of national security, it's game over.' Nothing any Dutch politician could say would carry any weight, least of all cause George Bush to change his mind.

The acquisition was approved in late May 2001. That was not due to Jorritsma's discontent, nor an act of compassion from Bush. What sealed the deal was the backing of Intel: their strong links with the United States Department of Defense had given it the push that was needed. ASML complied with the requests of CFIUS and sold the parts considered too sensitive in the American's eyes, including Tinsley Laboratories.

Once more, ASML had found itself on the receiving end of what amounted to interrogations. The CFIUS talks were highly intense cross-examinations: fifteen experts from all the relevant US ministries would spend hours bombarding Dunn and Wennink with questions. After the second meeting Dunn was so disoriented he walked straight out without stopping to pick up his leather winter coat from the Pentagon cloakroom, only realizing in the car on the way to the airport. Sheepishly, he called the Pentagon to ask if they could send him his coat.

But the wheels of US bureaucracy are slow to turn. Close to two years later, just before he resigned from ASML, a package arrived. Inside was his leather coat, along with a greeting from the Pentagon. An unexpected souvenir from ASML's encounter with the hornet's nest in Washington. 'It was probably bugged,' Dunn grins.

ASML had managed to secure Intel as a customer via SVG. However, the delay in Washington meant the deal was closed amid the dot-com crisis. The stock price halved within a year, as did the revenue, and investors were demanding measures be taken. By the end of 2001, around 1100 employees had lost their jobs. Many ASML'ers couldn't understand why they had burdened themselves with SVG, especially in the middle of a crisis. The takeover had only sped up the inevitable: it had become a matter of when not if Intel would make the switch to Veldhoven. In their eyes, Dunn had caused unnecessary misery by obtaining a dying competitor that made exclusively 'old crap'.

Across the pond, there were just as many doubts among the new American employees. Who did these Dutch think they were to swan in like this? And where on earth is Veldhoven?

SVG had a branch in Wilton, a village typical of small-town America nestled in the woods of Connecticut. Although unassuming, important chapters in the history of lithography were written in this town. Wilton was once home to PerkinElmer, the company interested in Philips' wafer-steppers in the early 1980s. It had been manufacturing advanced lenses as far back as the Second World War, and in the late '60s was commissioned by the Department of Defense to design lithography machines that would produce chips for military applications. They also made the lenses for the Hubble Space Telescope but had to pay millions when NASA found out – after the launch – that the telescope was unable to focus properly and had to be upgraded. Eventually, they fell behind developments in lithography, and found themselves taken over by SVG.

Doug Dunn had been entirely preoccupied with snagging Intel, believing that SVG had nothing special in-house that other companies could not offer as well. The extensive expertise in Wilton begged to differ. They crafted catadioptric lenses, made up of a complex combination of lenses and mirrors. They also built wafer-tracks, the machines that apply the light-sensitive layer to silicon discs.

But ASML was not at all interested. They wanted to remain a one trick pony, focusing all their efforts on producing the lithography machine, the most expensive piece of equipment in a chip factory.

And so, in November 2001, large swathes of the technology at svg were declared redundant and development was ordered to desist. This went down horribly in Wilton. 'Something I had worked on for twenty years was suddenly worthless,' recalled Christopher ('call me Chip') Mason. Mason had been a long-esteemed researcher at the company, frequently lauded for his pioneering work. Yet he suddenly felt totally superfluous. It would take years before he could finally get on board with ASML's approach.

To reconcile the bad blood between the employees in Wilton and Veldhoven, ASML brought into production a full-color staff magazine: *Spectrum*. The second issue carried an interview with Martin van den Brink, who had since risen to be a member of the board of directors. He talked the usual talk about the need for speed and risk-taking in the chip industry, but Van den Brink knew he had other problems. He had to figure out how to forge one company from not only two lithography programs, but two groups of stubborn and bitter engineers.

For the interview he posed with his horse on the cover, clad head-to-toe in Western attire. Action photos of him galloping past the camera adorned the inner pages. The message: there was a cowboy inside every ASML'er, and Martin was already giving his one-trick pony the spurs.

The horse was named 'Harry', as was his previous owner – Martin liked to name his horses after the person he bought them from, for ease of memory. But the results of the photo shoot didn't sit well with him. He felt these pictures of him and Harry placed him unjustly on a pedestal. People might get the wrong idea that ASML was all about him, or worse, that he thought himself the center of ASML's universe.

13

THE TWO CASH COWS

Around 2001 the chip industry faced an important decision. What would be the next wavelength for lithography machines? The chip factories were pushing for lines thinner than 100 nanometers (100 millionths of a millimeter) as smaller wavelengths meant the ability to project far finer chip-structures. All the current technology offered was a broad-tip marker, and they were searching for a fine liner.

Every advance by ASML in reducing the wavelength was followed by adjusting the resolution of the projected lines. This meant improving the lenses in the new machines, with each step requiring a larger aperture. The physical phenomenon is described by the Rayleigh formula, and every tech-head in the industry knows it by heart. As soon as the physical border of the lens comes into view, it is time for a new light source. You can think of this as swapping the color, although at this point, they all remain invisible to the human eye which only sees rainbow-range wavelengths between 400 and 750 nanometers (or violet to red).

In the '90s, ASML had replaced their mercury lamps, limited to 365 nanometers, with lasers capable of producing deep ultraviolet light, initially at 248 and ultimately 193 nanometers. But the chip industry needed more. The limits of what was possible with 193 nanometer lithography were close to being exhausted. A new number was floated: 157 nanometers. Together with Zeiss, ASML invested money into research for this new technology, but the material for lenses capable of 157 nanometers proved to be very expensive. No longer expecting enough profit, Intel dropped out the race in 2003 and other chip factories soon followed suit.

This was a blow to the Brabanders. Their hefty investment in research had been in vain and most of the extensive preparatory work found itself flushed down the drain. ASML wasted no time grieving. They were already working on something more promising. Nonetheless, to fulfil requirements for a European subsidy, they still sent a 157-test machine to imec. The device was never meant for operation, nor would it ever be used.

This failure proved a costly lesson. The chip manufacturers had made down payments of 300 million euros for machines that, due to the spook in the market, ASML never followed through with. That money needed to be refunded, much to the irritation of the lithography manufacturer. Notes were duly taken in Veldhoven: going forward, it would be vital to ensure customers also have some share of the risk when pushing for the next leap in technology. Everybody should have skin in the game.

157 nanometers proved to be a dead end. However, there is one light source that carries a far shorter wavelength of just 13.5 nanometers: extreme ultraviolet light. It would require painstaking years of research before the industry could make use of this. In the meantime, the chip industry needed inspiration from elsewhere to keep Moore's Law alive. Fortunately, the solution was something ever-present in the life of a Dutch engineer: water.

In the 17th century, the Dutch mathematician Willebrord Snellius investigated how light rays refract as they pass through one material to another. The law Snellius derived was later published by his compatriot Christiaan Huygens, pioneer in theoretical physics and optics. Even today, their work is still a must-read for every engineer at ASML.

The advance this yielded was significant. By holding a thin layer of pure water between the lens and the wafer, you effectively get the same result as increasing the size of the aperture. This allowed the engineers to push past the limits of what was thought possible with 193 nanometers, all without needing to change the light source itself.

You can experience this for yourself by looking down at your legs in a shallow pool. The surface of the water refracts the light rays, and as a result your legs seem horribly short and your feet closer than ever. This everyday phenomenon was precisely the foundation from which ASML took the next technological leap. By applying water between the lens and the wafer, extra small details were able to be projected by the lithography machines. They called the technique immersion, or "dipping".

However, a different type of optics that combined transparent lenses and mirrors was needed. The task fell to Zeiss, who set about building such a system for ASML. Creating the desired effect required only a teaspoon of water, no more than the bottom of a shot glass. However, this puddle needs to stay completely still on a silicon disc rapidly firing back and forth. Anyone who has tried to keep a glass full of water steady as they run will know how difficult this is.

'We just couldn't come up with anything that would work' said Frits van Hout. When he returned to the company in 2001 he found the engineers completely stuck on how to manage the wet wafers. 'TSMC was desperate to make use of immersion, so they suggested using a raised lip to keep the water in place. Impossible.'

Eventually, the breakthrough came in the form of a mini-swimming pool held under the lens. With this ASML avoided having to immerse the entire wafer, and could keep it to only the part lined up to be exposed. A continuous stream of air blown over the disc, like a 'ring of air', was then utilized to keep the mini pool stable.

For this to work, however, no air could come between the lens and water. Furthermore, the layer of water had to be precisely the same depth throughout, which was difficult because the lens is naturally curved, not flat. In days gone by, engineers at ASML and Zeiss had flattened the last lens in the optical system to be able to check the alignment of the wafer. Although thought to be obsolete, the function had never been removed from the design. This accidental sloppiness then had proved itself extremely valuable now.

The first immersion-machine hit the market in 2004, immediately putting the Japanese competition at a disadvantage. The already expanding Dutch market share was pushed ahead even more by the introduction of another groundbreaking invention: the TwinScan. This new machine could measure for alignment and illuminate at the same time, performing a high degree of complex multitasking that shaved off invaluable time for chip factories.

This is how it works: before a new pattern can be printed on a silicone layer, the wafer must first be measured. This information is needed to align it before exposing it, so the new layer will fall exactly on the previous pattern. Already difficult, but the real problems stem from the degree of heat the wafer has to endure in the ovens. This can cause the wafer to warp, like a Pringle potato chip. What looks like a perfectly flat disc to the naked eye is revealed by a microscope to be more like a rugged mountainscape.

So, before any measurement can take place, the wafer is carefully suctioned into place, which removes the worst of the bumps. Sensors then record the remaining deviations, creating a detailed 3D map of the surface with all its peaks and troughs. The lithography machine then uses this map to adjust the focal plane during exposure, compensating for the deviations so the chip patterns are projected at an equal sharpness over the whole surface. Think of it like the autofocus on a camera, rapidly correcting the image at miniscule distances and depths.

Immersion and the TwinScan turned out to be a match made in heaven. Making this 3D map is best done with a dry wafer, and with the TwinScan you could undertake the wet exposure while the next disc, still dry, was already being measured. Just like doing the dishes with an extra pair of hands.

The tables of the TwinScan were driven by powerful motors, able to accelerate and decelerate in an instant. But directing the two simultaneously turned out to be far more complicated than imagined. The first TwinScan system ASML delivered in 2000 only carried the one wafer-table. It would need to wait some time for its sibling to arrive.

A sophisticated name was spun to gloss things over: the TwinScan 'Single'. But despite limping to market on one leg, ASML knew the machine would have no difficulty being sold. This new generation of lithography machines exposed wafers with a diameter of 300 millimeters, roughly the size of a vinyl record album. This was still a significant increase on the 200mm industry benchmark, allowing for more chips to be produced. Just like an album holds more songs than a single.

Once again ASML took the route of deliver first, improve later. This also worked in favor of the chip factories, allowing them to try out producing the most advanced – and most profitable – chips before competitors. ASML was happy to play along; after all, such an early delivery was also a sure-fire way to keep their own competitors out of the chip factories. As Martin van den Brink put it: 'If we wait until our machines work, then we're already behind.'

That strategy seemed to work. With immersion technology and the TwinScan, ASML gained valuable market share at the expense of Canon and Nikon. In the meantime, Veldhoven was already pouring money into research for the future EUV machine, as yet with no profit. But with their two cash cows ready to milk, the twin-tables and the wet wafers, the Dutch engineers hoped their heads would remain firmly above water.

14

JAPAN'S REVENGE

The change in ASML was evident from miles away. A new head office was rising in Veldhoven, a dark black and green tower stretching 83 meters into the sky. Although known as Building 8, as per their nomenclature, a near-death experience for the company during its construction would lead some to refer to it as the Gravestone.

In 2001, while ASML was preoccupied fighting its way through a year of turmoil, Nikon was plotting a surprise attack. The Japanese manufacturer had watched their market share dwindle and stood by as Japanese chipmakers like Seiko, Epson and Sony made the move on ASML's equipment. Fellow nationals opting for foreign technology was a disgrace few would bear lightly. It was time for revenge.

One December morning, Doug Dunn arrived to find a series of complaints on his desk. The Japanese competitor had accused ASML of infringing on thirteen patents, carefully preparing the charges for well over a year to the complete ignorance of Veldhoven. Overwhelmed, Dunn realized ASML had been caught with its guard down, and the prospects were not good. ASML had managed to patent some of its own technology, but as a young company this paled in comparison to the far more extensive portfolio of Nikon, which had been actively producing lenses and microscopes since 1917. And in conflicts over intellectual property, the party with the greatest number of patents almost always wins. Predicting the outcome is often nothing more than holding a ruler next to the stack of papers: the highest wins.

Nikon was merciless, filing the accusations with the ITC in Washington and a court in California in an attempt to hit ASML where it hurt the most: the American market. If the ITC recognized even one patent violation, ASML would no longer be permitted to supply chip machines to American manufacturers. After all they had sacrificed to break into the market, this would be a fatal blow to the Dutch company.

'They want to destroy you.' As Doug Dunn heard the words from his lawyers, his heart skipped a beat. Normally, the etiquette was to have a prior consultation between the companies on issues with patents before deciding whether or not to involve the courts. But Nikon had no interest in negotiating or settling. Dunn could already picture the headlines; the CEO busy erecting his prized new headquarters, forced to close the lot before he could even step foot on it. An 83-meter monument to the failure of ASML – a gravestone.

ASML did the only thing you can do in a patent war – strike back. It sued Nikon, and busied itself assembling a group of independent experts to explain the complex technical details to the ITC staff. After all, lithography technology was a complicated matter, and they needed to gain as much favor in Washington as possible. Intel and Micron also lent support behind the scenes in an attempt to stave off their own production issues should their supplier succumb to a patent battle.

Dunn tried to force a solution, inviting himself to Japan for a meeting with Nikon's CEO Shoichiro Yoshida. In his bag he carried a thirty-page weapon faxed to him by his lawyers before embarking on his flight to Tokyo: a copy of the preliminary conclusion of the ITC, ruling in favor of ASML. Now holding all the cards, he brought along his own interpreter to make sure the conversation kept moving and the Japanese couldn't seek respite behind any pretense of misunderstanding.

'You're not going to win this,' Dunn told Shoichiro Yoshida, but the CEO wouldn't hear it. His heels were firmly dug in. Dunn responded by laying the documents with the preliminary conclusion on the table, the sight of which caused Yoshida to become enraged with his lawyers. He turned back to Dunn – he needed time to think. The ASML delegation was invited out to dinner that evening; sushi, sake and small talk were on the menu. A meal out was not the time to talk patents.

Afterwards the offer from ASML to settle came through to the tune of 100 million dollars. A hefty amount, but for Dunn a price well worth the next five or ten years of conflict it would avoid. But the Japanese refused. They wanted to see the Brabanders on their knees.

Yoshida's fixation on revenge failed to pay off. When the ITC brought forward its final ruling a few months later, it turned out that one of Nikon's patents was itself invalid. A worker had taken it from their previous employer and resubmitted the exact same invention, rendering it null and void. The other claims of patent violations fared no better: none were recognized by the ITC. It was a resounding victory for ASML, and an enormous relief for Dunn.

The Brit was in the middle of a visit to Zeiss in Oberkochen when the call from his lawyers came through. 'Should I kill myself or should I cheer?' was all he could ask as he stepped out the room. Thankfully, cheering it was: the judge had ruled in favor of ASML on all counts. Dunn couldn't believe it: he had to ask several times for the lawyer to repeat the news. The lawsuit in California concluded with a mediation round that saw ASML settle for 87 million dollars, less than they had originally offered. They had quelled their Japanese competitor, at least for the moment.

The Nikon case was a rude awakening for the teams in Veldhoven. The company had paid far too little attention to its intellectual property in its early years, focusing almost entirely on innovation and not considering the need to record and secure their inventions. In the world of modern technology, this was pure lack of experience. Although Dunn would never deny this, he remained sympathetic to why this blind spot came about: 'ASML was still a young enterprise. Everything needed to be done at once. We had the smartest people that wanted to make the best machines in the world, and brought together the best ideas to do so. To then also have to record and write these ideas down in excruciating detail is annoying. How much time do people enjoy spending on their tax returns?' He shrugged. 'It's boring! We all know the feeling.'

Boring it may be, but protecting the knowledge you produce in this industry is an absolute necessity. ASML started in 1984 with no more than a handful of patents and licenses from Philips, which had prioritized protecting their precious CD player instead of filing patents for lithography machines. In the late '90s, ASML created its own department to manage intellectual property. Even then, new patent applications would take years to be approved. But ASML recognized the need to step up their game after Nikon's surprise attack, introducing a fellowship program that offered a better career path and salary for engineers that registered their ideas. 'Otherwise it's only the gray-haired managers getting to drive the luxury cars,' says Dunn, himself a gray-haired manager.

Three types of fellow can be found at ASML: fellows, senior fellows and corporate fellows. Workers are nominated for this based, among other things, on their patents. It is a closed selection process, however, the results of which Martin van den Brink and the head of the research department Jos Benschop announce at the company's annual technology day.

The best inventors (some of which have more than two hundred patents to their name) are commemorated by having their faces engraved on silicon wafers and hung on a series of large wooden beams, like a Mount Rushmore of the chip industry. It was Van den Brink's dream to assemble such a wall of famous inventors, just like the names of the acclaimed physicists he once saw adorning the reception hall of Bell Labs in New Jersey, the home of the transistor. The only prize missing from the Veldhoven collection remains a Nobel laureate.

As of 2023, ASML has registered more than 16,000 patents. A number of these have been developed in collaboration with suppliers that over time have needed to deliver increasingly complex parts to ASML. Zeiss is by far the most significant of these co-inventors. Former CEO Hermann Gerlinger referred to this alliance as 'the ultimate merging of machine and optics, in which ASML tells all their secrets to us, and we in turn share everything with them.' Coming from the historical German craftsman, it sounds almost romantic.

15

THE WISDOM OF ZEISS

'You're not talking to me like that, are you? Sir?'

The patience of the German police officer had run thin. He was looking at a totally unconcerned Hermann Gerlinger who was too busy yelling into his phone at Martin van den Brink. Their argument had started while the Zeiss CEO was behind the wheel, spilling over into an all-out shouting match even as the policeman ordered him out of the car.

'Just give me the damn ticket,' snapped Gerlinger as he pulled his papers out from his glove box. All the while, he continued his spat with Van den Brink, who was giving it back in German just as hard from over in Veldhoven.

The officer had enough. 'Hang up. Now.'

'One moment, Martin, I'm putting you on mute,' said Gerlinger. One tap and Veldhoven fell silent – no need to wait for a response. A few minutes and one fine later, the CEO was back behind the wheel and on his way. He whipped out his phone and hit unmute. '*So ein Scheiss.* Total waste of time. Now, where were we...'

Sparks never failed to fly when the technical directors of Zeiss and ASML crossed wires. They both lived for head-on confrontations, as they thought all good engineers should. That much at least was clear. Later, they would fondly laugh about the incident over dinner, brushing away any notion of ill feeling. 'You'll never survive in this business without humor,' Gerlinger said as he stepped down as head of Zeiss' semiconductor division in 2016.

As intense as the interactions between researchers on the optical systems were, the commercial relationship between Zeiss and ASML had turned cold. The problems escalated sharply following Dunn's exit in 2004. When his term as CEO ended, he elected to draw his pension, spending the rest of his time taking supervisory positions at chip companies. And so Veldhoven swapped the Brit for a Frenchman by the name of Eric Meurice. Previously an employee of Intel and computer manufacturer Dell, he had moved over from his position as vice president at French electronics manufacturer Thomson. He took pride in being able to tell people they were 'incompetent' in whatever language they preferred. It was a term employees at ASML would soon hear echoing the hallways on a regular basis, especially in discussions about Zeiss. A significant rift had formed between the longstanding partners as they once again found themselves embroiled in a row that was, as always, about money.

Once again, ASML wanted to double its revenue in the coming years and needed Zeiss to up its production of lenses to do so. However, Zeiss refused to let ASML's rose-tinted forecasts pull the wool over their eyes. Memories of Doug Dunn's merciless canceling of orders during the crises of 2001 and 2002 were still fresh, and the acquisition of the American SVG in the meantime had not helped smooth things over. SVG also manufactured lenses, leaving Zeiss with serious questions about the exclusivity of their partnership with ASML. The takeover had opened a door for ASML they would have much rather seen remain closed.

Suspicion hung heavy in the air. With the trust broken, ASML summoned a mediator: Guido Groet. Although now working at Meta, the technology company behind Facebook, in 2004 he had just returned to ASML from the US after managing the sale of surplus parts of SVG. After spending his first year in Veldhoven overseeing cuts as part of the expensive TwinScan production, a new task awaited him: bonding.

Groet was called to the twentieth floor. There, Martin van den Brink and financial director Peter Wennink laid out their woes regarding the fractured relationship between ASML and Zeiss. For Wennink it was simple: 'We need you to get us working well together, in good balance with one another.' But Van den Brink saw things slightly differently: 'Make sure they don't keep tricking us.'

To save their ailing partnership, Zeiss and ASML underwent a series of intensive meetings between 2005 and 2007, with Peter Wennink attending a commercial consultation in Oberkochen every three months on behalf of ASML. In addition, every quarter there was an 'interface' meeting directly about the technical cooperation between the two companies. These would alternate between Veldhoven and Oberkochen, and occasionally taking place at a neutral point halfway – typically a hotel in Frankfurt.

Mending such a break requires first bringing the fracture to light. Small teams from each company were brought together to air their grievances. As might be expected, the Dutch had no qualms putting their problems straight on the table. But with a little encouragement the Germans did the same, and the teams were then encouraged to present the reconciliation jointly to the entire management.

But Groet soon found he had been tasked with bringing together two vastly different companies. ASML attracted cowboys who wanted to shoot faster than their shadows, while Zeiss fancied itself a traditional scientific institute, taking time to think through all the variables before even considering acting. This was a recipe for trouble. Employees collided on all fronts, and the search for a common ground proved an endless task. Especially when the ASML'ers had a tendency to change course without consultation after the meetings had taken place. This drove the Germans mad.

Dieter Kurz, boss of the overarching Carl Zeiss AG, took up regular attendance on behalf of the Germans while Eric Meurice represented ASML. Guido Groet would record the agreements made during the meetings on a large screen so everyone could read along. Childish, but at this point any measure that could minimize misunderstandings was welcomed. Not that it helped; upon sending his first minutes to Meurice, he quickly received back a heavily redacted version with a note at the bottom: 'You still have a lot to learn, kid. Don't write down what was said, but what was meant.'

Zeiss, as ever, disagreed. With the management teams once again at each other's throats, the meeting had to be entirely redone as if it were a retake of at test in high school. As the two sides assembled once more, Groet kept a low profile while his bosses battled it out. He did so on the good advice of a colleague from Zeiss: when the elephants dance, you shouldn't stand between them.

Zeiss and ASML continued to bicker about who deserved what and if everyone was getting what they were entitled to. And the amounts under discussion were significant; in 2004, the value of the optics accounted for around a quarter of the worth of a lithography machine. Martin van den Brink was particularly irritated that Zeiss was unwilling to give guarantees on lenses costing millions of euros. If a chip manufacturer discovered optical errors that were hampering production, it was up to ASML to cough up the costs.

For their part, the Germans figured they were the ones running the risks while ASML banked the rewards. Veldhoven could quickly up production by bringing in new people or asking existing workers to stay longer at the factories, but the timescales for a lens manufacturer were far different. Zeiss had admittedly solved one serious bottleneck for ASML in the '90s when they switched from polishing by hand to using robots for the task. But still, glass for crystal must first 'grow', and investment for raw materials needed to be done at least three years in advance. Polishing and measuring the lenses was an equally laborious task, neither of which gained any speed by simply throwing more people at it. As the sages at Zeiss were fond of saying: a pregnancy lasts nine months, and it won't go any faster if you put an extra woman next to you.

Sore spots continued to emerge: ASML was used to promising chip-makers significant discounts to bring in deals. However, Zeiss would then also need to offer discounts on the lens, otherwise the cost would be sunk from ASML's profit margin, which was hardly flourishing to begin with. The Germans were also completely unwilling to accustom themselves to the wild market fluctuations of the chip industry, always pushing a fixed price for their products. But as Groet knew too well, the world they moved in was full of 'enormous whiners, constantly pushing for discounts and always complaining about the quality.' Nobody cared to conform to what Zeiss wanted.

Ultimately, the crux of the matter boiled down to one key question: could ASML and Zeiss share the risks and profits fairly? Groet brought in a mathematician to crunch the numbers, and after two years of agonizing negotiations, ASML and Zeiss finally agreed and signed a new contract in 2007. They could now regulate guarantees and sudden adjustments in orders. ASML agreed to pre-finance a third of the value of the lenses, meaning Zeiss ran less risk when purchasing materials.

Van den Brink sought an end to the never-ending conflicts and floated the idea of taking over Zeiss. But this was unthinkable for the Germans: the lenses they made for lithography machines were their crown jewels. And so there would never be an official bid. Zeiss, solely owned by the Carl Zeiss Foundation, also kept ASML and their money at arm's length on matters of expansions and real estate. There was to be no Dutch hand in the German kitchen – for now.

The technical consultation rounds between Zeiss and ASML were dominated by Van den Brink. These meetings saw numbers of fifty persons from each company attend, arranged in a single horseshoe shape across the room with their eyes locked on each other. The engineers took it in turns to give presentations while the technical director had his nose cemented to his computer, his eyes only occasionally glancing up at the mention of a topic that caught his ear. Postures would stiffen as the room fell still: Martin had been roused.

The teams at Zeiss would balk the second Van den Brink's temper got out of hand, despite this being both inevitable and frequent. But his technical and strategic insight garnered a high level of respect, and the outbursts became accepted as evidence of his intense commitment to Zeiss. As Guido Groet saw, this was not wishful thinking; 'Martin would unleash a whirlwind of fury if I hadn't been over to Oberkochen for two or three weeks. He also thought I should be speaking German, as I'd then better understand what they meant.'

'If I'm angry at a German, I'll swear at them in German,' Martin would later confide. 'It's the better way to get the message across.'

The closer you get to the work floor, the more Zeiss and ASML start to feel like one company. Project teams are a mix of Brabanders and Germans, with dozens of ASML personnel at work in Oberkochen each day. Together, they set about building the heart of a highly complex machine, a process that cultivates a bond between both sides of the aisle. After a long day, the engineers often come together at Landgasthof LäuterHäusle, where the Dutch invasion joins their Zeiss colleagues in raiding the salad bar.

Despite this, ASML's most important supplier continued to prove a weak link in the chain. In 2007, ASML found itself prey to furious chip manufacturers who had not received their ordered TwinScan machines. Veldhoven had done their part: fifty machines were ready to be shipped, except for one vital part. This time the illuminator was to blame, the component that guides the laser in the machine, manufactured by Zeiss in the town of Wetzlar, just north of Frankfurt.

Tempers were high and everyone was quick to point the finger, but the cause of the delay remained unclear. 'Why are you not already in Wetzlar helping them?' Van den Brink snapped at the startled Groet. It was an order hardly disguised as a question. So Guido Groet immediately took himself to Germany, camping out for a month to find the kink in the cable. The trail eventually led to delays with a special optical filter, only available from one source in Russia.

Groet flew to confront the supplier: 'Where are those filters, everyone is waiting for you!' But the Russians were completely nonplussed by the problems they were causing. 'Every time we ship something to Germany, we need to bribe a customs officer. So, we save the filters until we have fifty, then we only need to do it that once.'

16

A LIVING ORGANISM

That's when the shit hits the fan, as Frits van Hout puts it. Or in more polite terms: 'When Zeiss say they're ready with the lens, that's when our problems truly begin.' As soon as the optical system is completed, that's when ASML needs to integrate it with the rest of the machine. You can design the perfect lithography machine on paper, but in practice the end result will always deviate from this. With the best will in the world, the only thing you can know for sure is that any plan will fall short.

Martin van den Brink has his own one-liner for this: 'It's not about preventing errors, but how well you manage them.'

ASML's machines are far too complex for one person to understand in their entirety. The first wafer steppers at Philips required a team of ten to be assembled, and by the time Van den Brink and Van Hout started in 1984, already more than a hundred technicians were working on the devices. Managing this was a science in itself, and so the system design was divided into sections and different teams were allocated to work on these tasks in parallel. The collaboration between all the ASML engineers itself became an inscrutable machine. But just like a beehive, what appears to be total chaos is actually the bustling activity of everyone knowing and executing their own role, almost perfectly.

When a new chip factory requires an investment of billions of dollars before any chips are even close to being printed, everything revolves around value for money. The rule of thumb is that around 30 percent of that capital investment is needed for the lithography machine, the essential tool for transforming cheap and plentiful silicon into valuable chips. The billions will only flow back in if that device delivers the right number of wafers per hour with enough error-free chips. The first chip manufacturer to master this with the latest technology will pay off the expensive machine in no time, a game ASML played like no other.

It's all about large volume and small details, so in order to deliver the right equipment for a client's needs ASML would get deeply familiarized with its customers. Martin van den Brink always wants to know from the bosses of the chip factories precisely what products they have in mind, from which he can devise the technology to make this happen. Whatever he comes up with becomes the driving force of ASML's roadmap, shaping the marching orders for the whole company.

The first task in designing a new machine is for the system architects, who in consultation with the chip manufacturers determine what requirements the scanner must fulfill and what that might cost. For instance, if a chip manufacturer wants a machine that produces 290 rather than 270 wafers per hour, the architect may recommend using a more powerful laser, installing faster motors for the wafer or choosing a lens that can be swapped out at a later date.

The job then falls to the engineers in the Development and Engineering department to actually carry out these designs. This department is the nerve center of the whole company. Thousands of engineers specializing in hardware and software work together in D&E to pick the best technologies to bring these ideas to life.

A lithography machine depends on three properties: the fineness of the mesh that constitutes the integrated circuit, the precision with which the layers in a chip are laid on top of one another, and the movement speed of the wafers (in other words, how much they can feed the machine). How these all work together needs to be carefully negotiated by all parties. It is an ongoing discussion, even within ASML.

The art lies in finding a good balance between time, specification and costs, otherwise known by Frits van Hout as 'The Holy Trinity'. If the technical requirements are too demanding, you run the risk of building a machine no one can afford, or implementing a production process so complex that you fail to build a machine on time at all. The research departments naturally tend to choose the technology that offers the very best resolutions, and so can create the finest lines. But an improvement here comes at the cost of time: the finer you go, the slower everything has to run to maintain accuracy. Then you have to answer to the chip factories, ever fixated on increasing the speed of production. '"Keep on stamping! We'll never get the smallest resolution so just stamp wafers!" is all we then hear from them,' according to Van Hout.

The scanners don't have to be perfect – there's always room for improvement, as regularly happens with rolling upgrades for components and new machines. They just need to be good enough to get the job done.

Designing a machine at ASML is not approached as if it were a perfectly predictable static entity that can be captured by a good blueprint. Rather, the whole process is regarded as cultivating a living organism, continuously adapting to technical setbacks and attuning what you're creating to the everchanging circumstances it finds itself in. This is not a case of choosing one of many paths up the mountain; this is the only way it can be done. On a microscopic level, no part is identical, no motor runs exactly as fast as the other. Materials vibrate: gases are emitted and parts expand when heated. Every swirling dust particle counts and every single nanometer of difference in a hole or screw has consequences. But as the creator of the whole system, ASML has the know-how to compensate for an unexpected turn of events in one corner of the machine by adjusting what would seem to be a completely separate part elsewhere.

The architect is also responsible for the 'error budget', which represents the acceptable margins of error for all the different components. These margins are divided like a pie of which each team gets a piece. Your allotted slice is how much you can deviate, no more. The tighter the deadline, the tighter the margins: bars in these cases are set extra high for all components in order to leave more slices of the pie to be freely allocated afterwards, wherever needed. It is the art of 'overspecifying'.

In the meantime, the most important design choices are studied and verified separately to make sure engineers don't take too much risk, or take a completely wrong turn. This is all done in parallel, for the fastest results and the lowest cycle time – the clock is always ticking at ASML. The goal: to find as many errors as possible and iron them out before the machine is sent on its way. If you can avoid having to build each part to do this, all the better. With more experience and subsequently more accurate theoretical models, the teams at ASML have learned to read and predict almost intuitively what will happen in a machine when you put all the pieces in place.

As the person who oversees the entire life cycle of a new machine, from the drawing table to the factory, the project manager arguably carries the greatest responsibility. The cycle is broken down into fourteen decisive moments, such as the first prototype or the first delivery to the manufacturer, and the responsibilities are further divided according to areas of expertise. Different project leaders busy themselves with the mechatronics, or the wafer-table on which the silicon disc lies or the mask-table that holds the chip pattern, while a different team of experts concern themselves with the millions of lines of code that direct the machine, constantly correcting and bringing all the different moving parts in line.

This makes the product development manager (or PDM'er) the executive of a series of projects, landing them the tricky task of balancing numerous budgets while fostering cooperation between groups. This is a tough responsibility. 'From the very start at ASML, if the word 'project' was involved, then it needed to happen.' This, according to Frits van Hout, is the ultimate mark of importance in ASML. Departments were king at companies like Philips, but in Veldhoven this is flipped on its head. 'Projects involving new machines are our lifeblood. Anyone not in line with this would be quickly put in their place.'

A manager at ASML confirms this. 'The program wields the power in this company,' emphasizing the word 'program' like it was the name of some deity with a capital 'P'.

As the machines grow in complexity, so too does the project structure. More target dates, milestones, more people, more meetings, more abbreviations. Technicians jump from one project to the other, chasing problems as they come up. Moments to bask in successes are few and far between.

'What's it like developing machines for ASML? Might as well be developing crack, it's that addictive,' says Markus Matthes, former head of D&E. 'We work so fast that we don't even have the specs ready when we start to design. Now that's a thrill.'

Matthes previously worked in the automotive industry, a risk-averse culture that starkly contrasts with ASML. 'I was done with all the incessant rules and cost restrictions of the car world. This place is every engineer's dream.'

Dream it may be, but Martin van den Brink has a knack for snapping heads back to reality. His 'reviews', the discussions on the progress of the technology, largely involve constant reiterations of the importance of avoiding 'flamboyant' overengineering. As he points out: 'Our machines are equipped with enough valves and pipes. There's no need for them to be unnecessarily complex or costly.' He often asks, 'Do you do this at home too? Beneath every toilet there's a pipe made of cheap plastic. So why do we insist on having one made of stainless steel?' Nothing is safe from scrutiny, and every choice needs to be justifiable.

Gregor van Baars, associated with the Dutch research organization TNO, worked in close partnership with ASML on the development of their new machines. 'They dissect the machine into manageable pieces, assigning each person a specific section of the puzzle,' he explains. 'Then it's just a matter of extensive drawing and calculating, with constant discussion and coordination. It's the pinnacle of hardcore engineering.'

The most challenging aspect is maintaining harmony among all the scientific disciplines involved: 'Imagine someone devises a smart new motor. Someone from the thermal group will then raise concerns about the increase in the machine's temperature due to the more powerful heat source. Effective communication and a solid grasp of the other fields involved are the only way to make this work.'

According to Van Baars, ASML excels in identifying and resolving hiccups in the machines. 'An entire army of engineers is immersed in a kind of crime scene investigation to find the source of the errors, and figure out exactly how to correct or compensate for them. After a while it gets difficult to distinguish what were meant to be solutions within this web and make sure these don't interfere or even counteract with each other. That's why they have an astronomical number of engineers. It's insane.'

But as Frits van Hout explains, it's not a case of one-size-fits-all when it comes to engineers. 'A mechanical engineer can create and design structures, whereas an electronic engineer designs circuits. And physicists may "understand" everything, but ask them to actually do something and see how useful they are.' Spoken as a true physicist.

The technicians at ASML are expected to continually challenge one another, to never blindly accept what someone has said simply on the basis that they hold a higher position in the company. Egos need to be checked at the door, and for good reason. As Frits van Hout points out, this flatness gives a degree of security and protection essential to the smooth running of such an intense operation. 'Even as the boss, if you're completely in the wrong with a decision, you can at least be sure someone will say something about it.'

'When it comes to allocating available budget and workers, the ASML'ers compete against one another. It's a company that works in an extremely informal manner,' wrote Theo Verkaart, a researcher from TU Eindhoven who analyzed the production process at Veldhoven in 2013. 'There's no uniform approach, and project leaders tend to hide what they actually have in reserve, only to then demand higher requirements during the budget negotiations.' Screaming bloody murder is the only way to get things done in this company: if you're not making yourself heard, good luck getting a share of the pie you need.

ASML's customers are just as unpredictable: chip manufacturers are prone to abruptly altering demands, changing orders or suddenly asking for extra options and new features. 'You turn away for a second, and suddenly they all want a new plaything for their machine,' as Van den Brink puts it. He tends to choose the simplest words for the most complex parts.

In between juggling these requests for alterations, it falls to the program managers to keep everyone on track to hit the deadlines. They not only ensure the prototypes are ready, but also oversee the procurement of parts and spares.

Another vital consideration is whether the factories actually have the capacity necessary for the assembly of the machines. Despite the depth of ingenuity and engineering prowess involved in this process, the most obvious problems can be the easiest to overlook: will the machine fit in the flight container and through the door of the factory? Some chip-factories had to demolish an outer wall when ASML's newest machine turned out slightly larger than expected.

The lifecycle of a new lithography machine doesn't end upon delivery (otherwise called the NPI, or New Product Introduction). The approach here between the lithography manufacturers differs wildly. ASML's machines still require extensive remedial work, while ASML's competitors in Japan always aim to deliver machines the same way they deliver their cameras; finely tuned, and ready for immediate use. You just need to plug it in.

The latter may seem the obvious choice, but ASML's 'perfect enough' approach has its advantages. With this method, the chip manufacturer can begin their own testing much quicker, allowing them to fine-tune the device to the particularities of their environment and get it on its way to fulfilling its purpose: exposing wafers all day, every day. And that's a different ball game.

17

A LEGION OF NURSES

Ominous shadows fill the desert plains in Arizona. Scattered amidst Native American reservations and the Phoenix mountains lay a series of fabs, built by companies like Intel, Motorola, and NXP, with two brand-new chip factories from TSMC set majestically against the horizon. Although the 'Valley of the Sun' enjoys about three hundred days of sun a year, the daylight never penetrates the sterile cleanrooms of these imposing structures. They remain completely sealed off from the outside world. Nothing or no one is allowed to jeopardize production.

You only have to look up in a cleanroom to find out how well a chip factory is operating. Along the ceiling runs a stream of robots from one machine to the other, rattling back and forth with their trays full of wafers. But as soon as there's a malfunction the stream stops, leaving the machines standing like a line of impatient motorists on the wrong side of a traffic accident.

A blockage like this is critical: the heart of the factory, the lithography machine, can no longer beat. On a normal day, the quickest devices usually spit out two or even three hundred wafers per hour, and one wafer of chips can fetch up to 250,000 dollars. To a chip manufacturer, their actual heart may as well be on the line when a scanner stands still.

Todd Garvey is one of nine thousand customer service employees working around the world to keep lithography machines ticking. Operations are run from their base in Arizona, home to ASML's American office since 1984. The cleanroom uniform is a dust-free bunny suit that leaves only the eyes exposed. It wouldn't be out of place in a hospital, and neither would Garvey. He sees himself as one of ASML's nurses, tending to his patients throughout the day and night.

Service engineers like Garvey are responsible for keeping a fleet of forty to fifty machines in the air. It takes years to qualify for this, and this is why ASML starts training maintenance staff long before construction on a new fab begins.

You need to have a strong bladder to work in the chip factory. Getting changed for a quick bathroom break takes so long it's hardly worth the effort. 'Just try not to eat or drink too much,' advises Garvey. But good luck with that when you're in the middle of another one of the grueling twelve-hour shifts him and his team work. They alternate hours for three consecutive days, followed by a few days off.

When his friends ask what he exactly does in the chip factory, Garvey has his answer ready: 'I work on a highly expensive camera that photographs the same image over and over on a disc that moves at three to four hundred kilometers per hour. And it has to be razor-sharp, every time.'

Garvey has felt like a father to these machines for the past 25 years. 'They're all my babies. When a client ordered a machine, it would be me that went to Veldhoven to see how the system was coming along. I'd watch as it grew from individual modules to a full wafer-producing machine, and watch as it was broken down again to ship out. I'd then fly with the device, my baby, the whole way to the chip factory.'

Walk into any cleanroom, and you'll find the lithography machine is always king. The most expensive tool is also responsible for the most critical part of the production process, so it's vital that it's kept running at full power at all times. The other machines are less of a strain on the wallet and handle the rest of the steps, such as etching, heating, and applying new layers to the wafers. In between all this, the discs are also constantly measured to check the layers of the chips are still properly aligned.

Lithography machines will work between 98 and 99 percent of the time if they receive regular maintenance. Just like on a highway, with planning you can easily minimize disruption by redirecting tasks and traffic to other production lines. It's the crashes, the unexpected 'tool down!' warnings that deliver the most economic damage. And no siren will sound to tell you. They're usually disconnected: there's enough noise in the factory as it is.

If a malfunction is expected to last more than 48 hours, it is better to switch the wafers to a different production line and take the reduced yield on the chin. This leaves the robots waiting patiently in line while the ASML employees scramble to diagnose and revive the patient.

'It's like needing to solve a difficult puzzle,' says engineer Gang-san Kim. 'When you find the solution the relief is enormous.' You need nerves of steel to handle these delicate devices. Chip factories might be fully automated, but you can never fully escape human mistakes: loose cables, a missed bolt, falling tools, a fingerprint or scratch on a lens. But the worst thing to happen in a cleanroom is water leakage or damage to the mask. This is the unique blueprint with the chip structure, and it costs hundreds of thousands of dollars to replace.

As soon as something is wrong with the masks, the top bosses in the factory swarm around the machine. 'Too many captains, not enough crew,' as Kim says. The managers watch on anxiously while he delves under the hood of the machine to find the problem. They dare not get involved – they know the body of wires and lenses is far too complex for them to interfere with.

It can take weeks to untangle the Gordian knot. And if ASML's legion of nurses can't work it out, the specialists in Veldhoven are summoned. Time is everything, so the longer a problem persists the higher up the chain of escalation it goes, all the way to the original designers themselves.

Wim Pas remembers his white whale clearly. The site manager for the TSMC fabs north of Phoenix ran into trouble with a notorious immersion device; it would inexplicably produce faulty chips for two hours after every restart, and then run seamlessly as if nothing had happened. It took months of research to figure out why. The second the machine stopped, five droplets of water would fall on a layer of glue, causing it to expand by just a few nanometers. This was all it needed to throw off the chip-pattern. And once the moisture evaporated, the glue would shrink, leaving no trace of any error with the machine.

Problems like this only come to light in the harsh reality of the factory floor. Even with years of meticulous planning, half the issues these machines face could never be imagined. This is exactly why ASML leaves the fine-tuning of the design for when the engines are running. It is also the only way to find which parts wear out too quickly. As Pas says, 'It's only here that everything wrong with the design reveals itself.' Then you have to hope the spare part is available – with a device comprised of so many different components, it's almost impossible to predict and prepare in advance for what will be the first to go.

ASML's sales department takes care of negotiations with the chip factory over which improvements fall under the warranty and which upgrades they have to pay for. The service engineers steer clear of any financial discussions. Their day-to-day work on the floors of the fabs is pressure enough. They're on the ground, right in the line of fire: they can do without the distractions.

The lithography machine is eventually optimized using special 'recipes'. Like a Formula 1 car getting a separate tuning for each circuit, the machines are carefully fine-tuned to the type of chips that are being produced. Chip manufacturers want each device to operate at 'full capacity', but as Wim Pas explains, not every machine is identical. 'Imagine you buy two identical cars. But one can reach 150 kilometers per hour and the other 180. It's my job to convince the chip manufacturers to be happy about having a faster car and not to moan about the one that stops at 150.'

Just as Coca-Cola won't give away its secret recipe, formulas for the chips manufacturers production are kept close to their chests. However, if you tinker too much and create problems with your machine, Veldhoven will be in touch to find out why.

Unforeseeable complications aren't limited to the mechanics of the machines. Despite their best efforts, the cleanrooms can't always keep the outside world at bay. Earthquakes and atmospheric pressure fluctuations due to thunderstorms can easily disrupt the lithography process. Or cows. Intel once faced an inexplicable drop in yield every night for a few hours, with researchers running in circles until they finally realized the cause: cow farts.

Every night between 1 and 2 a.m. the wind would change direction and methane gas from nearby dairy farms found its way into the cleanroom through the air purifiers. The extra gas from their sleeping neighbors was enough to affect production and dropped the percentage of flawless chips produced in this time window. Filtering the gas wasn't possible, so Intel had to pay for three farms to relocate. Since then, everyone scouting a location for a chip factory knows to keep an eye out for cows.

You can hardly hear modern lithography machines over the racket of the air conditioners. The old timers, such as the PAS 5500, are recognizable by the metallic grunt they make as they wake up: 'The Roar' as the ASML'ers call it. If you hear this sound during boot-up, it means everything's good to go. Little Easter eggs are also hidden in the ASML software: those in the know can kill time on some systems with a game of Snake, the classic from the old Nokia mobile mobiles. Days can be long in the cleanrooms.

But stranger things can happen in the chip factories. About twenty years ago, a lithography system in a fab in Arizona kept experiencing malfunctions. 'There was no technical explanation,' according to an engineer from the factory. 'And it wasn't just ASML's gear. All the systems had problems. The factory manager was on the verge of a breakdown, until someone pointed out that the factory was built on an old Native American burial ground. He decided that must be it: the fab was cursed.'

A shaman was summoned. Right away something caught his eye: the concrete obelisks planted by the entrance of the factory resembled tombstones. He gestured; if they wanted to appease the spirits, removing those would be a good place to start. The shaman proceeded, donning a cleanroom suit and inspecting the production line. After a long silence, he turned back to the manager. 'The spirits are attracted to red,' he hinted, and quietly left.

It was decided. 'If the spirits want red, that's what we'll give them.' The manager's eyes fell on a cardboard box, used as packaging for a lens from ASML. It was the brightest of reds. He folded it into a triangle resembling a tipi tent and placed it on the lithography machine.

As if by magic, the problems disappeared. The red box stood on the machine for years – no one was allowed near it. When the chip factory later ordered a second machine, they asked the ASML'ers, 'Could you also put a small red tipi on that second machine?'

Sure.

PART III

BUILDING
THE IMPOSSIBLE

Dawn breaks, but Vincent Nguyen is already wide awake. Standing at the foot of his bed, the young blogger runs through his equipment one last time. 'Two extra batteries for my mobile phone and three for my video camera.' Nguyen suspects he'll need them. If the rumors are true, he won't want to miss a second.

It's Tuesday January 9, 2007, and after months of anticipation the presentation of Apple's latest gadget is about to go live. Word is they've invented a device that can do it all: call, email, music, videos – everything. And now, at MacWorld 2007 in San Francisco, the wait is finally over. Nguyen slips into line at the Moscone center, that snakes its way up to the entrance on the first floor. It has all come down to this. Behind those doors, history awaits.

The floodgates open. Vincent sprints into the hall, closely followed by thousands of other visitors. Nguyen knows he has to act fast to claim the best spot. By now Apple is more like a cult than a computer maker, and everyone wants a close view of the company's enigmatic leader. The hall is buzzing with anticipation. It's electric. Steve Jobs steps out to a standing ovation, sporting his trademark jeans and black turtleneck. The founder, CEO, and front man lives for these moments. He is the undisputed king of product presentation, and this is his stage.

For the first time, the iPhone appears on the big screen. The audience is ecstatic. With the entire crowd hanging on his every word, Jobs turns on the charm. This is no old-fashioned telephone with cumbersome buttons and 'baby software', he says. This is a fully-fledged computer. Who needs more than one button – we have a touch screen that can do the rest. Magic, all in the palm of your hand.

An astounded 'whoa' resonates as the Apple Boss opens the slide to unlock screen. A smattering of stunned laughter and applause sweeps across the hall. No one can believe what they're seeing. With one swipe of his finger, Jobs has opened the door to the future.

He smirks. 'Wanna see that again?'

Six months later and on the other side of the country, a long line has formed at the Apple store in New York. It's June 29, 2007, otherwise known as release day, and Vincent Nguyen is once again right at the front of the line. He is one of the first to come running and cheering out of the store, a black bag raised triumphantly in his right hand. Apple employees form a guard of honor, applauding as he steps out into the sea of cameras. The photo of Vincent with his iPhone is beamed across the world: the ultimate recognition for the most loyal of followers.

The introduction of the iPhone marked the start of a revolution in mobile technology that would irrevocably alter daily life. When Google followed in Apple's footsteps and released the mobile operating system Android, the phone cemented its place as the most important computer in the lives of millions of people. Soon there was an app for everything, and pockets gradually got lighter as every accessory to our lives was integrated into the one device: ID's, tickets, bank cards; even your entire social life was now at your fingertips. As soon as billions of eyeballs caught sight of those screens that fateful day in 2007, they never really looked away.

The revolution that began with the iPhone also changed the chip industry. The smartphone is itself a 'killer app', an indispensable tool that demands ever increasing memory, processing power, and sensors. The need for continuous internet connection led to more capable modem-chips, which in turn opened the door to an unprecedented explosion of data, even faster mobile networks and the ubiquity of cloud services. Thanks to your phone, offline is no longer an option.

In 2006 Intel, who was supplying the chips for Apple's computers, was asked if it could also supply the processor for the iPhone. It declined: the margins in mobile chips were far too small for such a company. This was a blunder of historic proportions. Considering there are now 1.5 billion iPhones in circulation, with the latest device costing somewhere around a thousand dollars, Intel shot themselves in the foot.

The first iPhone received a chip based on ARM technology. Although more efficient with its power than the processor in a PC, you would still be lucky if your phone made it to the end of the day without an extra charge – and there's no magic in lumping a dead block of aluminum around in your pocket. The battery life needed to be extended, so Apple decided it would design its own chips. As Jobs preached, you can't have good software without its own dedicated hardware. In 2008, he acquired the chip company PA Semi, and Apple developed its first chips for the iPad and iPhone. The strategy worked, and since 2020 Apple Silicon has been so fast that the company now uses their own chips in laptops and computers. With a battery life that dwarfs its predecessors, the MacBook no longer needs Intel to stand on its own two feet.

Apple also profited heavily from TSMC's new production techniques, as the Taiwanese manufacturer became the first to figure out how to create chip structures using 5-nanometer technology. If you're wondering how small that is, look at your hand and count to five. Your fingernail grows at a rate of one nanometer – one millionth of a millimeter – per second. Whatever you did – or didn't – see is what TSMC needs to work with.

Although the circuits on the chip are actually farther apart, there's still only one machine in the entire world that can manufacture these ultrathin lines. Apple knows all about this, because in 2010 the headquarters in Cupertino were repeatedly visited by ASML's engineers. There, they explained the physics-defying machine currently under construction in Veldhoven: a machine capable of delivering an even more powerful engine for the iPhones of the future.

18

AN INVISIBLE MONOPOLY

The chip industry grows through shrinking. The more circuits crammed per square millimeter, the more valuable the disc of chips that rolls out of the factory. With every step down in scale, a chip of the same size becomes more powerful, more efficient, and better value for money. That opens the door to new uses and applications for the chips, which in turn means more profit for manufacturers.

But Moore's Law keeps knocking. Well before the turn of the millennium, the semiconductor industry realized it needed a new light source for lithography machines if it wanted to keep doubling the number of transistors every two years. No one imagined it would take two decades for this quest to yield results. 'The source was always a problem,' noted Martin van den Brink in 2023. 'In fact, it is still a problem.'

The second half of the '90s was a race to reach this milestone. With deep ultraviolet light cranked to its limit, Canon, Nikon, the American SVG, and ASML all started researching which technique would have the most potential when it came to printing even smaller structures. Three options came to light: printing with ions, writing patterns with electron beams (e-beam) or 'printing' with extreme ultraviolet light (EUV). ASML figured that EUV lithography, with its wavelength of between 10 and 100 nanometers, would be the most profitable. Manufacturers don't want a hundred machines that produce one wafer per hour. They want one machine that can spit out hundreds. All ASML needed to do was figure out how to make that happen.

The Sun's corona, 93 million miles away, is the closest place you can find extreme ultraviolet light in its natural form. On Earth, however, generating EUV requires extremely sophisticated technology. One way is to shoot a powerful laser beam at a tiny droplet of hot tin. This creates a plasma, an energy charged form of gas, far hotter than the surface of the sun. In this process, invisible light with a wavelength of 13.5 nanometers is emitted. If you can catch this with a mirror, you can direct it into a lithography machine to project a chip pattern. Sounds simple: you just have to build a sun.

The preparatory research into utilizing EUV for chip production took place across three continents. Initial experiments were run in the 1980s by scientists at NTT in Japan, with the United States and the Netherlands following suit soon after. Finally, in 1990 Professor Fred Bijkerk from Twente succeeded in creating an image using EUV light. A good start, but still a ways away from being able to print an entire working chip with it.

In 1997, Intel assembled a consortium of tech companies and initiated the 'EUV-LLC' research program. It included Motorola, amd, the Department of Energy, American national laboratories: all titans responsible for the birth of the industry itself. When the Cold War began to heat up, these labs tried to keep the Russian threat at bay by staying one pace ahead in the technological race. The scientists at these institutes were working on new semiconductor tools and nuclear devices. Both were important weapons in the eyes of the us, but with the collapse of the Soviet Union, America's hunger for the technology started to dwindle. The Iron Curtain had fallen, taking with it any sense of urgency for the Americans, and government budgets for research into semiconductor technology were gradually scaled back. If Silicon Valley wanted to follow through with this technology, it was going to have to drag itself over the line. In these years, Intel stepped up and became the most important backer of EUV-LLC. In April 2001, a prototype device capable of creating lines only 10 nanometers across finally appeared in the Lawrence Livermore National Laboratory in California. However, it cost 250 million dollars to build, and the consortium expected it would take another 250 to 750 million before it would be ready for mass production. Plus, it would take time: the general consensus suggested it would be 2005 before an EUV-produced chip would roll off a factory production line. That estimate turned out to be off by fifteen years.

ASML was already keeping an eye on the ball in the earliest years of EUV technology. In November 1995, Steef Wittekoek, together with Fred Bijkerk and Richard Freeman of Bell Labs, took a EUV-workshop at Zeiss. 'Lots to be done,' was the verdict scrawled in his notebook. It would have to wait.

In 1997, Jos Benschop, the head of ASML's research group, revisited whether EUV was a feasible option. After a series of initial tests, it turned out that Zeiss was able to develop the extremely smooth mirrors needed to guide the EUV light. The balance was shifting: enough pieces of the puzzle had fallen into place for this impossible machine to become a reality. And so, with financial support from European and German governments, in 1998 ASML partnered with Zeiss and started the Euclides consortium for EUV. Before long, Philips, TNO and the German Fraunhofer Institute were also on board, and in 1999 the European and American EUV initiatives decided to join forces. This was perfect for Intel: it was already pushing for more lithography manufacturers to join EUV-LLC so it would have a choice of different suppliers when the technology was ready. The American SVG already had a license, but when Nikon and Canon came knocking, Congress put their foot down. There was no way they were going to allow the Japanese companies to profit from American tax dollars.

As long-standing allies of the US, the Dutch had no trouble securing approval. But to actually get the license, ASML still needed permission from the committee investigating foreign investments in the US. And so, in 1999, Martin van den Brink began talks with Ernest Moniz, who was then undersecretary of Energy.

With his wavy silver-gray pageboy haircut, physics professor Moniz is instantly recognizable. He granted Van den Brink the license, on the condition that ASML builds a factory in the US to deliver the American EUV machines and prioritize the use of American suppliers – something he proudly recounted to the EE Times in February 1999. But the

Dutch company would never meet these conditions, nor did it ever intend to. Van den Brink wasn't too sure about EUV at that time, he recalls. 'My story to Moniz was quite simple. EUV meant a huge risk for ASML and that is why we would only accept this deal on our terms.'

Negotiations were dragging on in the dark library of the Department of Energy. 'Stop saying "no" and just give them what they want,' his lawyer advised. 'We can edit this deal later.'

Van den Brink treated the Americans to a fancy dinner after work, seeking a change of atmosphere with a nice view of the White House. But he had to leave before the final agreement was signed. 'Tomorrow morning, I expect to see the contract with the right conditions on my desk in Veldhoven,' Martin ordered, and caught the last British Airways flight out of Washington. While Moniz was proud of 'keeping high-paying jobs in the US', ASML was already putting its own plan into motion: the previously mentioned purchase of the American competitor SVG, complete with its EUV license, for 1.6 billion dollars. Once the Dutch plan to annex SVG was approved, the game was over. Only one Western lithography manufacturer was now in charge of developing EUV machines. Japan was still trying with its own research program, but without the American patents, Canon and Nikon never stood a chance.

This was how, under the careful eye of the cfius watchdog, ASML gathered a virtual monopoly over EUV. But the technology was still very much in its infancy, and in the race to keep up with Moore's Law, there was no guarantee ASML had its money on the winning horse. EUV light was, and still is, extremely difficult to generate and sustain in an industrial environment. The invisible rays are absorbed by almost all materials, even the air, which means the lithography machine needs to have mirrors in place of lenses and can only operate in a vacuum.

Martin was keenly aware of this when he encountered Rob van Aken, ASML's in-house architect, in 2001. 'Hey Rob, can you make an entire factory in a vacuum?'

Van Aken was startled: 'Not really. Don't people need to work there? Can't see that happening without oxygen.'

'Yeah, damn,' replied van den Brink, his brow furrowed. 'Guess we'll have to figure this one out ourselves.'

19

NEVER TRUST
THE DROPLET

'The First Light'. Chip manufacturers love to use this term when they turn on a lithography machine for the first time. It's a reference to astronomy, usually reserved for telescopes capturing their first murky picture of some distant galaxy. But Hans Meiling doesn't see any stars. He sees bananas.

It's January 2006, and ASML's project leader is spending his Saturday reviewing the very first exposed silicon wafer from the alphatool, an early prototype of the EUV machine. In the early days of EUV development the lamp was still weak – you could only barely make out the still image from the scanner on the wafer. It looked like a series of fuzzy semi-circles in the vague shape of a banana. Once Meiling noticed this, he couldn't see anything else.

Hans was one of the driving forces of EUV, all the way from its first steps as an ambitious research project right up to the moment the first machines started up in Taiwan and South Korea. He no longer works for ASML, but still wears a grey sweater with the words 'ASML, A RELATIVELY OBSCURE COMPANY' in large print across the chest. The quote from the BBC holds a special place in his heart: they had no idea just how desperately this obscure company was in search of its ray of light.

Around 2006 ASML was working on EUV with a team of 275 people, a large part of whom came from Philips, TNO and Zeiss. The operation was tucked away in a building by Eindhoven airport, which allowed the research group to work on EUV in peace – albeit under the watchful

Early lithography technology at NatLab: the Silicon Repeater 1 from 1973 and the PAS 2000, photographed at the start of the 1980s.

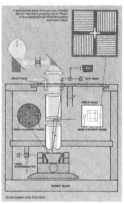

This Philips brochure on the PAS 2000 convinced Martin van den Brink, during his job interview in 1983, to join Philips.

Wim Troost was in charge of lithography technology at Philips and led ASML from 1987 to 1990. This photo was taken in 2022, the year in which Troost turned 97.

Gjalt Smit, pictured here in a photo from 2023, was the first CEO of the joint venture ASML, from 1984 until 1987.

Arthur del Prado, founder of ASM International and co-founder of ASML, receives the prize for Entrepreneur of the Year from Dutch prime minister Ruud Lubbers in 1983.

Willem Maris, ASML's CEO from 1990 until 1999.

Frenchman Eric Meurice was in charge between 2004 and 2013.

The Brit Doug Dunn led ASML from the end of 1999 until 2004.

Building 1, designed by Rob van Aken and opened in 1985, needed to look as futuristic as the tech companies in Silicon Valley do.

Frits van Hout (left) and Martin van den Brink, pictured in 1986 on their way to Phoenix, Arizona for a week full of meetings with American customers and suppliers.

In 1986, Frits Philips visited ASML, although he initially had trouble finding the site. Seated across from him are Wim Troost and Gjalt Smit (right).

Developers' work meeting, 1989. In the center: Steef Wittekoek, who led the research department. The flip chart shows the names of the European research programs Jessi and Esprit.

October 1999: Martin van den Brink explains to developers how ASML will make the transition to larger sized silicon wafers.

Peter Wennink (second from right) first worked as an accountant for ASML. In 1999, the year this photo was taken, he became financial director.

At first, wearing a facemask in the cleanrooms wasn't compulsory. From the late '90s onwards, ASML imposed much stricter requirements to prevent contamination of the machines.

A modern memory chip from Samsung. Due to the reduction in scale, more and more transistors fit onto a small chip surface.

A silicon wafer, consisting of multiple chips. This is a wafer from Intel, with Xeon chips for servers.

$$CD = k_1 \cdot \frac{\lambda}{NA}$$

The Rayleigh formula, printed on the wall of ASML's headquarters in Veldhoven, determines how small the details that a lithography machine can print are. The calculation is: the wavelength divided by the numerical aperture of the lens, multiplied by the k_1 factor. That factor is an indication of the complexity of the entire chip production.

eye of Jos Benschop and Martin van den Brink. As Meiling recalled, 'The first years were still totally unburdened by commercial pressure; it was wonderful.' All the time in the world to get absorbed by an overwhelmingly complex task, with nothing to go off but a few assumptions? Sounds like every engineer's dream. In his words, 'EUV was new and hard as hell; everyone wanted to be involved.'

But the dream couldn't last forever, and with the new year came new pressure. Martin wanted to have proof of a functioning machine by February to show at SPIE, the annual conference for chip manufacturers. Only photos of chip structures with a resolution of less than 40 nanometers would do, but the team were still counting theirs by the hundred. The race was on: Hans Meiling's team had only a few weeks to whittle this number down and refine the floating bananas into something presentable. Pumped up on adrenaline, the team pushed through long nights to complete a task that would normally take months. On the day of the presentation the latest images arrived from Veldhoven: 35 nanometers.

These very first EUV machines worked with a so-called discharge lamp, which generated such little power it took hours to expose a single wafer. Nevertheless, ASML sent alphatools to the research institute imec in Leuven and a lab in Albany, New York. It was only ever a temporary solution: Van den Brink knew the discharge lamp would never be powerful enough for the real job.

'How did we create the EUV light? By spinning two wheels in a bath of molten tin and adding a spark. If you wanted more light, you needed to spin faster, but this was just like biking quickly through the rain. It splattered in all directions and everything got dirty.' If ASML wanted to move forward, they needed to find another way.

Hopes fell on Cymer, a San Diego based company that already supplied lasers for conventional lithography machines. Cymer was working on a droplet generator capable of forming a 30-micron droplet of tin at a rate of 50,000 times per second. If you then shoot at it with a heavy CO_2 laser in a vacuum, you can create a plasma that radiates that golden wavelength of 13.5 nanometers.

That's the plan at least. Now they just have to do it in a chip factory.

In 2004, Intel invested 20 million dollars in Cymer to accelerate development of the EUV light source. But the company was not in the mood to be rushed: it did not want to be forced into a corner by heavily investing in a shaky technology with only one potential customer, who was from the Netherlands of all places. It was too risky: if they went for it, it would be on their terms.

Meanwhile, ASML had a not-so-secret weapon to keep its finger on the pulse in San Diego: Steef Wittekoek. The pioneer from the Philips era had been a member of Cymer's scientific advisory board for the past eight years and had held countless meetings about EUV during that time. He could see San Diego had plenty of smart employees willing to go out on a limb and experiment with interesting ideas, sometimes even with success. But the quality was inconsistent. Industrialization was Cymer's weak point, as engineers at ASML knew too well. The teams were horrified by the prototypes coming in from San Diego: these mechanical aberrations were a stark departure from the technology they were used to getting from their other suppliers. But the challenge of capturing extreme ultraviolet light in a lithography system is hard to match. The machine doesn't have to be pretty: it just has to work.

Cymer soon discovered that the intensity of the light source increased if you first flatten the droplet into a disc. The laser was now rigged to deal two separate blows. First, a gentle tap to flatten the droplet into a pancake-like shape, followed by an intense blast that heated the tin to two hundred thousand degrees, transforming it into plasma. Impressive, but that was only just the beginning: now they had to figure out how to do this fifty thousand times per second. The laws of physics groaned under the weight of ASML's progress; every step they took towards making the light source strong and stable was a battle against the limits of what was considered physically possible. Reflection caused a particular set of headaches. As soon as the CO_2 laser fired, the tin droplet would bounce a portion of the laser light back, all the way through a few hundred meters of pipes and mirrors to the heart of the laser itself. As soon as it touched that heart, the device would burn out. Game over.

The EUV lightsource

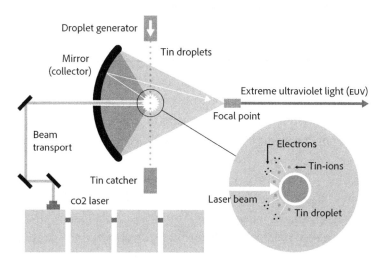

Two separate laser pulses strike a tin droplet up to 50,000 times a second, creating a plasma that generates EUV light.

The engineers searched for a solution the only way they know how: through trial and error. After numerous rounds of brainstorming, building and testing, ASML came up with the idea to integrate the tin droplet into the broader laser system by using it as a mirror itself. However, the laser light needed to refract back and forth several times to achieve the required strength, and by that time the miniscule droplet of tin had already vanished. Martin van den Brink realized he hadn't considered the ultimate limit: the speed of light. 'It took five years for us to realize: you couldn't trust the droplet.'

ASML was back to square one. The German manufacturer Trumpf, supplier of the laser, had to tackle the problem together with specialists from Veldhoven and San Diego. By this point, the laser apparatus for the EUV machine already consisted of more than 450,000 parts. Figuring it could handle a few more, the engineers devised a way to divert and cut off the reflected light before it could return to its origin. It took until 2008 for the trick to work, but by then the celebration was dampened: a new set of obstacles had already crashed the party. Starting the light source 'cleanly' turned out to be a challenge – just like a cold diesel engine emits a thick plume of soot first thing in the morning. The tin droplet also left a residue on the mirror after every explosion. This mirror is the 'collector' that gathers the light together, so as this layer thickens, the power decreases. This meant it needed to be constantly removed and cleaned, leaving the chip machine standing idle for long periods. It would be years before ASML would get this problem under control.

This whole process also required an extremely large amount of energy to retain enough light to actually print the chip patterns – far more than regular scanners. During its journey through the lithography machine, the light beam comes across 10 mirrors, each absorbing 30 percent of the light. Martin van den Brink quickly did the math: 'It starts with 1.5 megawatts from the grid, that yields 30 kilowatts in the laser, and that creates 100 watts of EUV light. Of this, about 1 watt ends up on the wafer.' The only thing these machines seemed good at was running at a loss, but at some point, they needed to turn a profit. So step by step, ASML upped the power. When it comes to illuminating on such a fine scale, only the most brutish lasers will do.

But more power also creates more heat. This causes the mirrors to expand, which in turn causes small deviations that immediately need to be corrected with small motors. Even the EUV mask, which carries the blueprint of the chip on it, is itself an extremely sensitive mirror. And like a 5-star–resort guest demanding nothing but perfection, even the slightest speck of dust on that mirror is unacceptable. But how do you keep all this clean? The machine might operate in a vacuum, but molecules can still penetrate the sealed chambers and settle on the mirrors. This led ASML to impose extra high demands on the cleanrooms the EUV machines need to be built in. Only ten dust particles of 100 to 200 nanometers in size can be tolerated in one cubic meter of cleanroom air – more than a thousand times cleaner than the air in a hospital operating room.

Hans Meiling already calculated back in 1998 what EUV would cost the chip manufacturers. According to his numbers, ASML was vastly underestimating the financial consequences of the new technology. In retrospect, he figures this was for the best. No respectable CEO would sign for a project that would take twenty years, without any promise of success or interim profit to carry it through. That's not taking a bet, that's bananas. This is also why the Japanese competition dropped out of the race: not because their engineers were any less capable, but because Nikon and Canon were simply not prepared to continue pumping so much money into EUV.

The real race against the clock began in 2006. Immediately after his SPIE presentation, Martin van den Brink sold the first EUV machine to Samsung from his room in the Amsterdam hotel The Grand, agreeing to deliver it by 2010. This was a daring deadline for commercial introduction: Samsung had demanded starting off with a machine that delivered 100 watts of EUV light. ASML was not even hitting 5.

From that moment on, Van den Brink required daily updates on the light source. Even during vacations – nothing was more important. One summer, frustrated by the lack of signal, he left his apartment in Italy in search of a suitable mountaintop to make the call from. Over the following two hours, it became clear just how much the issues at Cymer in San Diego had started to pile up. Every solution was causing new, bizarre problems. His heart sank. Van den Brink knew more money was needed to bring an end to the monstrous project. But where do you source capital when the financial world is collapsing, and dragging the chip industry along with it?

20

THE THREE MUSKETEERS

In September 2008, the world came to an abrupt halt. American investment bank Lehman Brothers filed for bankruptcy, pulling the emergency brake on the world market and sending it into complete chaos. The banking world had been a house of cards, built, ironically, on real houses with unreliable mortgages. With a global credit crisis now in full swing, there was no capital for chip manufacturers to invest in new technology. The world market shut down, and Veldhoven was left in the cold.

For the most part, ASML had a knack for anticipating the upcoming peaks and valleys in the chip industry. But no one could have expected this. 'Never before have we witnessed such a sharp and sudden fall-off in lithography system demand,' CEO Eric Meurice bluntly stated in his press release on December 18, 2008. It was now ASML's turn to hit the brakes. Work ground to a halt in the factories assembling lithography machines. With 6900 permanent employees and a 1600 strong temporary workforce, 1000 jobs needed to go.

ASML jumped on a reduced working hours program from the Dutch Employee Insurance Agency, UWV. That program promised to cover 70 percent of the affected workers wages, easing the pressure on companies while allowing them to protect their workforce. 1100 production workers, mainly from the factory floor, had their hours cut. But no one got away unscathed: every employee was also made to forfeit half of their yearly bonus, or their '13th' month's pay.

'The Big Down'. This was Peter Wennink's name for the crisis his company had landed in. But for all the panic surrounding them, Veldhoven was well positioned on 1.3 billion euros in reserves. Compared to their suppliers and chip manufacturers, they were in a remarkably good place. However, as Wennink made clear in a talk with analysts, they didn't want to be 'the central bank for the rest of the industry'. ASML kept investing, and the shareholders continued to receive dividends.

Dutch politicians soon noticed, and it didn't make for good news. The chip machine maker was receiving 15 million euros from the government in unemployment funds while paying out 83 million euros to investors. Politicians were astonished: it was basically disguised state support. ASML pushed back, arguing that paying dividends helped to prevent stable shareholders from leaving. But the damage was done, and the stock price was cut in half in a matter of months. Now the anxiety kicked in. The last thing they wanted was to become the latest punching bag for a hedge fund or short sellers to speculate on. This would inevitably make it vulnerable to hostile bids, a situation ASML was eager to avoid at all costs.

Since it did away with priority shares in 2006, ASML had left itself with only one line of defense against unwanted takeovers: the preference shares foundation, established in 1998. Fortunately, they never had to call on it, but there was still consistent interest from outside the company. On two occasions, ASML could have fallen into American hands. Around 1999, Applied Materials, a manufacturer of etching machines, considered entering the lithography market and canvassed ASML to gauge interest in a takeover. Both companies initiated a joint venture in electron lithography in 1999, but it turned out short-lived. Another American chip machine maker, KLA, wanted to acquire ASML when after the turn of the millennium the share price dropped. Veldhoven rejected the offer, and with that, the discussions ended.

Despite the initial panic, ASML pulled through to 2009 without falling into any serious danger. Six months later, the demand for chips and lithography machines began to pick up. They made it. The Netherlands was still fuming about the state aid fiasco, but Eric Meurice refused to give it air. He was already focused on bigger things: expanding the market share of lithography machines for processors and memory chips from 50 to 80 percent. If he managed to pull it off, this would direct most of the money generated for research into new technology straight to Veldhoven's front door. 'You'd have to be breathtakingly stupid to screw things up then,' as a former manager eloquently put it. They were slowly stacking the deck: by continuing to invest in research during a time of crisis while the Japanese competition remained cautious, ASML was building out a lead.

The company decided to focus on its collaborations with the handful of large chip factories that could afford the increasing investments in new technology. The plug was pulled on niche projects: so died the dream of using lithography machines for the production of LCD screens. The market had potential, but Martin van den Brink wasn't about to lose good engineers to flatscreens. He needed every available hand to help with the mountain of technical problems EUV was facing. The time left to fulfill Samsung's demand of 100 watts of power was quickly running out, and another major customer had decided to make life even more difficult.

Still unconvinced that extreme ultraviolet technology worked, TSMC decided to begin testing an e-beam machine, a piece of tech from the Dutch start-up Mapper. ASML had long written off e-beam for the mass production of semiconductors. True, if you write the fine chip structures with electrons you no longer need the expensive masks. But the speed of output is far too low for large scale work, and glacial in comparison to what EUV was promising. And this wasn't about to change: as the fineness of the chip structure increases, the printing only gets slower. Nevertheless, in 2010 TSMC came out saying it was convinced that Mapper's technology was a future standard. Veldhoven thought this was nonsense. They may as well have said grass wasn't green.

That same year, Hans Meiling turned into the parking lot at Infinite Loop, the entrance to Apple's headquarters. It was unusual to visit a 'customer of a customer', but Meiling figured the largest tech company in the world was worth an exception. After all, he thought, they invited him. Maybe Apple was considering up starting its own chip factory and wanted to hear about the EUV-machine.

But there was a bigger reason for the visit: the interest of a major customer like Apple could persuade TSMC. Meiling did let the Taiwanese know he was heading down to Cupertino. The relationship was fragile as it was – he didn't need them to find out through the grapevine.

A second meeting with Apple soon followed. ASML's ploy to build trust in the market for EUV technology paid off, and TSMC ordered their very first EUV machine soon after. Deeply impressed by the technical leadership of the Taiwanese, Apple dropped Samsung and from January 2013 TSMC took over the supply of its mobile devices. It marked the start of a symbiotic relationship between the two tech giants, built on a foundation from Veldhoven.

There was still one hurdle for ASML to overcome to get EUV ready for production. The small group working on the light source in San Deigo had been unable to increase the power of the laser. In a call with Martin van den Brink, Cymer's technical director laid his cards on the table: 'Look – this EUV light is unimaginably more complicated than a regular laser. In the past I used to just wait until everyone else left at five and figure out the problems on my own. But this, this is something else. We can't crack this.'

In 2012, Van den Brink's patience finally ran out. He wanted to take over Cymer and gain full control over the light source, hoping more money and more brain power would finally clear the blockage it had created in Europe. But Eric Maurice stubbornly refused. The world according to the CEO had a strict natural order: ASML is the architect that designs and assembles the systems, suppliers remain suppliers, and acquisitions only cause headaches. At least, that was the gospel according to Eric. He didn't want to go any further than a non-binding joint venture. For Van den Brink, this didn't go far enough.

'Goddammit Eric, if we don't take over Cymer we'll never get there,' fumed the technical director as they faced off over the idea. But Meurice couldn't be moved. In search of an ally to help push the takeover through, Martin immediately went to financial director Wennink's office. Peter blindly trusted Martin's technical judgement, but he needed some numbers.

'On a scale of one to ten, how good is our chance at getting EUV up and running?

'Between six and eight,' replied Van den Brink.

'Okay, let's go.'

At the next board meeting, the two teamed up and went for the kill. The Frenchman finally conceded: Cymer needed to be acquired. ASML couldn't cover the costs of the takeover and the extra EUV-research on their own, but thankfully, Eric Meurice and Peter Wennink had a plan.

At the start of July 2012, ASML announced a remarkable deal: the three largest customers were granted a stake in the company to release funds for research. Intel invested 3.3 billion euros into ASML in exchange for 15 percent of the shares. TSMC and Samsung followed suit with smaller parts, up to a combined maximum of 25 percent. But they would not be shareholders with voting rights or a chance to vote people on the board of directors. Only one hand gets to steer the course at ASML.

The plan was forged over the course of a single brainstorming session in Wennink's office. He became the driving force behind what became known as the Musketeer project, a reference to the French adventure novel *The Three Musketeers* by Alexandre Dumas. This time, the three protagonists were slightly different. There was Intel, the market leader in processors, Samsung, the largest manufacturer of memory chips, and TSMC, the world's largest semiconductor foundry. The three companies were united by a shared interest: they were all dependent on the innovation coming from ASML.

'One for all and all for one!' A nice idea, but the chip companies were not that tight-knit. Intel was making plans to use silicon wafers with a diameter of 450 millimeters instead of 300, a larger standard that could fit more chips. But ASML, like most chip machine manufacturers, had no faith in this format. All the devices in the chip factory would need to be adapted, and this disruption would cost more than the extra yield could ever make up for. The numbers were all wrong. If Intel wanted a '450' lithography machine, the Americans needed to pay for it. Even then, ASML would only deliver these machines if at least one other manufacturer was on board – this is why they also asked Samsung and TSMC to acquire a stake. The companies agreed on the condition that a sizable portion of the money would be allocated to EUV. The research funds were split: 553 million euros were earmarked for a machine with larger wafers, and 828 million for the development of EUV technology.

During the summer months, the entire ASML leadership traveled the world to unite the musketeers in this collective mission. Intel demanded the most preparation, earning this musketeer its own project name: 'Polder'. In turn, the Americans came up with a password for the agreement: 'Stroopwafel', a sweet treat from the Netherlands. Finally, Intel's operational director Brian Krzanich signed the papers in a hotel in Palo Alto. Over at TSMC, the signature of founder Morris Chang was required to purchase 5 percent of Veldhoven's shares. Samsung acquired a stake at the eleventh hour, taking 3 percent. In all fairness, their CEO had been sick.

In total, ASML sold 3.85 billion euros worth of shares, receiving 1.38 billion to invest in the development of new technology. In addition, 1200 high-tech jobs were created in Veldhoven. This was a huge amount for a company with 4000 engineers, and a massive boost for the Brabant region.

However, the plan still needed to be approved at the shareholders meeting. While minority stakes from clients are not unusual in the chip industry, what ASML was about to present would be a tougher pill to swallow. In exchange for compensation, existing investors were being asked to contribute a portion of their stake. A synthetic buyback of shares: a clever construction devised by Wennink to avoid diluting the value.

A barrage of critical questions followed from major investors such as Capital Group, Fidelity and BlackRock. Wennink weathered the storm, and in September 2012 the shareholders finally agreed. A month later, they announced the acquisition of Cymer for 1.95 billion dollars in shares.

However, the deal would take an unexpected turn for the freshly ordained shareholder Intel. As promised, ASML worked on the '450' machine for a year. But Van den Brink was done playing games. If Intel wanted it, they needed to place an order and pay for it. The Americans were reluctant and felt they had been called out. 'Are there no other manufacturers who would like to buy a '450' machine?' 'Well, geez, this was *your* idea,' sneered Van den Brink.

In early 2013, Van den Brink arranged a meeting in California between the technical directors of Intel, Samsung and TSMC. For the first time, the three musketeers could look each other in the eye. It was no longer one for all, but two against one. TSMC and Samsung went straight for the jugular: they saw no sense in the larger wafers. This surprise attack knocked Intel's boss off his feet. After decades of American hegemony, Asian chip manufacturers were now the ones calling the shots. And there was nothing he could do about it.

The 450 project was brought to an abrupt halt and the remaining budget freed up, giving ASML an extra 300 million euros to get EUV up to speed. That money came in at exactly the right time.

21

JOANN'S HANDS

Please, do be careful when you shake hands with Joann. She has the most remarkable fine motor skills, honed through years of work in ASML's cleanroom in San Diego. Hunched over a machine in complete concentration, she carefully wraps two wires around what is known as "the nozzle". That is what they call the spout at the heart of the EUV light source, responsible for shooting tin droplets through a hollow needle at a rate of fifty thousand times per second.

Only Joann and one of her colleagues have the ability to wind and solder these virtually invisible wires. It's a delicate task few could ever master. 'Even watchmakers can't do this,' says their awestruck boss, 'and there's no way to automate it.'

It is not a trivial matter: the nozzle regularly gets clogged during day-to-day use in the chip factory. When that inevitably happens, the only thing to do is to swap it out for a new one. It's hard to imagine, but without the fingers of Joann and her colleague, the EUV machines at Samsung and TSMC would grind to a halt. In the year 2023, two pair of human hands keep the world's most advanced chip production lines in motion.

The EUV laboratory in San Diego is expanding that same year, as is every ASML facility. Lithography machines are in high demand, and extra space is needed to test the prototype light-source for the new generation of EUV machines. If you want more power, you need to shoot a higher frequency of droplets, and it is up to the engineers here to figure out how. For all the mind-bending physics that take place in a lithography machine, this part is exactly as it sounds. And for once, you can even see it: in their test set-up, you can watch the rapid fire of molten droplets, like tiny dots silently floating in a metal tube.

The door to another cleanroom swings open to reveal 'The Monster', as it is affectionately known among the staff. This metal behemoth, standing several meters tall, surrounds the vacuum chamber where the plasma goes to ignite. The whole light source exudes an otherworldly aura – like an engine block hoisted straight out of a spaceship. Nearby, an engineer closely inspects a wafer full of tin splatters in her hand. With these discs, they can check whether the heart of The Monster is still beating reliably. Somewhere deep in the steel bowels of the beast lies the nozzle that Joann soldered, and in the chamber next to it sits the laser, ready to begin blasting away.

Elsewhere in a sealed control room, three engineers examine the latest results. They can finally cheer: the lab has successfully generated 600 watts of EUV light. But there's no chance to take the foot off the gas. Everyone's already talking about the next milestone: 1000 watts.

Ten years earlier, Martin van den Brink didn't even dare to dream of such numbers.

In 2013, the EUV source's power output was far too low to support profitable chip production. The droplet generator needed to have perfect timing and deliver a perfect droplet every time for it be useful. But the components were small and fragile. They constantly leaked, got clogged or simply broke off under the high pressure. Most of the droplet generator was still hand-made by Cymer and it was virtually impossible to test the part in advance. This made for completely unpredictable yields: in the initial phase of production, half of the droplet generators didn't even work. It would take years to industrialize this work and get it ready for mass production.

As soon as the acquisition was made, ASML cleaved Cymer in two. It was a strict division of assets, designed to prevent any conflict of interest. The result of the split is clearly visible on Thormint Court, a dead-end road to the north of San Diego where the company is located.

Look to one side and you'll see the 'old' Cymer, ticking along with the production of regular lasers just as before. They even still supply to competing chip machine manufacturers like Canon and Nikon. Not that ASML minds – more important is what is on the other side of the street. There you'll find the closely guarded EUV facility: this is where the real action is, and access is strictly ASML-only.

With the takeover complete, Martin van den Brink immediately hauled a significant part of the light-source development over to Veldhoven. In the space of a few months, there were already over 1000 engineers working away at ASML and laser manufacturer Trumpf – four times the size of the team in San Diego. There was no time to waste in trying to convince the American Cymer employees to 'the new way of thinking,' as Van den Brink called it. When it comes to industrializing complex technology, you need the ruthless Dutch touch.

The very first EUV experiments at Cymer were conducted by Australian engineer Danny Brown. Before landing on tin droplets, all kinds of metals were subjected to the lasers in his lab in an effort to generate the special light. 'Thankfully, somehow, nothing exploded. But nothing worked either.'

Once ASML took the reins, Brown found himself under enormous pressure to increase and stabilize the power output. Every year ASML was publishing a list of the largest technical obstacles, and every year, Cymer was number one. San Diego quickly had to get accustomed to Dutch engineering style: they would drill straight into any weak spot, like a dentist dealing with a rotting tooth. And there was no time wasted on anesthesia. It was direct, blunt, and in the eyes of the Americans, often downright rude. As a result, the new partners became increasingly reluctant to report setbacks. Unfortunately for them, hiding a problem out of fear was the quickest way to hit a nerve in Veldhoven. When Frits van Hout took over the project in 2013, he felt this all too well: 'Cymer were forever promising it'll get better. It was always "it will be done next week" and then, of course, it wouldn't happen. It drove us crazy – they wouldn't ever just give it to us straight.'

Van Hout arranged retreats to a hotel in Kasterlee in Belgium in an effort to bring the project leaders and departments closer together.

With Veldhoven fifty kilometers away and all the pressure and obstacles out of sight, they could calmly evaluate the state of affairs over a series of lunches and dinners. Every month they were also joined by an engineer from San Diego, and two times a year a similar session would take place in San Diego. They needed this to work, and it could only be done together.

Getting EUV technology up and running was already complex enough, but ASML made it even more challenging by kickstarting the next generation of EUV machines. These systems had a larger lens aperture, known in technical terms as 'High NA' systems. This was understandably frustrating for the teams from Cymer, and the retreats became battlegrounds where managers bickered over available budgets. With the lens manufacturer Zeiss' lengthy preparation time, these machines were still about ten years away from hitting the market.

According to Van Hout's calculations, the development of EUV was costing ASML 10 million euros per week, and it had yet to pay them a single cent. Meanwhile, the outside world was reacting with skepticism to every delay publicly announced by the company. Competitors were quietly hopeful: it looked like the fire that had carried ASML so far was set to burn out.

Pressure mounted on the project leaders: every arduous step carried the weight of the company's future. Now more than ever they needed to pull together, so the senior management decided to go on an outing with someone skilled in herding lost souls: a local Brabant shepherd. The ASML'ers were tasked with guiding the sheep into the pen themselves, with the occasional helpful nudge from the yelping sheepdogs. One sheep in, three sheep out: after having worked on EUV for so long, the process felt all too familiar.

The EUV designers were given a somewhat less biblical outing – stress prevention courses. The management knew the greatest risk was people working too hard and burning out before the machine could get up and running. Van Hout tried to convince the technicians of this when he told them they shouldn't go at it 'like idiots'.

The course leader was met with a group of enthusiastic, bright people all around the age of thirty. A handful were clearly on the verge of burnout, and the rest were busy wrestling with their own perfectionism: the worst thing you can ask an ASML'er is to choose between delivering on time or delivering quality.

They began with a little food for thought: 'Stress itself is not something that happens to us, but how we respond to something that happens to us.' An image flashed up on the screen. It's an overburdened donkey, struggling with a heavily laden cart but refusing to give up. They all know that feeling.

One of the stress prevention tips seemed tailor made for the participants. 'When a supervisor says, "I want to speak to you in ten minutes," your heartrate skyrockets. We all know why – you've immediately assumed they're angry.' The tip: think of nice things instead. 'Trick your brain by imagining a laughing baby, or a tropical paradise. Push that image of a barking boss out of your mind – think of a puppy wagging its tail with joy!'

When it came to the light source, every step forward felt as if it was followed by two steps back. One of the worst setbacks was in the expensive optical system. The lithography machine regularly needed to be stopped to replace the mirrors, as they were extremely vulnerable to contamination from carbon deposits. These would settle on the surface, dirtying them and eating away at the power. The machines had to pump continuously to remove unwanted matter from the vacuum chambers: one stray fingerprint was enough to require an extra 24 hours of pumping. Only when a chemical analysis confirmed everything was back below the contamination threshold could the EUV light be flicked back on.

In addition, it turned out the mirrors developed blisters. The coating consisted of dozens of wafer-thin layers, which were actually a stack of mini-mirrors to deflect unwanted light frequencies. Much like your own skin during a long day at the beach, these layers would burn easily, and the consequent blisters caused the light to rapidly lose power. The result: fewer wafers per hour, and more angry clients. Graciousness is not the name of the game when there's this much money on the line, and customers were not happy with Veldhoven.

Samsung and TSMC were already using prototype machines in 2013, running trials to iron out any problems before embarking on full-scale production with EUV. As part of this, the chipmakers expected all problems ASML found to be reported immediately, but Veldhoven had its own strategy for these bad-news conversations. The engineers wanted to first identify a 'course of solution' for any acute problems before alerting the impatient chip manufacturers. In the experience of Hans Meilling, 'if you immediately tell your customer about a stumbling block but you have no idea how you're even going to try and solve it, that's the easiest way to make a bad impression.' And as he sees it, this isn't a matter of being dishonest: 'Obviously you should not talk complete nonsense, but you don't always have to disclose everything you know. That is different from not telling the truth.'

The delay in EUV development dragged on for years. The struggle with the light source was stressful for everyone. Even Van den Brink acknowledges this. There were moments when he also wondered if they would ever get on top of it. 'But it's just like your time in the military – when you're in the thick of it, it's terrible. But in retrospect, it's the best time of your life.'

Not that he was ever in military service – he was exempt. Probably for the best: good luck getting Martin to follow an order.

22

YIN AND YANG

As a boss at ASML, you have little say. For CEO Eric Meurice, this was an unexpected culture shock. Direct orders were taken more like starting points of a conversation, and that was not at all the Frenchman's style. Like his favorite historical figure, Napoleon, he preferred to be the center of power – to the point of being downright intimidating, as his employees frequently experienced. If you crossed him on a bad day, his responses would be harsh and blunt. But outside of working hours, Meurice cut a far more relaxed, even entertaining figure. He was the first to open the conversation at dinner: 'What can't we talk about? Sex, politics and religion. Well then, which one should we get into first?'

'The Dutch have one big disadvantage – they're not French,' joked Meurice as he left in 2013 following the end of his second term. He wasn't shy with his opinions: 'Dutch people just aren't quick to accept a clear leader that is willing to ramp up the pace.'

Believe what you like about the Dutch, but ASML clearly has a leader: Martin van den Brink. 'CEO' might not be on his business card, but he's without doubt the rock the company relies on. He's the one setting the technical agenda, helping to write patents and determining the strategic acquisitions. It is his name that commands respect throughout the entire chip industry. And if one of his plans gets blocked in the boardroom, he'll dig in and stick to it until he gets his way. When it comes down to it, it is clear who has his hand on the wheel.

An autocracy with a hint of anarchy grew around Van den Brink, a culture in which everyone has the freedom to propose a better idea.

As he said himself, 'at ASML, you should have the feeling that you can change something. It's the people that make the difference.'

With around 13,000 employees in 2013, this made ASML a challenge to manage.

As Eric Meurice's contract was coming to an end in 2012, the board of commissioners began to wonder who could succeed him. Did ASML really need another outsider to keep Martin in line? The commissioners knew they already had a potential leader within the executive board – the personable Peter Wennink. By many, he was already viewed as CEO. As chief financial officer, he was outwardly the most prominent figure in the company, he knew the suppliers in the region on a first-name basis, and spent his time advocating for the interests of the Dutch manufacturing industry in The Hague. Only by looking at his lanyard could you know his official role.

Since 1999, an ever-deepening bond of trust had grown between Wennink and Van den Brink. They knew exactly what they had in one another. They oversaw acquisitions together, visited clients together, and stood shoulder to shoulder in the face of the fury of the French CEO. These harsh confrontations bonded them. When Meurice and Van den Brink clashed, which happened often, Wennink was the one who kept things together. He shone when it came to building bridges. But this was also tiring – after all, it's never a good idea to keep two roosters in the same henhouse.

In Wennink's view, ASML didn't need another boss from outside like Meurice. It was better off without any 'big dogs' trying to put a leash on Martin to satiate their ego. He didn't want to have to deal with someone 'who barks and pisses at every tree they come across', and neither was he excited about reprising his role as a mediator. He would rather just do it himself. But not without Martin. In the end, both Van den Brink and Wennink expressed an interest in leading the company, but also said they would accept the other as leader if that was the decision. The board could see that they were both essential to the company. They complemented each other perfectly. 'They're like yin and yang,' as one commissioner put it.

And so, in 2013, ASML appointed two president-directors. Wennink became president and CEO, Martin van den Brink president and technical director. An unusual setup, but there was no doubt about their individual roles. The CEO steers and Martin sets the course – that's just the way it is at ASML. Wennink knew this. As he said, 'With Martin, you have the golden ticket in the palm of your hand. Are you really going to mess with that?'

Wennink came up with a simple formula for their salaries: combine the previous CEO and CFO's salaries and divide it by two. It was less than Eric Meurice received, but they would more than make up for it soon enough.

Over the course of the next six months, the duo worked out a plan for the future of ASML. But the collaboration wasn't immediately all smooth sailing. Wennink was initially unsure in his new role, a feeling exacerbated by his colleague's tendency to meddle with everything. Van den Brink's extensive knowledge of the chip industry, combined with his fiery temperament, proved overwhelming. For a non-engineer like Wennink, every visit to Martin's office felt like a test.

The two presidents revived a tradition from the time of Willem Maris and put on a yearly barbeque for ASML's top management. As the only directors with yards spacious enough to set up a tent for 150 people, it was alternately hosted at the homes of Van den Brink and Van Hout. Wennink had a more nondescript house in the suburbs of Veldhoven – although it still boasted a wine cellar.

Wennink never doubted Martin's technological instinct. 'With Martin, the goal is always clear. We know what machine we're going to deliver next year, and we know what we'll be doing in ten years. It's easy – there's no discussion about it, and that makes life simpler.'

But leading as a pair is tricky. You need keep your ego in check, and there isn't any room to wing it with what you tell the outside world or other ASML'ers. Peter and Martin do not always agree with each other, but what matters is that they learned to understand each other, inside and out. Often, they knew exactly what the other was going to say before they had even said it.

Every few weeks, the two would take a long walk in the Kampina, a nature reserve in Brabant. The space afforded them a quiet moment to catch up, whether about work or how their kids were doing. It is the same area where you can often spot Van den Brink on a morning bike ride in the nearby woods. He has two children from a previous marriage and two stepchildren with his third wife, while Wennink has two children from his second marriage.

Wennink is the one who wants to keep everyone on board. He understands the confrontational culture of the technical teams: 'The clashes are not so much about ideology but about technology. It is about showing who is right – everyone wants to be the smartest in the room.' He wanted to make ASML into a place where everyone felt comfortable, not just the hardened engineers. And to him, constantly shouting and yelling is pointless. 'People just get used to it. They'll say, "Yeah, sure, whatever.' I can also get emotional – but if it only happens every now and then, it's much more impactful.'

But there's no yin without yang. And Van den Brink had no reservations about showing his anger. Sometimes, people left his office in tears. 'Who the hell invited that loose cannon!' he exclaimed out of nowhere during a meeting, angered that a competitor was at a presentation for clients. Once a team member explained, his anger evaporated just as quickly as it came on. He just wanted to know what was going on; not letting it go would just be a waste of time. A joke followed to clear the air.

Most meetings with Martin never got past the first page on the agenda. He would hijack the conversation almost immediately, sometimes talking for three quarters of an hour about what he had just read in the paper and leaving fifteen minutes for the topic on hand. He knew what he was doing: one gift he received from a colleague was a Delft Blue tile, inscribed with one of his regular closing remarks: 'We didn't see many slides, but we grew mentally.'

Martin made a habit of challenging everyone who sat down with him. Even if he was fully on board with your proposal, he would take the opposing stance to test your conviction. Sarcasm was a favorite weapon, often used as soon as he had an inkling of doubt. 'Interesting. And that definitely works just as well as your previous idea?' he would cynically ask.

Most ASML'ers grew accustomed to his outbursts. It was just a part of life in Veldhoven. The real thing to worry about was if he kept looking at his laptop. Bad news: apparently, you're not important enough to pay attention to.

His colleagues consistently praise his aptitude for abstract thinking. You can see this in action: when speaking with intense concentration, Martin keeps his eyes clenched shut for seconds at a time. As his focus deepens, his right hand instinctively goes to his forehead, three fingers raised in the air – as if he is pushing his thoughts back in to keep them from wandering off.

But as sharp as he is on technical details, Martin can be remarkably absentminded in his day-to-day life. When traveling, he was prone to grabbing the wrong suitcase from the conveyor belt or simply forgetting his belongings altogether. 'Oops. My laptop is still on board,' he exclaimed while navigating customs at a Korean airport. He had simply walked off the plane without his personal items. As one colleague joked, 'the Dutch consulate in California has a stack of spare passports ready for him.' Martin's unwavering focus on ASML left little room for anything else. If it is not on his mind, it does not exist.

While Martin was forgetting about the outside world, Peter Wennink was actively pursuing it, representing the company at shareholder meetings, to suppliers, the media and any politician that would listen. The two still managed the relationships with chip manufacturers together, as they had been doing for years: meeting after meeting, flight after flight, continent after continent and then, as always, back to Veldhoven. For Wennink, personal engagement is everything in the chip industry: 'It's never the lawyers that arrange a deal. It's the people that need to make the decisions. The ones that sit by each other, look each other in the eye and say, "I trust you." That's how it happens.'

Yet during the early years of their partnership, confidence in EUV was waning. Technical problems were pushing back the introduction date, and a disastrous presentation in Silicon Valley in 2014 only made

Working of an EUV machine

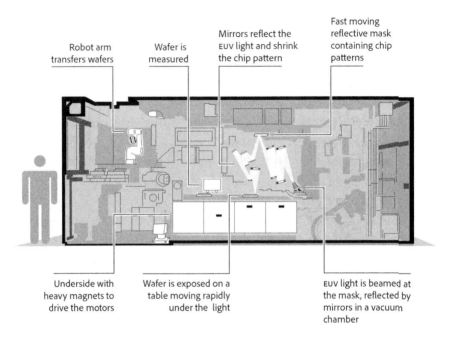

Robot arm transfers wafers

Wafer is measured

Mirrors reflect the EUV light and shrink the chip pattern

Fast moving reflective mask containing chip patterns

Underside with heavy magnets to drive the motors

Wafer is exposed on a table moving rapidly under the light

EUV light is beamed at the mask, reflected by mirrors in a vacuum chamber

thing worse. ASML's development machine had broken down, leaving TSMC pessimistic about the project. 'Moore's Law is dead!' jeered the American analysts in their comments. They were celebrating like kids in a schoolyard: you could almost hear the 'Naah-nah-nah-naah-nah!' as they wrote the headlines.

The mood was solemn as the ASML delegation gathered for breakfast in San Jose the morning after the presentation. Martin van den Brink tried to limit the damage by leaking technical details to the media, claiming that the EUV machine at TSMC only had a minor problem and would soon be up and running. ASML needed the world to trust that Moore's Law was alive. Still, Samsung was waiting to receive the promised light source – one powerful and reliable enough for chip production. At least 100 watts, as agreed upon.

The risks were piling up for ASML. Even though the regular EUV machine was still not functional, preparations were already underway for the next generation of machines, the so-called High NA systems. This required a multi-billion-euro investment from Zeiss, as the lens manufacturer had to build a whole new factory and fill it with extremely expensive equipment to meet the new technical demands.

However, these plans didn't leave ASML's supervisory board jumping with joy. They were hesitant to invest in yet another non-functional machine. Nonetheless, Wennink and Van den Brink managed to secure approval, and in November 2016 ASML invested one billion euros for 24.9 percent stake in Carl Zeiss SMT, the semiconductor division of the lens manufacturer. With this investment, the Germans had access to 760 million euros to develop the next generation of EUV mirrors in Oberkochen. They could start pouring the slabs, and the engineers were already licking their lips at the prospect of their new futuristic playground.

But Martin van den Brink faced another challenge. He needed to immediately start looking for customers for the new machine, which at this stage was only a blueprint. In 2017, he arranged for a private tour of the Van Gogh Museum in Amsterdam so he could speak with the chip manufacturers among the sunflowers. But Samsung had no interest in a High NA machine. 'Make sure you get the promised 100-watt light source up and running first. Then we'll talk,' the Koreans responded.

At the end of that year, Wennink and Van den Brink flew to South Korea for a meeting with Kinam Kim, the head of Samsung's semiconductor division. As they stepped off the plane, Martin glanced at his phone. Grinning like the Cheshire Cat, he showed the message to Wennink. It was an email from the Australian engineer Danny Brown, radiating relief: 'We have 100 watts!'

San Diego had finally pulled through. But to truly convince Samsung, they needed to have an EUV light source fully up and running in Korea, not just in some shaky testing system on the other side of the world. And the collector, the mirror that captures the EUV light, was still getting contaminated far too often. That is simply not workable in a chip factory that needs to run around the clock. 'So really, we did not have anything,' said Van den Brink. He was never one to count his chickens before they hatched.

One Saturday morning just before Christmas, Samsung's technology chief arrived in Veldhoven. He wanted to see results. 'You go on ahead,' Van den Brink had to tell his wife. He was about to leave with his family on a ski vacation, but the light source was still malfunctioning. Desperate to find a solution, the technical director and his teams in San Diego held daily calls with Martin to solve the issue of the blackened mirrors. ASML had until March 2018 to get Samsung's machine working, but there was no good news to give the visitor. Meanwhile, another deadline was fast approaching: Van den Brink had promised the supervisory board he would secure orders for the High NA machines before the first of the year, otherwise his plan would halt. A request for a three-month extension was made: one more quarter to decide the commercial fate of EUV. Van den Brink didn't dare provide any guarantees about its success. He could already hear the smug analysts taunting him all over again.

In the meantime, Intel was actually considering buying a set of High NA machines, but the asking price was half a billion dollars higher than what the Americans were willing to pay. Van den Brink's jaw hit the floor. 'Holy cow. Well, if you guys really want those machines, we'll split the difference.' Intel agreed, although the details still needed to be worked out. Van den Brink rallied his sales team; they needed to bulldoze this enormous financial hurdle as soon as possible, and with that he set off to Taiwan to reel in the next High NA customer.

At first, TSMC showed no interest in this newest generation of machines. But when Van den Brink and Wennink flew together to Taipei in February, the Taiwanese were convinced. 'It's a leap of faith, but we're jumping together,' Wennink poetically promised them. That very line persuaded Morris Chang to purchase TSMC's first EUV machines. And if the implementation of new technology proved a challenge, ASML would ensure that backup machines or alternatives were available to keep production going.

Samsung proved to be a tougher case. The Koreans had been waiting seven years for a working EUV machine, and they were out of patience. Martin van den Brink wrote a personal email to Kinam Kim: 'Give us one more month – just until April. Then it'll happen.'

A completely coincidental discovery pushed EUV over the tipping point. In February 2018, an engineer noticed something strange: 'Isn't it odd how the mirror becomes clean again when we open the vacuum system to change parts?' Antoine Kempen, a chemist on the team, had an explanation: it was likely because of oxygen entering. A rapid series of tests followed, and their suspicions were confirmed: if you add a bit of oxygen to the vacuum in addition to the hydrogen, the mirror of the light source stays functional far longer.

At the end of March, Van den Brink traveled to Korea to show that EUV was ready for production. 'We didn't tell Samsung anything, only that the machine needed a tiny upgrade. One extra pipe with oxygen, and the problem was solved.' Satisfied with the result, Samsung immediately signed the contract for the High NA machine.

Van den Brink awarded Antoine Kempen the honorary title of 'fellow' for 'groundbreaking work in the fight against contamination in EUV technology.' Thanks to his little puff of oxygen, ASML could breathe a sigh of relief.

23

THEY WON'T GO HOME

NanoCity. Sounds small, but 40 percent of the world's digital memory is born here. When you exit from highway 311 towards Samsung's memory chip factories in Hwaseong, it's hard to imagine that South Korea was once incredibly poor. Exhausted by Japanese colonization and ravaged by the Korean war, for a time it was even worse off than its sibling to the North. But since 1970, the GDP per Korean has grown from 600 to 40,000 dollars. Thanks to the strictly planned economy of the military dictatorship and mega-corporations like Samsung, LG and Hyundai, the country transformed into an industrial powerhouse. 20 percent of the South Korean economy now relies on the revenue of one single company. Hence their nickname: this is the Republic of Samsung.

The colossal fabs are covered with a series of red, yellow and blue panels, each several meters high. It evokes the colors of the iconic Dutch painter Piet Mondriaan – but, as a Samsung employee points out, this isn't art. It's an enlarged rendering of the patterns found on the memory chips, for the storage capacity of your phone or the working memory of your laptop, that are produced in these buildings.

Upon entering the Samsung factory, you are greeted by a plaque inscribed with ten guiding principles for its employees. 'Reach beyond your goal' is one of the commandments. Founder Lee Byung-chull admired the wisdom of the Chinese philosopher Confucius and was inspired by the rock-solid discipline of Japanese factories. Under his successor Lee Kun-hee, Samsung's shifted its focus towards the West and became the market leader in telephones. Kun-hee believed that Korea's biggest conglomerate needed to swiftly adapt to new markets, touting his favorite slogan: 'Change everything, except for your wife and children.'

NanoCity, situated just south of the capital Seoul, has a fully operational production line open for visitors. 'This one is as big as three soccer fields, but we also have ones spanning the size of eleven,' the guide explains, gesturing towards the cleanroom behind her. Shielded off by a large glass wall, visitors have a panoramic view over the entire space. There is little to see except machines. Humans pose too much of a risk: they bring in dirt and dust particles that harm production. Nevertheless, an invisible team of thirty employees is on standby, ready to intervene should any issues arise.

Robots and automated carts transport stacks of wafers, each containing up to ten thousand memory chips. It takes six weeks for one disc to undergo every step of the process, after which it goes to a different factory to be cut up into individual chips.

Chip machine manufacturers like Applied Materials, Lam Research, Tokyo Electron and ASML have branches located nearby Samsung so they can promptly respond when called upon. The guide points to the back of the hall where the scanners are located, bathed in a sea of yellow light. 'The color aids the lithography process, just like developing photos in a darkroom.' A golden halo for the factory's most expensive piece of equipment.

The chip division is the most lucrative arm of Samsung Electronics. But demand for memory chips fluctuates heavily, leading to dips in the market that hit Samsung's revenue hard. In addition, computer memory chips have a slimmer profit margin compared to advanced computing processors, which is why the Koreans are so intensely focused on efficiency and high throughput. Once they get EUV up and running, and the machine spends less time idle, they stand to save valuable production time.

At the end of 2018, NanoCity was filled with large yellow construction cranes as work began on a new eight-story factory. The start-up cost: 15 billion dollars, with an additional injection of 11 billion dollars. Samsung was effectively building two fabs on top of one another, as it also wanted to use the EUV machines for making memory chips. White and blue containers with ASML's logo were already piled up, ready to go.

Through tireless effort and military-style discipline, Samsung and SK Hynix, formerly part of Hyundai, conquered the chip world. And they expect nothing less from their suppliers. Working in South Korea means, 'pushing hard, harder, and then even harder', in the words of one ASML'er.

ASML's sales director Sunny Stalnaker was born in Korea and deals extensively with Korean technicians. She is quick to answer when asked what sets these chip factories apart from other customers: 'Simple. Their laser-sharp focus.' The Koreans are fixated on getting the most of out of their lithography machines, and do not tolerate setbacks.

When the Asian currency crisis hit in 1997, it plunged Samsung and SK Hynix deeply into debt. It required billions of dollars in support from the International Monetary Fund to help the South Korean economy recover. According to Stalnaker, the chip factories survived on sheer willpower: 'All Asian chipmakers pay attention to costs, but none of them push like the Koreans – they work unbelievably hard.'

For instance, as soon as there is a problem with a system, the Samsung employees in charge stay onsite until the machine is up and running again. 'They don't even think about going home before a problem is solved. If you asked them, they'd probably just laugh.' You can see this dedication has rubbed off on the ASML'ers in South Korea: the office comes complete with beds, so you can take a power nap in between speaking to enthusiastic chip manufacturers.

'A sharp knife calls for a good cook,' or so the saying goes at Samsung. They aim for nothing less than total mastery over the recipes for producing chips with lithography, the employees at ASML have noticed. 'When there's a problem with a machine, you get bombarded with their analyses, down to the smallest detail,' says Stalnaker. 'They're not necessarily relevant, but you need to run through it all to get a grasp on all the facts. And in the meantime, you have to answer ten thousand questions. They want updates every hour, even if nothing happens in that hour.' In the early nineties, Japanese lithography makers often covered up their machines during maintenance, to prevent Korean customers from seeing the internal components. ASML, on the other hand, laid everything bare for all to see.

The Koreans have a 'killer mentality,' as Frits van Hout says. In his years leading ASML's support department, he frequently found himself alone face-to-face with of a group of shouting Koreans. However, there was no point trying to match their tone. 'They're all under enormous pressure from their bosses. And as soon as you find the solution to their problem, you have a friend for life.'

As a token of gratitude and on behalf of ASML, Van Hout was presented with South Korea's Hendrick Hamel award. Hamel is probably the most famous Dutchman you've never heard of. Back in the seventeenth century, the life of this bookkeeper from Gorinchem took an unexpected turn when, while working for the Dutch East India Company, a shipwreck accidently landed him in Korea. His travelogue opened the doors for foreign trade, and he has been celebrated as a folk hero in Korea ever since. He's almost as popular as Guus Hiddink, the soccer coach who led the South Korean national team to great success. More than three hundred years later, ASML is still enjoying the fruits of Hendrick Hamel's adventure. According to the Central Bureau of Statistics, in 2023, Dutch exports to South Korean totaled 12 billion euros, with 'specialized machines' contributing 6.3 billion euros. And the bulk of these machines came from Veldhoven.

Martin van den Brink remembers the aggressive atmosphere in Korea during the years that ASML first supplied Samsung: 'A lot of suppliers were used to bending to Samsung's will, but we were still too small to meet all their demands.' In the nineties, ASML outsourced maintenance in Korean chip factories to local intermediaries to bridge the cultural gap. When it set up its own service organization, it looked to primarily hire Korean workers, as they were used to the strict hierarchy and long workweeks of fifty hours or more. The high level of education in South Korea proved to be another advantage, with relatively large numbers of women pursuing technological studies. And even at school, the pressure to perform at your best is extremely high. According to Sunny Stalnaker, that's just part of Asian culture: 'Singapore, Korea, Hong Kong, Taiwan or Japan: in all these countries children are up until midnight, studying.'

ASML managed to get the EUV light source for Samsung up to standard, albeit seven years later than agreed. Almost simultaneously, their Taiwanese competitor TSMC started with the production of EUV chips. However, only one could be first, so the Brabanders needed to come up with a trick to allow each of them a spot in the limelight. TSMC became the first with a machine that could expose more than 150 EUV wafers per hour, and Samsung secured bragging rights over the most powerful light source. By this point, ASML was already on the verge of surpassing the 250-watt limit.

For a while, the Far East were the only guests at the party when it came to producing chips using extreme ultraviolet light. In 2018, American chip manufacturer GlobalFoundries pulled the plug on two EUV machines in Malta, New York after they failed to achieve an economically viable level of production. Intel was being surpassed by their competitors in Asia on every front and would only start using EUV for chips after 2023.

American politicians are inclined to perceive chip technology as something that was snatched from them by Asia, just as 'their' extreme ultraviolet light source was taken over by a Dutch company. Van den Brink sees it differently: 'The development of EUV has been going on for 25 years. They did the first five years, but we've done the last twenty.' Put simply, the Asian chip manufacturers took the lead thanks to their willingness to take greater risks than the American competition.

In August 2019, the first smartphone with an EUV-produced processor hit the shelves: the Samsung Galaxy Note 10, based on 7-nanometer technology. Martin van den Brink received a device as a gift – a small thanks from the same boss who often drove him to despair. At the end of 2019, TSMC delivered a comparable chip for the Chinese company Huawei's phones. Apple soon followed , and in 2020 an EUV-chip made with TSMC's 5-nanometer technology was installed in the iPhone.

The descriptions that chip manufacturers use for these technological generations or 'nodes' need to be taken with a grain of salt. The physical dimensions of the smallest circuits and connections on the chip are, in practice, five to ten times larger than advertised. A nanometer was once just a nanometer, but accuracy has never stopped a good marketing slogan.

Neither does 'EUV chip' tell the whole story. Every processor is built in dozens of layers: if you cut a chip in half, you'll uncover all sorts of different lithography techniques stacked on one another, just like the rings in a tree trunk. Only a handful of the layers with the most critical circuits are exposed using EUV. For the patterns of the other layers, conventional machines do the job.

In December 2020 ASML celebrated the sale of their one hundredth EUV scanner, but the technology was still far from being mature. The machines in the factories required drastic upgrades and fixes: whenever the laser was taken out for repairs, the whole operation would stand still for weeks, or even months. This meant a large number of back-up machines needed to be on standby at all times.

Chip manufacturers are also keen to exaggerate problems with the machines. They cannot replace a multi-million-dollar scanner for a competitor's version at the first sign of trouble, so instead they prefer to keep ASML on its toes by emphasizing the setbacks and presenting long lists of complaints. The engineers are bombarded with PowerPoint presentations containing hundreds of slides – one for each missing screw and each delayed spare part.

But by far the most noise is made over contaminating particles that cause deviations on the silicon wafer. Issues here are quickly passed on to ASML specialists who can help optimize production. It is a stressful job, according to one of the employees in Asia. You're meeting customers during the day, conferring with the designers in Veldhoven in the evening, and taking video calls from San Diego in the early morning. It feels like a non-stop meeting that leaves you with at best five hours of sleep per night. 'Unless an unexpected problem arises. Then it's even less.'

The mirror, which collects the light from the exploding tin droplets, requires regular cleaning. Initially, this task needs to be done every few weeks, eventually extending to every few months. ASML developed a carwash-like system, equipped with a high-pressure cleaner specifically designed for the collectors. With so many EUV machines already running in Asia, it is far more convenient to run this process in that region, rather than constantly having to fly the mirrors back and forward to the Netherlands to be cleaned.

This is why Linkou, ASML's Taiwan branch, cleans more than two hundred EUV collectors each year. Even the dirty mirrors from South Korea are sent to Taiwan, where they end up in Cathy's cleanroom cabin. She's just graduated as a mechanical engineer and is busy working on a new subject: a mirror with caked on blobs of tin, as if a sloppy painter had been messing around with putty. Cathy sets the timer: twelve hours of cleaning with CO_2, and the mirror is ready to go back into a machine.

The majority of mirrors find their way back into a scanner owned by the largest customer, TSMC. After all, Korea may provide the digital memory, but the world runs on the computing power from Taiwan.

24

MATES WITH MORRIS

It's five in the afternoon in Hsinchu Science Park. Every time the traffic light turns green, a swarm of scooters leaves the TSMC campus. They squeeze past trucks filled with gases and chemicals, as well as the construction traffic for 'Fab 20'. That is the newest gigafactory, and from 2025 it will start producing chips to within an accuracy of 2 nanometers. It's a massive installation that barely wedges between TSMC's other buildings.

There are many ways to spot an employee from the Taiwan Semiconductor Manufacturing Company: the T-sticker on their scooter's mudguard, the orange keychain around their neck, or the transparent bag they carry. The latter is mandatory to prevent people from smuggling out trade secrets. Taking your smartphone inside with you is not an option here.

The chip factory runs around the clock, with the production employees alternating in twelve-hour shifts. TSMC was aiming to hire an additional six thousand people in 2023, but with a birthrate as low as Taiwan's, finding talent is a challenge. It now tries to attract high school students to work there for a few hours a week and become the latest recruits to the 'TSMC army', which already counts troops about seventy thousand strong. The Taiwanese chipmaker is a powerful link in the chip industry, manufacturing processors for Sony's PlayStation, Apple's iPhone and the graphic chips for the American chip manufacturer Nvidia, used for running artificial intelligence applications. In addition, Tesla and the datacenters from Amazon, Alibaba and

Microsoft source their computing power from Taiwan. In 2022, TSMC supplied more than half of the world's chips and 90 percent of the most advanced processors.

In light of the staggering costs of building a state-of-the-art chip factory, chip designers prefer to rent capacity from specialized 'foundries' like TSMC. Even Intel outsources some of its production to the Taiwanese while its own EUV production isn't running at full capacity.

Morris Chang, the brain behind TSMC's formula, is the embodiment of globalization. Born in 1931 in China, he studied mechatronics in the US and worked for Texas Instruments before moving to Taiwan. As previously mentioned, he started the Taiwan Semiconductor Manufacturing Company with support from Philips in 1987. Since then, he has carried a black notepad in his pocket, always ready to write down new wafer orders. He's also inseparable from his pipe and completely disregards the smoking ban in TSMC's offices, much to the surprise of the ASML'ers. No one dares to point it out.

Chang stepped down as CEO in 2005, but in 2009 he returned at the ripe old age of 78 to bring the company back on course. He disagreed with his successor Rick Tsai, under whose lead TSMC produced chips for solar cells and LED lighting. Chang wanted to capitalize on the mobile revolution. In 2013, he reeled in Apple as a customer, securing ASML a mega-order worth more than 3 billion euros in the process. Chang resigned from his position after the introduction of EUV in June 2018, but has remained extremely influential well into his golden years. Taiwan may not be a monarchy, but this doesn't stop foreign politicians from regarding Morris, the 'king of chips', as industrial royalty. He's also a source of inspiration for Taiwanese entrepreneurs like Lisa Su and Jensen Huang, the leaders of successful American tech companies AMD and Nvidia. They were both born in Tainan, the city where TSMC now produces their chips.

Chang's motto, in his own handwriting, is displayed on the wall at their headquarters in Hsinchu. Loosely translated, it reads: 'Behind great obstacles, a bright future awaits.' And there are plenty of them, as the four thousand ASML'ers who work in Taiwan know all too well.

Since TSMC is the company at the forefront of EUV technology, it is also the one exposing that technology's problems.

In Martin van den Brink's office sits a plaque from TSMC, that reads: 'EUV, April 2018'. It is his pride and joy. 'That was the breakthrough,' he remembers. 'It all hinged on one thing: will it work, or will it fail?'

It worked.

However, in 2018 the new lithography machines were not working nearly as well as hoped. Mysterious particles that floated around in the machines were causing headaches and were decreasing the number of usable chips per wafer. And at TSMC, the yield is sacred: every fraction of a percent counts when you produce more than 15 million wafers annually, each containing several hundred advanced processors.

Because the lines in EUV are so extremely thin, any amount of contamination has consequences. ASML keeps track of the number of errors that TSMC discovers in a 'particles per week' tally. The Taiwanese practically explode with anger if tin particles end up on the mask. The fallout is immense: any mistake there is repeated on every wafer, with every step of the exposure. It is possible to cover the masks with a protective film, or 'pellicle', which keeps the particles at a distance and unable to do any harm. Think of it like a smudge on your sunglasses that you can still see through. But no matter how thin, this extra layer will always block out some valuable EUV light, meaning it'll take longer to expose the wafers. Every solution has its price in the world of ASML.

Thanks to the new machines, TSMC no longer needs to use double or triple exposures to draw fine lines on chips, at least for the time being. This saves money and time, but the learning curve is steep. It's not an exact science, but rather a matter of trial and error, and adjusting accordingly. They gather data on 'wafer movements' from an early stage, as their data analysts use this information to improve the yield. To fill the database faster, TSMC also orders as many machines as possible from ASML. This kills two birds with one stone: every machine in Taiwan means one less for a competitor in South Korea. Veldhoven has limited production capacity, especially for the latest generation of scanners, and chip manufacturers gladly take advantage of this shortage.

ASML's field engineers are up to their eyeballs in assisting TSMC in optimizing the factory. At the same time, they have their work cut out for them convincing their colleagues in Veldhoven to help. Such discussions are often tense, and tempers flare between the ASML and TSMC departments. The designers in Veldhoven tend to suggest that TSMC isn't using the EUV-machine properly, or that other machines in the chip factory are causing contamination. If a manager at TSMC abruptly ends a Teams call in anger, the local ASML team knows it is up to them to pick up the pieces.

'TSMC has a good balance between helping and pushing,' says Frits van Hout. The two companies come together quickly when it comes to sorting out technical problems. There's a cultural click: Taiwanese people generally speak English well and have the same 'outsourcing mentality' as ASML: if someone else can do it better, let them do it.

The culture at TSMC is more hierarchical as compared to ASML, but less militaristic than in South Korea. The research departments bear the brunt of the workload, leaving their experts feeling that they are the ones doing the heavy lifting by helping ASML solve problems that will benefit their competitors down the line.

Hsinchu, located on the northwest coast of Taiwan, is TSMC's hub for working on new technology for chip production. Two groups of engineers, labeled the red and blue teams, take turns refining the new 'nodes'. Once the new manufacturing technology is ready, the mass production of wafers in cities such as Tainan or Taichung can begin. This area used to be filled with rice fields and fruit trees, until the chip giant started planting megafabs and gigafabs. The noise they produce fills the entire area and sounds like a taxiing plane that never seems to take off.

Even though an EUV machine is about the size of a city bus, the associated construction spans several floors. TSMC's main floor, which is more than 10 meters high, houses lithography systems, measuring equipment and other types of chip machines. Below it is the 'sub-fab' and the 'sub-sub-fab', with racks full of electronics, the laser, and machines that regulate handling of the cooling water, gases, and chemical components. You can see the impact of these EUV machines in the data on Dutch exports to Taiwan: between 2016 and 2022 the figure almost quadrupled from 3.1 to 11.6 billion euros. It is a hefty investment – but it pays off. Since 2019, TSMC's yearly revenue has more than doubled to around 70 billion dollars. It now commands 60 percent of the entire foundry market, making it four times larger than its closest competitor, Samsung.

One key to the success in Taiwan lies in TSMC's strict separation of its clients. Engineers assisting one client, such as Apple, know nothing about the chips Nvidia makes. ASML employees must also adhere to this strict confidentiality: explicit permission is needed to email any documents, and taking a quick photo of what was drawn on the board during a meeting is strictly prohibited. Some of the measurement data from the factory can be accessed remotely via a secure connection. There's no time to waste on trivial trips to the cleanroom.

However, TSMC can't always fend off risks from the outside world. Dotted around the chip factory are red poles where TSMC staff gather in case of emergencies. And the Taiwanese chip giant is far from immune to severe natural disasters. In September 1999, a powerful earthquake temporarily shut down the factories, and the subsequent chip shortage sent a financial shockwave throughout the industry.

After every major earthquake – which Taiwan counts by the dozen every year – ASML technicians immediately rush into the factories to inspect the machines. The scanners have advanced air suspension to absorb the shocks, and these are incredibly sensitive. The system shuts itself down if the ground trembles too forcefully, which then means an entire reboot. Sometimes, simply hitting the power button is enough, just like reviving a frozen PC. But as soon as any one of the more than twenty indicator lights on the machine turns red, the whole system needs to undergo a thorough examination.

About 40 percent of ASML's revenue comes from Taiwan. However, no matter how close the relationship between TSMC and ASML, the Taiwanese are not amused when the Dutch speak too extensively with other customers about the possibilities of EUV. ASML's top executives occasionally visit Qualcomm in San Diego, and Apple's employees are known to stop by in Veldhoven every now and then. Because

TSMC wants to retain control, this only heightens their paranoia about potential leaks of technical knowledge.

Meanwhile, Taiwanese employees are regularly approached by Chinese tech companies like Huawei and SMIC. They can easily earn three to five times their current salary in China, but would enjoy far fewer freedoms than in democratic Taiwan. The most prominent of them and one who does make the move is Liang Mong Song, the TSMC research director who first leaked sensitive company secrets to competitor Samsung and then joined the Chinese competitor SMIC in 2017. In the eyes of his former colleagues, he committed a double betrayal, and it won't be long before the rest of the world realizes how crucial Liang's knowledge is to China's expanding chip industry.

In addition, Taiwan faces a far greater threat from China. The Chinese Communist Party considers the island a renegade province, and with a single military action could annex or block the world's most advanced chip factory. However, TSMC relies on Western knowledge and companies like ASML, so the boycott that would occur after an annexation would lead to an acute shortage of fast semiconductors and plunge the global economy into turmoil, China's included.

The leaders of the Chinese Communist Party will never risk this catastrophic scenario – or so the Taiwanese hope. They see the factories of Morris Chang as a 'silicon shield': as long as the world relies on computing power from Taiwan, the island is protected by the TSMC army. That is the theory. In practice, economic logic rarely outweighs political interests in Xi Jinping's China.

25

THE CAMERA THAT
NEVER EXISTED

Oerle, Zeelst, Meerveldhoven: nestled between these tongue-twisting tiny townships in the municipality of Veldhoven, a powerful monopoly was emerging. Years of investment in an improbable technology was yielding serious results, and in 2017 ASML reported over a billion euros in revenue from the new EUV machines. Meanwhile, ASML's market share in conventional lithography systems had climbed to 90 percent.

One company had been watching this rise through gritted teeth: Nikon. Right up until the '90s, the Japanese technology group had been the market leader in lithography machines – until ASML came, saw and conquered. But there is still a way to turn things around when you've been kicked off the throne: sue the new king.

In April 2017, Nikon initiated another patent lawsuit against ASML. To their dismay, Carl Zeiss SMT, the German lens maker's semiconductor division, was also dragged in. The Japanese accused them of violating eleven patents in the Netherlands and filed simultaneous complaints in Germany and Japan. If the courts ruled in Nikon's favor, ASML would have to cease the production of machines in Veldhoven. Once again, the survival of the company was at stake. Market leader or not, a looming ban on production was the last thing they needed. But this time, the attack did not come as a surprise.

ASML still vividly remembered Nikon's claims from 2001. That lawsuit came out of the blue and ended in 2004 with a so-called cross-licensing agreement. Nikon, ASML and Zeiss effectively signed a ceasefire so they could continue using each other's technologies without being dragged to court. The deal cost ASML 87 million dollars and Zeiss had to pay Nikon another 58 million dollars.

Part of the cross-licensing agreement expired in 2009, and when ASML reached out to discuss an extension, the Japanese were silent. In 2013, as the remaining agreements were about to expire, ASML knocked on Tokyo's door again. Once again, Nikon didn't respond. The Dutch were willing to pay a reasonable amount to continue the licenses, but Nikon wasn't interested in an extension of the existing deal. It wanted a chunk of ASML's revenue. In 2017, this amounted to more than 9 billion euros. Nikon was looking to receive potentially hundreds of millions of euros it would then be able to use to recoup its own lithography research costs. The Japanese EUV project had stalled in 2009, effectively gifting ASML a monopoly over these machines. A lingering resentment had simmered among the Japanese ever since: they had failed to win the first patent battle, and it had cost them their leading market position.

Veldhoven, in turn, harbored a strong antipathy towards anything even remotely associated with the Japanese competition. You wouldn't see the old-school ASML'ers with a Canon or Nikon camera. They would rather buy an Olympus or Sony – after all, Japan did produce the best cameras in the world.

This gave Eric Maurice an idea – and a brilliant one, he might add. In 2011, two years before the Frenchman stepped down as CEO, he approached Martin van den Brink with a plan. As soon as the Japanese filed their first complaint about lithography machines, ASML should use camera patents to hit Nikon where it hurt the most. Meurice could feel the storm brewing, and he gave a stark warning to Van den Brink: 'You're gonna have a problem Martin, that's why you need to attack them on their own turf. Make sure you get those patents.'

Van den Brink often clashed with Meurice, but he knew the Frenchman was clever. He took the warning to heart and consulted with Ton van Hoef, who managed ASML's lithography patent portfolio. Patents needed to be acquired, and preferably not in plain sight.

According to the database on company.info, in October 2011, a company called Tarsium B.V. was established. It was a shell company set up by ASML to stay under the radar of Nikon's lawyers. On paper, Tarsium was officially registered in Amsterdam and in a residential area in Eindhoven. The name appeared to be derived from 'tarsier', the wide-eyed nocturnal primate native to islands of Southeast Asia that hunts insects under the cover of darkness. Between 2012 and 2014, Tarsium acquired nearly 10 million euros' worth of patents for digital photography, including from Hewlett-Packard, Xerox, MediaTek, and the American patent aggregator Intellectual Ventures. The first patent, obtained in November 2012, described a method for selecting faces in an image. Convenient for quickly snapping a group shot.

When the cross-licensing deal expired in 2014, ASML enlisted the help of Willem Hoyng, partner in Amsterdam-based law firm Hoyng Rokh Monegier and specialist in intellectual property. The conflict with Nikon became the biggest case of his fifty-year career. Hoyng quietly set about assembling a team of twenty lawyers, and for a time, everything remained calm. In 2015 and 2016, mediation attempts between ASML and Nikon once again failed, and the inevitable legal battle ensued. The new patent war had started, and as soon as Nikon fired its first shot on April 24, 2017, ASML deployed its secret weapon. On April 28, Tarsium transferred the accumulated patents to ASML and Zeiss, and on the same day, those companies sued Nikon.

The outside world was surprised to hear the counterclaim also targeted cameras. Wasn't this all about lithography? CEO Peter Wennink denied that Veldhoven was infringing on Japanese patents, explaining ASML's counterclaim in a press release: 'We have no other choice but to file these lawsuits. Nikon never took the negotiations seriously. We will defend ourselves with every means at our disposal.'

The lawsuits were beginning to stack up globally. But first, ASML had to defend itself against the Japanese allegations in the Netherlands. Willem Hoyng went to meet with Martin van den Brink. Right away, Martin asked him, 'Ah, so you're the famous lawyer – what chance do we have of winning these cases?' Hoyng estimated perhaps as high as 80 percent. Van den Brink exploded. 'We have more than fifteen cases going on. Have you calculated what 80 percent of 80 percent of 80 percent is? Keep going and I won't be able to pay you by the end of it all.

I want the fifteenth root of 80 percent! Until then you'll be here every Friday afternoon to keep me up to date.'

And so nearly every Friday, just as requested, the lawyers met at ASML. Meetings with the intellectual property department took place first, followed by a mandatory brainstorming session in Van den Brink's office. They figured it was not in Nikon's interest to actually shut down ASML's production: they just wanted money. A lot of it. But Martin van den Brink wasn't about to let himself get cornered by a competitor.

The Dutch judge saw the stack of cases on his desk grow by the day, filled with words like 'onderdompelinglithografiebelichtingsinrichting', the 46-letter Dutch word for an immersion lithography exposure device. Exasperated, he summoned the lawyers of both parties. If this was just about money, surely it could all be resolved a bit faster. He forced a discussion between Nikon and ASML, but Nikon had no intentions to negotiate: they wanted to win a case first so they could corner ASML and ask for more money. The subsequent meeting in San Francisco lasted less than two hours, and the lawyers were on a flight back to Amsterdam that same day.

The first four of the Dutch patent cases ruled in favor of ASML and Zeiss. But this was no cause for celebration. The company was on the line with every case: lose just one of the next hearings and they would lose everything. Zeiss, now fully intertwined with ASML, was the most concerned. The companies were united in their legal battle against Nikon, but they were dependent on the tempo of the court, which was progressing at a snail's pace, according to Van den Brink. In a patent dispute, you need momentum to force a breakthrough.

A year and half later, the breakthrough finally came. In August 2018, the American International Trade Commission ruled that Nikon had infringed upon the camera patents owned by ASML and Zeiss. Suddenly, Nikon's camera division was facing an American import ban, and the Japanese were getting nervous.

As the complaining party to the ITC, ASML and Zeiss had to demonstrate that they were suffering real economic damage, which meant there needed to be a camera available for sale in the US that used the patented parts. To everyone's surprise, in the fall of 2018, Zeiss announced the ZX1. It was a compact digital camera with a fixed lens and large touchscreen: jet black, angular, with built-in photo editing software and internet connection. There was even a catchy slogan: 'Shoot, Edit, Share'.

The industry press was perplexed. When Zeiss had last made cameras, they still required roll film. Digital camera sales had plummeted since the iPhone's arrival, with most people just using their phones to take photos. Was Zeiss seriously planning on entering this declining market now?

Zeiss promised the ZX1 would be available in early 2019 – although they refused to reveal the price. A team from the American division built some prototypes, and Zeiss announced the ZX1 at the Photokina fair in Frankfurt. It was a grand affair, with the employees welcoming the gathered media with applause. It was like the world had been turned upside down. In December, a YouTube video appeared featuring a German photographer trying out the ZX1 for the first time, taking snapshots while wandering around the sushi shops in the Little Tokyo district of Düsseldorf. Another jab at the Japanese.

Nikon became concerned. With four lost cases and a threat from the ITC to their name, the Japanese buckled and decided they wanted to negotiate a new agreement at a more reasonable rate. The parties were brought together by Edward Infante, the American judge who handled the previous confrontation between Nikon and ASML. On January 23, 2019, Nikon, ASML, and Carl Zeiss released a joint statement to the press: the deal was done. The Germans and Dutch paid Nikon 150 million euro (of which ASML paid 131 million) for the use of their patents until 2029, and ASML had to cover a 0.8 percent royalty on every immersion machine sold. It was a fraction of the percentage Nikon originally demanded.

In retrospect, Nikon overestimated its own position. When you put smart engineers in two companies that develop the same product, the same ideas can easily emerge. Many of the patents Nikon gathered were granted too effortlessly by the European patent office, but it was undeniably the psychological blow of the camera patents that secured the knockout.

In October 2019, the shell company Tarsium disappeared from the face of the earth. And what came of the ZX1, with its 'Shoot, Edit, Share'?

A handful of prototypes landed in the hands of reviewers. A few videos and blogs praised the metal lens cap and silent shutter, as well as the included shoulder strap. But they all wondered the same thing: when would the camera finally be available for purchase?

For a brief moment in October 2020, it seemed like it could be ordered from an American online store for a mere 6000 dollars. However, the ZX1 was never actually sold, let alone delivered. When photographers enquired about it, Zeiss' official response was: 'We are very critical about the finetuning of all aspects of our camera.' And that is where it ended. In 2020, Zeiss referred to the ZX1 as a 'concept camera'. As if it had never existed, as if it had only been built to make Nikon's life difficult.

But the ZX1 didn't leave without a trace. Back in his office, Martin van den Brink rummages through his awards and other memorabilia to retrieve a white box. A name is embossed on the front: Zeiss ZX1 – still wrapped in plastic, with the manual untouched. He holds the camera up to his eye and grins.

'Brand-new. No idea if it even works – I've never taken a photo with it myself.'

26

A GOLF BALL
ON THE MOON

'Sorry, you have to take your pants off too.' Zeiss' top technical executives Peter Kurz and Thomas Stammler don't mess around. Whoever steps foot in their heavily secured cleanroom needs to wear not only a dust-free suit, but also fiber-free underwear. After being blasted for twenty seconds by an air shower, you can then enter the production hall in the south German town of Oberkochen. Here, Zeiss works on what lies ahead.

ASML's next generation of EUV machines goes by the nickname High NA. These colossal scanners span 14 meters and feature large mirrors up to a meter wide. The optical system by itself consists of twenty thousand parts and weighs twelve tons, making it seven times heavier than the optics for the current EUV machine. With this growth comes a new price tag: while a 'normal' EUV system costs around 200 million euros, the new variant is expected to be double that.

The value of High NA lies in its ability to print chip structures with a precision of 2 nanometers and smaller, a reduction in scale made possible by the higher opening angle of the lenses. In technical terms: the numerical aperture (or NA) increases from 0.33 to 0.55 – the difference between Low NA and High NA.

ASML's suppliers have been working on parts for this new machine for years. Zeiss needed to begin production early on due to the extensive preparation demanded by lens fabrication. This prompted ASML to take a stake in Zeiss in 2016, which used the investment to kickstart the research process. It took five years to figure out all the ingredients required.

Zeiss's advanced laboratory sits between the mountains in Oberkochen, constructed on a thick layer of vibration-free concrete. There, with the help from ASML, the lens maker developed the measurement technology needed to manufacture the new mirrors. EUV mirrors are not flat like the mirror in your bathroom. They have complex shapes – think of the distortion you get from a mirror at a funfair. The difficulty is being able to measure whether the surface is smooth enough all around to reflect the light without disturbance. 'If you can't measure it, you can't make it,' as the Germans say.

Kürz and Stammler walk down the stairs into a scene straight from a James Bond movie. The center of a cavernous room holds two gleaming steel cylinders, each as wide as a submarine and sealed off by massive vault-like doors. Figures clad in blue cleanroom suits carefully shuffle around the space-age technology. These cylinders contain a vacuum with the same chemical composition as the lithography machine and are used to check the mirrors for deviations. Here, they count by the atom. A data center in the left corner processes the terabytes of measurement data for the calculations. Behind the cylinders, a yellow robot systematically takes mirrors from a rack. They are far too heavy to be lifted by a human, and far too valuable to drop.

Even the smallest deviation will be visible in the wafer, so the mirrors are constructed from a material that is virtually unaffected by temperature fluctuations. Thankfully, Zeiss is able to draw on knowledge from its former aerospace division. While satellites and chip machines seem worlds apart, they both need to perform their tasks under extreme conditions.

For months, the surface is polished by robots, after which Zeiss shoots off the remaining atoms one by one. More than fifty ultra-thin reflective layers are then applied, and the mirror is ready. 'If you lined it up right, you could hit a golf ball on the moon with one of these,' says Thomas Stammler. And he has more comparisons: if you could stretch the mirror from a High NA system until it was the size of Germany, the largest irregularity would protrude at most 20 micrometers from the surface. That's less than the thickness of a single human hair.

It is perfectly normal to feel dizzy in this place. Not because of the sterile air, but because the mere thought of the extremely complex tools needed to make the chips destined for the phones of the future can make you lightheaded. A machine invented in Veldhoven, manufactured with parts from all over Europe and shipped to chip factories in Asia and the US, where it produces silicon wafers full of processors and memory chips that, in just a few years, will end up in the palm of your hand.

Fortunately, Jan van Schoot stays on top of it all. As ASML's system architect, he was involved in the design of the original EUV machine, as well as the new High NA generation. The machine needs to undergo a large number of adjustments to meet the demands of the new optical system. As he says, 'you're constantly creating new problems', and it is up to him to solve them.

The light is bounced throughout the entire EUV system: first from the light source to the mask, then from the mask to the silicon wafer. Each mirror absorbs 30 percent of the light rays, and the new High NA machine has two mirrors fewer than the first version. This effectively means more light and a faster exposure, which saves valuable time for the manufacturer.

So why not make a machine with these large mirrors in the first place? As Van Schoot explains, ASML does not like to jump straight into the deep end. 'The equipment for measuring mirrors is getting increasingly complex. Each time we ask ourselves how far we can push it and how much risk we're willing to take. With the first optics, we took it as far as we could with the available technology.'

Chip manufacturers also need to be able to keep up the pace. The area in which the light beam is razor sharp is now slightly smaller on the new system. Think of a portrait photographer who only brings your eyes into focus and leaves the rest of your face blurred. As a result, deviations on the surface of the wafer require extra attention, and the layers applied by other chip machines need to be even thinner.

Another problem: the EUV light falls at a steep angle on the mask in a High NA system, causing only a small fraction of the pattern to be properly reflected. An anamorphic or 'widescreen' mirror is used to fit more patterns on the mask, but the field of view is smaller and the chip design has to be adjusted to accommodate this.

And then there's 'dead time', ASML's morbid term for the valuable seconds when the wafers are not being exposed. The speed of the wafer tables has been ramped up to cut this down: they now accelerate to their position under the light with a force more than ten times that of gravity. Faster than a fighter jet. This is not even the quickest part of the machine – the mask with the original chip pattern moves four times as fast. To keep these forces in check, a counterweight races in the other direction.

This combination of brute force and atomic precision is controlled by software. Computing power is also needed to calculate the positioning of the mirrors, with a series of sensors constantly monitoring how they behave and how this affects the image on the wafer.

Thomas Stammler swings open the door to a new production hall, where the EUV mirrors are assembled in series. A knocking sound from a worker nonchalantly hammering a piece of optics with a rubber mallet echoes through the hall. But no one's alarmed – even in the world of high-tech, low-tech tricks are known to come in handy. The mirrors ultimately hang in the system in such a way that no force is exerted on the material. There is no escaping gravity, but the mirrors still seem to be 'floating', according to Zeiss.

In a nearby room, robots practice with dummies to pre-program the movements. The actual High NA mirrors are already in the making, albeit in various stages of completion. It takes an entire year to fabricate and perfect a single mirror.

The entire system of mirrors will soon end up in the 'optical train'. The complete lithography machine is an awe-inspiring monolith, as tall as a two-story house and filled with futuristic technology. The cleanroom also needed to expand to accommodate the sheer size of it. You can tell from looking at the Zeiss campus where the High NA optics are assembled – it's the tallest building in the area.

Zeiss itself has roughly a thousand employees working on the new technology. Regular meetings with ASML help to keep the collaboration running smoothly. With the knowledge from Veldhoven now completely intertwined with that from Oberkochen, transparency is everything. 'It's worse than a marriage – we can never get rid of each other now,' jokes Martin van den Brink. And at Zeiss, they make exactly the same joke. The terms of the marriage are simple: Zeiss provides optics only to ASML, and ASML exclusively uses optics from Zeiss. They completely share the intellectual property, and the old slogan 'two companies, one business' still holds true. Neither side has any desire for a complete takeover. The Germans want Carl Zeiss SMT to remain independent because of the money their semiconductor division brings in, with revenue growing from 1.2 billion euros in 2016 to 3.6 billion in 2023. It is the result of a fruitful long-distance relationship, and there is no interest in rocking the boat anytime soon.

Zeiss may have been prepared, but the High NA machine failed to meet the intended introduction date of 2022. ASML and their suppliers were swamped by a rapid rise in demand for other types of scanners, forcing them to push back the schedule for these latest machines. To save time, the Leuven-based research institute imec immediately used the first High NA machine in Veldhoven for production tests, with couriers shuttling the exposed wafers back and forth to the cleanrooms in Belgium. Breaking down and rebuilding the system in Leuven would have cost an additional year, and the chip industry couldn't afford to wait. Intel stands first in line to receive the inaugural High NA system. Seven freight planes were needed to transport the machine from Veldhoven to Intel's research base in Hillsboro, Oregon. It's the world's biggest copier, weighing 150 tons. It will be at least 2025 before these machines begin producing chips.

27

A TOUCH OF VOODOO

You may think a lithography machine with a price tag of hundreds of millions of euros would be able to make perfect copies of chip structures. Think again.

The mask, which carries the original image of the chip, does not leave an exact replica on the photosensitive layer. The chemical processes that occur on the wafer create rough and messy lines. However, with mathematical models, you can calculate how to shape the mask so that, despite these deviations, a pattern emerges that will transmit the electric signals on the chip without fault. You can compare it to the beauty filters on TikTok or Instagram, which correct the 'imperfections' on your face to make you look like a model. However, making a mask takes much more time than snapping a selfie, and it takes weeks for the pattern of the chip to be converted into a flawless image.

Computational lithography, as this technology is called, is an indispensable link in the production of chips. Martin van den Brink knew this when he charted out ASML's long term strategy in the late '90s. As chips become smaller, so does the room for error, and at a certain point using software to make these adjustments is the only way to keep producing chips that work.

The Dutch company gathered the required expertise through a series of acquisitions. In 1999, they took over American start-up MaskTools, and in 2006 ASML paid over 270 million dollars for Brion, a company with branches in Silicon Valley and China. Brion developed software that simulates the operation of lithography machines to create masks.

The production of a complex EUV-mask costs more than half a million euros and takes a huge amount of time to calculate. If you use smart software to accelerate this development, you save yourself a lot of money.

ASML also developed its own measuring instrument, the Yieldstar, which traces errors on wafers with a camera. And in 2016, it bought the Taiwanese company HMI for 2.75 billion euros. Their machines check the wafers by taking random samples with an electron beam. Each of these applications generates vast amounts of data, all of which is then stored on large computer systems in the chip factory itself. It's a vicious cycle: more computing power is needed to design and manufacture chips for more powerful computers.

Silicon Valley is the birthplace of the semiconductor industry, yet the last major chip factory in this region closed its doors in 2009. However, the specialists in chip software remained in California and soon found their place among the new tech giants.

ASML Silicon Valley is located on West Tasman Drive in San Jose. Brion's and HMI's Asian origin is immediately noticeable by the giant dragon made out of balloons in the lobby, positioned proudly next to the wall displaying the company's patents. Chinese New Year is an important holiday here, as is the Dutch celebration of King's Day on April 27. Just to make sure, the ASML'ers also celebrate Cinco de Mayo. Yu Cao, the co-founder of Brion, thinks it fosters a sense of community.

'Silicon Valley' is different to the other ASML locations. Eric Meurice, the CEO who signed the acquisition of Brion in 2007, urged the founders not to let Veldhoven control them too much: 'If ASML tries to push you into their corporate structure, ignore it. And otherwise, just give me a call.' Veldhoven has a rigid project organization entirely focused on building scanners, and this does not match how HMI and Brion operate.

Brion supplies its optical proximity correction software, or OPC, to companies that are also located in San Jose like Samsung and GlobalFoundries. The measuring technology of HMI faces far more competition than ASML's lithography systems do. But when put together, these three elements – measuring technology, correction software, and the scanner – form the pillars of 'holistic lithography'. It is an ecosystem carefully built by ASML to reduce the margins of error throughout the chip factory and increase its effectiveness. The applications division, as this branch is known within ASML, now generates billions in revenue.

However, ASML is just one of thousands of tech companies clustered together in Silicon Valley. This is why the trams in San Jose were plastered with huge ASML logos throughout 2023 – every little bit of recognition helps. Just like all tech companies in Silicon Valley, ASML is constantly on the hunt for talented software specialists. Employees visit technology conferences and universities in the US to explain what this Dutch company and its seven thousand American employees do. It even has an advertising campaign on TV. A catchier slogan for people not already working in the industry would have been good – at least according to software specialist Ahmad Elsaid. 'You know the first thing my wife asked me? What on earth does "pushing technology one nanometer at a time" mean?'

In San Jose, ASML faces tough competition in the quest for talent. Between 2018 and 2020, a substantial number of workers left for other nearby companies, such as Google and Facebook, while others also ventured into software development for Apple, Waymo, or even Tesla's self-driving cars. While big tech companies in Silicon Valley might offer higher salaries, ASML is a more interesting employer to physicists. At least, this is what Chen Zhang believes, an employee at the Brion division: 'Here, we operate on the dividing line between fundamental science and economics, and you get to learn something new every day.' Zhang studied atomic, molecular and optical physics – this is why she prefers to work on optimization software for chip machines, rather than beauty filters for TikTok.

The primary language in San Jose is English, but you'll often hear Mandarin as well. ASML Silicon Valley is in close contact with hundreds of colleagues who develop software in Shenzhen, and ASML has a team of 1500 people who maintain measuring equipment in chip factories, among other things.

In one of San Jose's cleanrooms, a brand-new HMI system is being inspected, the hood open like a car in a garage. The device uses electron beams to scan for defects on the wafers. This version has a Dutch touch: the electron sensor is supplied by Mapper, a company based in Delft. After the start-up went spectacularly bankrupt at the end of 2018 – more on that later – ASML was able to acquire the e-beam technology along with one hundred experienced technicians. Mapper dreamed of building a competitor to Veldhoven's scanners, only to watch their promising multibeam technology end up in an ASML product. The scientists from Delft are now collaborating with San Jose on a radically enhanced version, slated to be ready by 2025 and capable of handling the unbelievable amounts of data required to inspect the wafers in detail.

In San Jose, everything revolves around data. The datacenter for performing the heavy calculations is located next to the cleanroom. Currently, the software runs on regular processors or CPUs (central processing units), but the new versions will also make use of the cloud and operate on fast graphics processors, convenient for applying artificial intelligence to the data sets.

The explosion of measurement data has made it impossible to capture all the variables at play into predictable formulas. Therefore, Brion uses AI to understand the interplay between the light beam, the mask, and the chemical reactions on the wafer. The technique used for this is machine learning, in which neural networks look for patterns in an enormous set of data.

In machine learning, the computer draws conclusions that you can't replicate. The software can even predict in advance how you should set up a lithography machine to get the best results, prompting Martin van den Brink to coin a term for it: voodoo software. 'No one knows exactly what goes on with machine learning', he expresses. 'But if you rely solely on AI, you're not adding any extra value. Then you don't need to understand what it's doing anymore, and that's where the problems start.'

Van den Brink believes technology should be something you can calculate and understand. From the very start, ASML built its designs on the laws of physics and mathematical models. Even the most complicated optics from Zeiss are ultimately a calculation, so you know that what you make is correct and, in the end, that it also works.

'Martin hates laziness,' clarifies Jim Koonmen, the head of operations in San Jose. 'He can't stand it if you say, "I can't make sense of the model, so I'll just train a computer and hope for the best." He challenges the people here: why do you choose machine learning over modelling that uses the physical principles?'

Overdependence on dark magic is risky: if you do everything with voodoo software, you'll no longer differ from your competition. Van den Brink sees it as a valuable addition, but only as a final step to speed up reaching a solution. 'We need to distinguish ourselves. If we don't include the added value of our physical models, then anyone can do it.'

He compares it with generative artificial intelligence, such as ChatGPT, which can create readable text in seconds, but doesn't add anything new. 'As if you asked ChatGPT to write a book about Martin van den Brink,' he says. Ultimately, the software from San Jose is the glue that binds all the components of the machine together: without it, one would never be able to optimally align the lighting system, the mask and the lens.

But software has its drawbacks. Top of the list: it is easy to copy. In 2014, six former Brion employees made off with trade secrets, stealing – among other things – two million lines of software code, algorithms and manuals via email and used the details to start a competing company in Silicon Valley. When Samsung wanted to terminate its contract with Brion because a new competitor with a suspiciously good product had emerged, alarm bells sounded at ASML. This new company was called Xtal, pronounced 'crystal'.

In 2016, ASML filed a lawsuit against the former employees. It took Yu Cao, founder and technical conscience of Brion, dozens of hours on the stand to explain the complex evidence. When the judge and jury then examined the Xtal code behind closed doors, it became evident that algorithms had indeed been copied.

ASML was awarded 845 million dollars in compensation in 2019. But with Xtal long bankrupt, there was nothing to recover. The high amount was intended as a deterrent, a serious signal for anyone else considering sneaking off with trade secrets.

Incidentally, Xtal founder Yu Zongchang started a Chinese counterpart around the same time. His company, Dongfang JingYuan Electron, is still in business and even receives subsidies from the Chinese government. ASML urged its customers to steer clear of Dongfang, yet leadership decided not to publicize the lawsuit. After all, they thought, it involved less than 1 percent of ASML's revenue, and both the stolen information and the contract with Samsung were safely secured.

That decision completely backfired. The Dutch newspaper Het Financieele Dagblad reported on the lawsuit and pointed the finger at the Chinese government, suspecting them of orchestrating the data theft. Much to the dismay of ASML, this turned the affair into a political issue. The company expressed disappointment over the 'conspiracy theories' in a press release, citing: 'No evidence has been found for this.' This did not keep ASML from being thrust into a new arena: the world of geopolitics. And there, everything Chinese is regarded as suspicious.

Due to the tech war between the US and China, an invisible barrier runs through the ASML facility in San Jose. The US government does not cooperate with issuing new employment contracts, and some employees, due to their nationality, are not allowed to work on EUV programs or other advanced technology intended for Chinese companies. The hundreds of people working for ASML in China are concerned about the ramifications of new export regulations on their home country. There is one advantage though: 'ASML is in the news so often, at least my parents in China now understand which company I work for,' says Chen Wang.

The media and politicians are discovering how crucial ASML is to the major chip factories. The eyes of the world are beginning to focus on 'that company', as the Dutch tech giant is called in the corridors of Capitol Hill. The mysterious company that, with over forty thousand people and a touch of voodoo, manufactures the most complex machine on earth. The genie is out of the bottle.

PART IV

IN THE SPOTLIGHT

The robot squeaks a cheerful tune called 'Dreamy Waterland', a Chinese folk song from the eighties. The approaching melody lets the Huawei employees know that they need to step out of the way: the self-driving cart, loaded with parts, is coming through.

It is the summer of 2017. About 21,000 people are at work at Huawei's factory in Dongguan, a city that emerged from the outskirts of the Shenzhen metropolis. The first floor is filled with fifty production lines that churn out 38,000 amplifiers every day for the cell towers of mobile networks. Go a level higher, and you can find Huawei employees assembling smartphones. It is monotonous work, so every two hours the staff are allowed a ten-minute break. Most spend that time staring at their phones, but twice a day they come together for a collective singing and dancing session – a chance to shake out the legs after hours on the production line.

In 2017, Huawei still had plenty of reasons to celebrate. The company was riding high on the mobile revolution, with hundreds of millions of Chinese citizens glued to WeChat. Thanks to this large market, as well as state subsidies and cheap labor, Huawei was able produce its technology far more cost-effectively than European competitors Ericsson and Nokia. Exports to Europe accounted for nearly 30 percent of their revenue, and Huawei was already going head-to-head with Apple's smartphone sales.

Huawei became a high-tech hit, and the Chinese undertaking stuck billions into the development of its own internet technology and software. In 2017, the European Patent Office received a total of 2398 patent applications from Huawei – more than from any other company. This bombardment of applications was down to one thing: Huawei was preparing for 5G, the latest technology for mobile networks. 5G allows for the large-scale connection of devices to the internet, making it an essential link for the future while society, industry and the economy continue to digitize. Control this network, and you control the world.

Born out of a military-academic project in the United States, the internet has always remained under American influence. It is no surprise that China has taken an interest in the underlying network technology: after all, the country has over one billion internet users – which is more than North America and Europe combined. Technological power is shifting from the West to the East, simply because the majority of the 5.3 billion internet users live in Asia.

The US watched the rise of Huawei with suspicion. The major American telecom providers are prohibited from using any Huawei equipment in their networks, with American policy makers claiming as early as 2012 that the Chinese company lies, cheats, and steals. Huawei's smaller counterpart, telecom company ZTE, is not considered much better.

However, providers in the EU are impressed by Chinese technology, which is far cheaper than what they are used to. Besides, the Snowden affair left a bad taste in the European's mouths. In 2013, whistleblower Edward Snowden revealed that the CIA was engaging in eavesdropping on a mass scale, using backdoors at the biggest tech companies as well as hacked phone networks and internet cables. Even European government leaders were being spied on by their own allies.

Snowden's revelations created a dent in the trust held in US technology. As a result, the largest telecom provider in Germany, Deutsche Telecom, built a public cloud together with Huawei in 2016, which was intended to become an alternative to the dominant American cloud providers such as Microsoft and Amazon. And just like that, Chinese technology was embedded into the veins of European datacenters and communication networks. The Americans were dumbfounded, thinking it was incredibly naïve.

Huawei, which loosely translates to, 'what the Chinese make possible', began in 1987 as one of the first independent technology companies in a special economic zone around Shenzhen. This city produces electronics for the entire world – all the ingredients to make a smartphone, computer or TV are readily available here. It is also one of the locations where the Taiwanese electronics giant Foxconn assembles iPhones for Apple, in mega-factories with hundreds of thousands of workers. Directly across from the Foxconn-complex lies the Huawei Campus, which houses tens of thousands of employees in massive dormitories constructed by the company. Right next door is the office of Huawei founder Ren Zhengfei, with a fabulous view over an enchanting lake with black swans. It's an image drawn straight from a fairytale.

China is the largest manufacturing hub for electronics globally, which makes it the world's biggest consumer of chips. But with the local chip industry still in its infancy, the country needs to import almost all of its advanced processors, the majority of which come from the US. Likewise, the memory chips that China incorporates into its electronics are predominately sourced from foreign companies. To reduce this dependency, Xi Jinping, leader of the Communist Party since 2012, wants to kickstart China's own semiconductor industry. With his ten-year 'Made in China 2025' plan, more than 100 billion dollars in state support has been reserved for the construction of new chip factories and the acquisition of foreign chip technology. China's goal is to be 70 percent self-sufficient in products from ten strategic sectors by 2025, including the most important building blocks for modernization – chips. Gone are the days when Chinese chipmakers were cumbersome state-owned enterprises: now, chip factories receive capital through national and local investment funds to stimulate innovation and entrepreneurship. Although a string of failures and corruption cases arose, this policy also resulted in successes like memory manufacturer YMTC. Founded in 2016, YMTC became almost instantly competitive and Apple considered sourcing a large portion of the memory for iPhones from this company. However, the deal was considered too sensitive in the US, and Apple had to back out.

China is also able to compete in the development of 5G chips for phones, via companies like Huawei's subsidiary HiSilicon or Unisoc. These companies were founded shortly after the turn of the millennium, just like the national chip champion SMIC. This foundry drew heavily from TSMC's playbook – to the extent that it lost several lawsuits claiming theft of Taiwanese patents – and made full use of the experience gained by Chinese 'knowledge workers' abroad. This is also part of Xi JingPing's strategy – entice high-tech experts from Western companies so they can serve their motherland.

Xi dreams of a Chinese renaissance by 2049. The People's Republic will have existed for one hundred years, and should have reclaimed its status as the world's most powerful civilization by then. China was still the richest country in the world at the end of the nineteenth century, but the US soon took the top spot. By the last decade of the twentieth century, China was beginning its transformation from a poor communist country into the world's second-largest economy. This rapid rise was due to their leader Deng Xiaoping, who modernized the country and partially opened it to the global market through economic zones like Shenzhen. For a long time, Western nations – in particular the US – thought that China would democratize if it could participate in global trade. The first American president to seek harmonization was Nixon, who made a historic visit to communist China in February 1972 in the hopes of forming a counterforce with party leader Mao Zedong against the Soviet Union. In the 1980s, President Ronald Regan relaxed existing export restrictions against China, and under Bill Clinton the US even launched advanced satellites from Chinese rockets. This event took place in 1996 and caused a stir, as it seemed to overstep the boundaries of American national security. However, Clinton brushed off the criticism, assuring the public that 'there was absolutely nothing done to transfer any technology inappropriately to the Chinese.'

Following years of negotiations, China became a member of the World Trade Organization in 2001. Many foreign entrepreneurs had already been lured in by the vast Chinese market and its availability of cheap labor. They brought capital and expertise, which has made China wealthier and more knowledgeable, but not any more democratic. Open criticism of the administration is prohibited, protests are suppressed, and the government fails to protect foreign companies against corruption and the theft of their technology. Chinese people are monitored with sophisticated surveillance and facial recognition systems, and their online behavior is analyzed and censored. For the Obama administration, China's growing economic and military power in Asia prompted a shift in foreign policy towards the Asia-Pacific region: China had become a threat to the American liberal world order and had to be contained, or even pushed back. American political parties may be deeply divided, but they agree on one thing: China's technological advance is a threat to the free world. And soon, this arch-rival will be more powerful than America in the field of artificial intelligence and cyber espionage.

To America, this sounds familiar. It stands on the threshold of another 'Sputnik Moment': in 1957, the communist Soviet Union became the first country to launch an artificial satellite, Sputnik, into Earth's orbit, in a display of technological superiority that deeply shocked the Americans. Now, just as in the space race between the US and the Soviet Union in the fifties and sixties, China and America are locked in a struggle for technological dominance. And with 5G, the US has once again been left in the dust. America was once a pioneer in network technology, but its telecom suppliers have either gone bankrupt or been acquired. Now, Americans are dependent on European providers and have to watch as those are outcompeted by Huawei.

In early 2017, the Obama administration began laying the groundwork for an answer to Xi Jinping's 'Made in China 2025'. However, the actual implementation of this strategy fell to Obama's successor – Donald Trump. But he had a different agenda: he first wanted to put an end to the trade imbalance with China.

On January 20, 2017, with his hand on two Bibles, Trump swore to 'make America great again'. And sure enough, the trade conflict between the US and China rapidly evolved into an all-out tech war, with Huawei as the initial target. The globalized chip industry was sucked into a geo-political conflict, and to the astonishment of Veldhoven, ASML found itself thrust into the spotlight. Tech companies soon became famil-iar with Trump's favorite weapons: unpredictable tweets and equally unpredictable export rules.

28

SHOOT FIRST, AIM LATER

Then came the atomic bomb.

In the words of the American media, on May 15, 2019 Donald Trump decided to 'go nuclear' in the trade war with China. He placed Huawei on the Entity List, a feared list by the Bureau of Industry and Security (BIS) of the Department of Commerce. American companies wanting to supply goods to the Chinese telecom company were now required to apply for a license, which was then assessed against national security criteria. It is a disguised export ban, preventing Huawei from purchasing new American software and chips – all the technology that is essential for making phones and equipment for telecom networks.

The Entity List had been successful before. In 2016, the export rule brought Chinese telecom company ZTE to its knees after it violated US sanctions against Iran and North Korea. With its chip supplies cut off, ZTE almost fell into bankruptcy, until the company admitted guilt in 2017 and settled for 1.2 billion dollars. While studying the ZTE documents, the Americans uncovered evidence suggesting Huawei had also turned a blind eye to the rules of the sanctions, and it was this trail of breadcrumbs that led to the arrest of Huawei's CFO Meng Wanzhou in Canada at the end of 2018.

A mention on the Entity List was intended to be the final blow against the Chinese giant. According to the US, the company was an undeniable threat to their national security: it allegedly engaged in the theft of trade secrets, conducted espionage for China, and was even said to be under the influence of the Chinese army. Tim Morrison, one of Trump's security advisors until the end of 2019, left no room for doubt about America's position: 'Huawei is the tool of the Communist Party. This company must be destroyed. Out of business.'

But the desired nuclear effect never happened. Within five days, the ban on Huawei was postponed by three months, gifting the Chinese company the chance to stock up on semiconductor supplies. In addition, Huawei's subsidiary HiSilicon produced the most advanced chips in TSMC's factories, which were not yet subject to US export regulations. 'We've let Huawei become too big,' sighed Morrison as he later looked back on the failed blockade. 'We could still surprise ZTE, but Huawei knew what was coming and was prepared for it.'

The Trump administration also underestimated the effect of export regulations on its own chip industry, as the unilateral export restrictions encouraged Huawei to search for alternative suppliers outside the US. This alarmed American chip companies, as they suddenly faced losing a third of their revenue. They warned the administration about the dangers of 'decoupling' their industry: eliminating the mutual dependency between Chinese and US enterprises would push the US even further behind, as revenue from China provided much-needed additional funds for the development of new technology.

But as a company, criticizing Trump's policies was a dangerous thing to do. One exclamation mark-laden presidential tweet could send their stock price plummeting in no time. The tech sector found itself knocking at the door of the Department of Commerce and searching for allies in the Pentagon. Their point was simple: if the US Department of Defense wanted superior weapons built with homegrown chips, it needed a thriving chip industry that would earn enough to stay ahead of the game and keep on top of the most cutting-edge technology. And so, behind the scenes, American chip manufacturers continued to secure licenses to export to China.

The Huawei case marked the moment when US export restrictions turned into economic weapons. 'It all started with Huawei's violation of the sanctions against Iran and North Korea,' a former staffer at the Department of State explained when discussing how he coordinated the measures against Huawei during the Trump administration. 'But then all kinds of layers of policy were thrown on top, because everyone was suddenly concerned about a company from China becoming the largest in 5G technology while having possible backdoors in their software.'

The general public never received a good explanation. 'That would be a waste of bureaucratic time. The Trump administration was good at making quick decisions and leaving us to clean up the mess.' This was typical of the Trump era: shoot first, aim later.

Responsibility for the Entity List isn't attributed to any one person or institution. It's a joint undertaking, compiled by four American departments: Defense, State, Energy, and Commerce. The Bureau for Industry and Security, which implements export controls, falls under the latter.

Coordination was lacking from the moment Trump won the keys to the White House. The President himself was surprised by his victory in the 2016 elections, and had not prepared any policies or selected experts for key political appointments within the departments. Lower-level officials suddenly found themselves grappling with significant decisions. Mess up, and you were fired immediately. Staff were wary of presenting too many issues to the president due to his inclination to act impulsively, often with the subtlety of a bull in a china shop.

Responsible officials deliberately kept their plans away from what they called 'Trump's madness'. With one tweet, he overruled a decision to put ZTE back on the Entity List and hinted that the ban on Huawei could be reversed if the US and China struck a trade deal. On February 18, 2020, he tweeted: 'The United States cannot, & will not, become such a difficult place to deal with in terms of foreign countries buying our product, including for the always used National Security excuse.' And then, in Trump's trademark style: 'THE UNITED STATES IS OPEN FOR BUSINESS!'

The tweet sparked widespread confusion among America's allies: the US had been urging them all to expel Huawei from their networks over security concerns. Now, it seemed to be the one holding open the door. In January, Republican politicians introduced yet another threatening bill, proposing that the US should cease sharing intelligence with countries that continued to use Huawei in their networks. The Netherlands was alarmed – two out of three mobile providers in the country used Huawei equipment in their cell towers and networks. The American ambassador to the Netherlands, Pete Hoekstra, tried to ease concerns in an interview with national newspaper NRC. 'We'll figure it out,' was about all he could promise.

Contradictions piled up as Secretary of State Mike Pompeo took a different approach. He wanted to split the internet in two and called on all 'freedom-loving' nations to join The Clean Network. This was the catchy name for an online world without China: a vision of a mobile network with no Huawei, smartphones without WeChat and TikTok, and a cloud without Chinese servers.

Meanwhile, one of Trumps economic advisors pushed for the rapid development of 'anti-Huawei' technology with Dell, Microsoft and AT&T. Attorney General William Barr envisioned the US taking a controlling stake in European network providers Ericsson and Nokia to 'weaken Huawei's drive to domination'. One day later, the White House dismissed his idea.

The world watched in astonishment as the wild schemes continued to trip over one another. Rationality was in short supply in Washington, overshadowed by a mix of clashing egos and an overeagerness to act. 'It wasn't like being in one henhouse, but three henhouses mixed together,' one Trump advisor later reflected.

In May 2020, Trump reached for heavier artillery and prohibited TSMC from producing advanced chips for Huawei. This was enforceable due to the Taiwanese use of American tools in their factories, such as design software for chips and chip machines. With this measure, the US extended its extraterritorial power to target Huawei. Every chip factory in the world used American technology, which meant every chip factory was brought under American export regulations.

With Huawei out the picture, TSMC instantly lost a significant portion of its revenue. The repercussions made their way to Veldhoven, as the Taiwanese immediately scaled back their orders for chip machines. What followed was a chain reaction no one saw coming. Out of fear that they could be placed on the US's banned list at any moment, other

Chinese tech companies started stockpiling chips en masse. This contributed to the chip shortage in the automotive industry, as they ordered not only the latest processors but also the less advanced chips used for smartphones. TSMC's order books were overflowing, and suddenly they were pressing ASML for lithography machines capable of a higher production output.

The Chinese fears were well placed. In December 2020, the largest Chinese chip manufacturer SMIC landed on the Entity List after allegedly producing chips for military purposes. The Americans came up with a new set of export rules: tools for advanced processors were no longer allowed to go to SMIC. Chip machines for older technology were permitted – at least in theory. This also affected ASML: without an export license, it could no longer supply spare parts from the US to SMIC.

Huawei was left gasping for air. With the American company Google no longer allowed to supply its Android operating system to Huawei, smartphone sales plummeted – no one wants a phone without YouTube or Google Maps. The Huawei name was tainted by the relentless accusations, and the export rules for chips cast doubt over the capabilities of future products.

The Chinese telecom company also lost ground in the EU after governments there tightened their network regulations. However, the approach was less aggressive than the American's. Europe didn't want to step too heavily on the toes of its trading partner China, a crucial supplier of vital raw materials.

All EU member states were left to decide for themselves whether to allow Huawei in their networks. However, there still was a European safety directive they needed to comply with. The EU spent months deliberating over this '5G security toolbox': to the policy makers in the US, this felt like they were watching the grass grow. They were able to add a company to their Entity List in two days, without telling anyone or providing a public comment. That's the American way.

Compared to the barrage of US actions against Huawei, decision-making in the EU was undeniably slow. Nevertheless, something was beginning to change. By the end of 2019, the Netherlands demanded that network providers should be able to easily remove suspicious equipment from their mobile networks if it originated from 'a supplier under the influence of a malicious party'. Any mention of Huawei, or China, was strictly avoided. The Chinese ambassador to the Netherlands, Xu Hong, responded in an announcement in the national newspapers. Without explicitly naming the country, he accused the US of 'politically pressuring' the Netherlands to cut ties with Huawei without providing any evidence to validate their claims: 'What they have done is anti-historical, and anti-civilization.'

In response to the intense scrutiny, Huawei took the initiative and presented the EU with a magnifying glass. A so-called 'red zone' with a direct line to Shenzhen was set up in the Huawei Cyber Security Transparency Centre in Brussels. This Transparency Centre was strategically placed between the embassies, the European Parliament, and European cybersecurity organizations. To enter the red zone, you first must pass through a secured door and metal detector, and then make your way along a row of rooms bearing the names of famous inventors like Shannon, Einstein and Tesla. This is how the Huawei employees see themselves – as inventors, not as extensions of the Chinese Communist Party.

Running along the floor is a data cable that, via a secure connection, leads all the way to the main office in Shenzhen. From this building in Brussels, experts were now able to delve into the source code of Chinese telecom equipment and sift through millions of lines of software to root out any potential backdoors and vulnerabilities.

However, source code is not the main concern. The 'tech war' transcends technology – at its core, it is a battle of economics and politics, of cultures and ideologies. European governments worry about a different type of connection to China. They fear the country is transforming into a totalitarian state, capable of forcing Chinese multinationals to spy for the Communist Party. And that poses a significant risk to the 5G infrastructure in the West.

As for the US, Huawei is an ideal target, but it is certainly no longer the endgame. The stakes in economic warfare are huge, and Washington is just getting started.

29

THE SPIRIT OF
THE MERCHANT

ASML makes no secret of doing business with the whole world. As soon as you walk into the headquarters in Veldhoven, you can see who is interested in a new lithography machine. If South Korean customers are visiting, you'll see a South Korean flag sitting on the reception desk – next to the Dutch flag, of course. When Chinese companies visit, a Chinese flag will be waving to welcome them in. Nice gesture, no effort. For ASML, all customers are equal. Only, the world doesn't work like that anymore.

In China, new chip factories are rising up everywhere, helped by billions in state aid. In 2017, Chinese customers ordered 700 million euros' worth of lithography machines. 'A new record,' Peter Wennink told his investors at the end of that year, predicting it to be 'a very clear growth opportunity' for them all. A few months later, Liang Mong Song, director of Chinese chip manufacturer SMIC, signed on the dotted line in Shanghai for their first EUV machine.

The supervisory board immediately pointed out the risks of this order. 'Guys, we're gonna have a problem here. The Americans won't allow us everything.' But the ASML management brushed off the concerns: they do not do politics in Veldhoven, and they had already been delivering to China's largest foundry, SMIC, for years. Hundreds of ASML's scanners were running in the factories of this valued customer.

In November 2018, the top management scheduled a trip to China with the supervisory board. There, they met with the mayor of Shanghai, the Minister of Industry and Information Technology, and the chairman of the National Development and Reform Commission – the latter of which directly advises Xi Jingping.

Peter Wennink traveled to China often, five or six times a year. He knew that if you are talking to Chinese customers, you will also often end up talking to the Chinese government. Intellectual property was a sensitive topic in these interactions. ASML would only export its most advanced machine to China on one condition: under no circumstances should the valuable technology be copied. The Chinese officials assured him that the country would behave itself with regards to intellectual property rights, and even wanted to adapt its legal system accordingly. Wennink felt this was a shaky promise. However, he believed it was better to maintain dialogue and keep one foot in the door. Wennink was never one for burning bridges.

As he explained in January 2019, ASML wanted to be part of China's growth. 'But as soon as we see flagrant infringement of our intellectual property, we're done. No way China will catch up to us in the next ten or fifteen years. They're light-years behind. Light-years!'

At the time, Wennink was still confident that the EUV machines could be shipped to China. He claimed he wasn't experiencing any pressure from American politicians, despite mounting anti-China sentiments in Washington. 'ASML sticks to the law. We can ship to China because we get an export license from the Dutch government. So if there's any pressure, it'll be between governments.'

And he was right. As soon as ASML applied for a Chinese export license in the Netherlands, the Americans kicked off their diplomatic campaign to keep EUV out of China. When the Dutch Prime Minister Mark Rutte and Donald Trump met at the end of 2018 during the G20 summit in Buenos Aires, the 'ASML question' was raised. Rutte remained pragmatic: he didn't want to be fazed by the chaos surrounding the American president. To him, it was more important to keep relations with the US on good terms. Rutte's strategy for talking to Trump: don't mention the uproar. Be all smiles, and concentrate on 'content'.

Trump's security adviser Tim Morrison subsequently made multiple trips to The Hague to speak with representatives of the Dutch government. The American diplomatic offensive was a joint effort by the departments of Defense and State, along with staff in the White House. Despite spending most of his time ridiculing international partnerships, Donald Trump decided to make an urgent appeal to the Netherlands on the basis of a multilateral agreement. According to Morrison, you would be wrong to think this was a case of the US exerting pressure on friendly nations: 'We all agree on how important EUV technology is. The Dutch government can take an independent decision on this matter.' Though preferably a decision America agrees with.

EUV is controlled by the Wassenaar Arrangement, the multilateral export control regime on conventional arms and dual-use goods and technologies. It was finalized in December 1995 in castle De Wittenburg in Wassenaar, an affluent town just outside The Hague. The negotiations went down to the wire; just before the celebratory dinner started, the French and the Russian delegates couldn't agree on the final text. Their argument was solved at the very last minute, in a corner of the castle's kitchen. In July 1996, the Arrangement became effective, and now 42 countries jointly regulate the export of sensitive technology. The Wassenaar Arrangement is the successor of COCOM, a multilateral committee that, until 1993, aimed to prevent communist countries from gaining access to military technology. It is the reason EUV requires a permit.

The Wassenaar Arrangement regulates the export of equipment that could be used for military purposes. This includes the most advanced lithography machines. Experts from participating countries gather annually in the Austrian capital of Vienna to determine which sensitive new technologies to add to the dual-use list. If the equipment becomes widely available, it can be removed from the list via consultation.

When the US granted ASML permission to acquire its American competitor SVG in 2001, the monopoly on EUV technology fell into Dutch hands. However, the Wassenaar Arrangement offers the Americans a way to influence which countries can use that technology. This would slow down Chinese innovation by limiting access to chips with a fineness of five or seven nanometers. If they wanted to manufacture processors on a large scale with even finer lines, they would need an EUV machine.

The Dutch cabinet found themselves wrestling with the issue: after all, this country had no choice but to be held accountable for its own tech giant. Although in principle Europe couldn't help – in the EU, export control legally is a matter for the individual member states – the pressure from their powerful ally America could not be ignored. Insiders described it as a 'turd' handed to the Dutch Ministry of Foreign Affairs. No matter how you handle it, you'll come away with dirty fingers.

The mess the Dutch found themselves in should not have come as a surprise. The Americans do not want an actual war with China, so instead seek to maintain control over Chinese technology by all other means. Chips are the oil of the modern economy, and if you follow the value chain, you quickly end up in Brabant – at exit 32 to Veldhoven-Zuid, to be precise.

Politics at ASML had traditionally been seen as a side issue. It came in handy for securing innovation subsidies or for arranging reduced working hours during times of crisis. But anything that diverted attention away from technology was considered unnecessary fuss and swiftly dismissed. This all changed in the summer of 2018 when the US blocked the export of American chip machines to the Chinese memory chip manufacturer Fujian Jinhua. Because the matter stemmed from a dispute with Micron, it received less attention than the widely reported campaign on Huawei. Nonetheless, Veldhoven was shocked by this move from the Americans.

ASML had already appointed a board member to strengthen government relations in early 2018, as other EU countries had been grumbling about subsidies granted by Brussels to the prosperous ASML. This board member was Frits van Hout, who represented ASML's strategic interests with policy makers through his government affairs team from 2018 until his retirement in 2021. When he saw his workload suddenly increase due to geopolitical tensions, he realized that a new game was unfolding.

According to Van Hout, ASML is not diplomatic by nature: 'We're very direct. If we mean no, then we'll say no. And yes is yes. End of story. Governments have to get used to that.' But ASML also had to get used to governments – sometimes, they also say no. ASML may dominate the market for the most important chip machines, but it no longer determines its own fate.

This still causes a huge amount of resistance. In Veldhoven's eyes, the people who make the rules don't understand how 'it' works – 'it' being the entire chip industry, with all its global dependencies, vulnerable supply chains and complex technology. It is a world that revolves around mutual trust, long-term agreements and free-market dynamics. The government cannot be allowed to disrupt this fragile ecosystem: most of all because ASML makes a lot of money from it, including in China, and it creates many jobs in the Netherlands.

ASML claims the US is mainly using the blockade of EUV to feed its own economic war against China. The technology is for manufacturing advanced semiconductors in larger volumes, with fewer tricks and fewer mistakes. These are chips for phones, not for fighter jets. As far as Veldhoven is concerned, fears about EUV being used for military applications are baloney – the weapons industry uses proven lithography techniques that have been on the market for years. In addition, most chips found in weapons are 'off-the-shelf' chips that can also be found in laptops, washing machines or cars, and are easy to purchase anywhere in the world.

But the US sees things differently. The American definition of 'military' goes far beyond conventional weapons. They fear the emergence of Chinese artificial intelligence, the Chinese supercomputers that are dominating the global rankings and the arsenal of superior cyber weapons that will be at Beijing's disposal. And there is one thing those all need: advanced chips.

Until 2021, decisions about the export license for EUV were the responsibility of the Minister of Foreign Trade, Sigrid Kaag. ASML traditionally enjoyed a far better relationship with the Ministry of Economic Affairs and Climate Policy, which between 2017 and 2021 was led by Eric Wiebes. However, he was preoccupied with the damage being caused by earthquakes related to gas extraction in the province of Groningen, so at the beginning of 2018 he handed over his industrial portfolio to State Secretary Mona Keijzer. Ultimately, her ministry had little say over export licenses. It could only advise, and via the embassy in Washington it tried to mitigate damage caused by the Trump administration's string of anti-China measures.

The final decision on the export license for EUV rested on Mark Rutte's third cabinet, in which the intelligence services, along with the Ministries of Justice and Security, Defense and General Affairs, outrank the Ministry of Economic Affairs.

This ministry traditionally championed a hands-off approach towards businesses, allowing them to take full advantage of world trade. As a neoliberal trading nation, the Netherlands rode the wave of globalization for over thirty years. This also meant they turned a blind eye to China's rise, preferring to defer the thorny political decisions to its companies. In the words of a Dutch diplomat, 'You could call that naïve, but it's earned us an unbelievable amount of money.' ASML is the embodiment of that mercantile spirit.

However, the Dutch perspective on China was shifting. In May of 2019, the Dutch Ministry of Foreign Affairs published a critical report on China, titled, 'A New Balance'. This report stated that China was guilty of engaging in unfair trade practices, cyber-espionage, and theft of technology. It also noted the deteriorating human rights situation, and raised questions about China's ambitions to become a world leader in artificial intelligence. The report doubted the feasibility of 'Made in China 2025', but it expressed a deep unease about where this might end: the emergence of China as a technological and scientific superpower that operates by its own rules, free from international conventions.

One year later, in June 2020, Dutch intelligence services warned of espionage attacks from China aimed at semiconductor companies. This came as no surprise: the high-tech sector had already been a target for years. For example, at the beginning of 2015, ASML found itself subject to a cyber-attack when hackers gained access to ASML's network through an account from their subsidiary Brion in Shenzen. An employee in San Diego smelled trouble as soon as the networks of ASML and Cymer were connected: someone was trying to get in with the wrong password. Alarm bells started ringing. Was there something wrong? Over in Veldhoven, it turned out there was.

Multiple security firms were brought in to assess the damage, and ASML's facilities in the United States also received a thorough examination. The investigation by these response teams, akin to a force of digital firefighters, went on for weeks. The hackers had built a backdoor and gained access to usernames and passwords, from which they had started to transfer captured information in zip files via computer addresses in Japan. The security experts were convinced that Chinese hacking groups knew what they were searching for: documents about lithography machines.

A team of officials from the Dutch General Intelligence and Security Service (AIVD) made an unsolicited appearance in Veldhoven. They received a cold reception, as ASML felt the AIVD'ers were just there to be nosy, especially when the intelligence services' cybersecurity specialists suggested ASML was too lax about the risks of economic espionage.

The breach brought the company face-to-face with a harsh reality. In 2015, the security of their networks was grossly inadequate. A new cybersecurity team took it upon itself to 'raise the dikes' and started to increase its collaboration with the AIVD. As a primary target, ASML has proven to be a valuable source of information for the intelligence services. When you keep a close eye on Veldhoven, you can learn a lot about the attack methods and capabilities of Chinese hacking groups.

Cymer was acquired in May 2013, and the breach was reported by the website *Tweakers* in early 2015. In theory, the hackers could have been snooping around the company network for a considerable amount of time. According to ASML, the breach was quickly halted, and there was no evidence that any valuable information was stolen. A brief press release stated, 'We cannot be certain about the identity of the hackers,' but one thing was for sure: ASML's servers had found themselves on the frontline of the cyberwar.

ASML long tried to avoid the geopolitical stage. In retrospect, Frits van Hout believes it was naïve to think they could avoid that dance. You cannot operate outside the spotlight forever when your machines print the building blocks of the modern world.

In January 2020, the diplomatic fencing finally became public. Reuters news agency reported that the US had asked the Netherlands to block EUV exports, and suddenly ASML found itself in the spotlight. The combination of Trump's trade war, the espionage cases and the debate over Huawei and 5G created a whirlwind of publicity, and Veldhoven became front page news.

As long as the export license remained officially 'under consideration', China would be unable to access EUV machines. Minister Sigrid Kaag encouraged ASML to explain this to the Americans so they would ease off their campaign, but the Trump administration was a challenge to deal with. Several online meetings with nearly twenty participants were arranged, with ASML, the Ministry of Foreign Affairs, and the Dutch embassy in Washington on one side and representatives from US departments on the other. No cameras, no introductions, just an impersonal barrage of questions.

Meanwhile, the US kept on turning up the heat. In October 2020, a confidential analysis written by the Dutch Ministry of Defense detailed how it had received 'an urgent plea from its most important strategic partner.' Its warning: with access to EUV lithography, the Chinese defense industry could develop smarter algorithms for missiles, drones, and cyber warfare.

The Netherlands ultimately denied ASML a license based on this advice, but it made sure to do so in terms that didn't explicitly prohibit delivery to China. Despite the diplomatic packaging, the result was still the same: no EUV machine was going to SMIC.

Rutte hoped this perpetual pause button would satisfy both super-powers. The Americans were pleased, but kept their sights trained on the Netherlands. If ASML were to unexpectedly get an export license for EUV, they had a plan B ready to fire. 'The bullet is in the chamber,' as one of Trump's hawks said in November 2020, one of the hardliners pushing the tough stance on China.

The US always has a so-called 'de minimis' rule in its back pocket. Like the sword of Damocles, this rule hovers over the entire international chip industry. As soon as there is even a scrap of American technology in a machine, the Department of Commerce can impose a licensing requirement on the entire device. The bar is normally set at 25 percent American technology: if it were lowered to 10 percent or less, it would put ASML in difficult waters.

The EUV machine consists of around 90 percent European technology, so it escapes falling under American export regulations. The scanners do have a light source that is partly made in San Diego – think of Joann's hands soldering nozzles or the droplet generator that regularly needs to be replaced.

The US wanted to know – down to the very last screw – what is put into a lithography machine, and the final destination of each component. To twist ASML's arm, American officials refused on several occasions to approve deliveries of spare materials from ASML intended for desperate chip manufacturers. Behind this tactic was the powerful National Security Council, which was fishing for a detailed list of components.

On behalf of ASML, Dutch diplomats objected to this underhand approach. It was verging on blackmail, and even members of the National Security Council questioned if this was any way to treat an ally. When it comes to China, apparently it was.

ASML reluctantly compiled a list, but added enough creative ambiguities to render it useless. One of the American experts chasing it later admitted that the NSC had a weak case anyway.

In 2020, ASML's annual revenue share coming from China was dwindling. Due to the restrictions on China, more of the high-cost EUV machines were now being sold to Taiwan and South Korea, which increased the proportion of revenue coming from outside of China. The Netherlands was not the only country to face issues following the EUV ban: after pressure from the US, Korean manufacturer SK Hynix was forced to back out after it ordered an extreme ultraviolet machine for a Chinese factory in Wuxi. ASML's second EUV license application was also scrapped.

Peter Wennink watched with regret as his company missed out on a potential market for significant growth. Even though his company had been forced to slam on the brakes in China, the Americans were putting their foot on the gas and capitalizing on their share of the trade. Chinese chip manufacturers were still able to produce more advanced chips with conventional DUV machines by using multi-patterning techniques. This involves executing multiple exposures in succession: imagine a printing press that doubles the number of words on a page by printing extra sentences between the lines of the initial print. However, this trick requires more advanced depositing and etching machines, and this technology mainly comes from American chip machine manufacturers like Applied Materials, KLA, and Lam Research. Those US companies were happy to see Veldhoven lose ground in China if it meant they would not miss out on revenue themselves. You can put a price tag on it: in a chip factory that uses DUV scanners and multi-patterning, 20 percent of the total investment goes to lithography machines. For EUV instead of multi-patterning, it is 30 percent. Considering a new fab can cost around 15 billion dollars, the stakes are high.

The EUV affair prompted ASML to strengthen its ties with governments by forging closer collaborations with ministries in The Hague and the US Department of Commerce, as well as establish its own representation in Brussels and Washington, DC. In addition, ASML built its own lobbying team in the US so it no longer had to solely rely on the Semiconductor Industry Association, the primary voice of American chip companies.

By the end of 2023, ASML's lobbying expenses in the US had grown from virtually zero to 1.4 million dollars. To compare, industry counterpart Applied Materials spent 2 million dollars that year to influence policies in Washington. ASML also increased its annual lobbying costs in Brussels sixfold to 300,000 euros. Although these budgets are still modest compared to other tech giants, one thing is clear: for ASML, politics is no longer a side show.

30

DEATH GRIP IN DC

The image of the man with the horned head dress was etched into everyone's mind the moment it flashed across the world's screens. On Wednesday January 6, 2021, Jacob Chansley, a.k.a the QAnon Shaman, stormed the US Capitol along with a group of rioters after refusing to accept the outcome of the presidential elections. Donald Trump had lost, and the violent rampage that followed left deep scars on the democratic heart of the United States. But despite their deteriorated relationship, both Republicans and Democrats still agreed on one thing: ever-advancing China was public enemy number one. Trump had discovered that he could use export regulations to constrain Chinese tech companies, and his Democratic successor, Joe Biden, set his sights on perfecting that weapon. After his arrival, the Americans decided they would no longer settle for the export ban on EUV machines. The White House wanted to grasp the Chinese chip industry by the throat, and forcing ASML to make further concessions would be the best way to do it.

Who in Washington writes the rules of the technology war? After passing through the security gates at Lafayette Square, do not take a left towards the White House. Take a right instead, past the West Wing where the president addresses the press, and go up the stairs of the Eisenhower Executive Office Building. This five-story structure of immovable granite – in French Second Empire style, as they call it – is home to the executive branch of the United States.

When the Executive Office Building was erected in 1888, the so-called Department of War moved in. That memory is kept alive by signs outside each office commemorating the government officials that worked within them. The halls are lined with a pattern of black and white tiles, repeating like an endless chessboard. Even when you whisper, you hear an echo.

This building houses the advisory bodies of the American president. The most influential entity is the National Security Council, which advises Biden on national security and foreign policy. The NSC has the most beautiful of all the offices, located on the second floor.

The Trump administration spelled chaos for the National Security Council: key figures abruptly departed, and a large amount of people were dismissed. Under the Biden administration, however, the staff expanded to more than 350 people, all united in orchestrating the plan to halt China's advance and boost the American chip industry with billions in state aid. The NSC also ensured that the relevant departments adhered to the established strategy. Geopolitics demands discipline, not a cackling henhouse.

Even before he was sworn in, Joe Biden pulled out all the diplomatic stops to coordinate export restrictions with allies. America started playing chess on several boards at once. In the Trade and Technology Council (TTC), a strategic dialogue between the EU and the US, discussions included export restrictions and stimulus plans for the domestic chip industry. Europe, like America, was developing a plan to support the local chip industry with tens of billions in subsidies. It was essentially a pot of gold to entice manufacturers to expand their production outside of Asia.

The United States were also trying to establish a 'Chip 4 alliance' with Japan, Taiwan and South Korea. However, Japan and South Korea share a complex history of war and territorial disputes, and trying to align these countries proved to be a challenge.

The closed trilateral discussions between America, Japan and the Netherlands, known as 'trilats', were particularly important for ASML. As the three countries responsible for supplying the machines and software essential to chip manufacturing, the trilats aimed to maximize Western technological superiority by depriving China of the tools it needs to build advanced chips. Following their success with the EUV case, the NSC turned its focus to another one of ASML's innovations – their advanced immersion systems. These systems make use of deep ultraviolet light, a field the company holds a 90 percent market share in. The chips made by these machines might not be as advanced as EUV, but they are still good enough to produce powerful processors for complex computing tasks – if you use the right multi-patterning techniques.

The Netherlands had known for a while that the Americans wanted to discuss export restrictions for these systems. In December 2020, Robert O'Brien, the last of Trump's four national security advisers, met with his Dutch counterpart Geoffrey van Leeuwen. In the US ambassador's Paris residence, O'Brien raised the topic of ASML's deliveries to China. Van Leeuwen figured the issue was a sidenote in a broader discussion about technical leadership.

Anyone who followed the influential think tanks in Washington, DC could have known that stricter measures were on the horizon. Biden's National Security Advisor, Jake Sullivan, was devising a strategy based on preparatory work done by two NSC members, Tarun Chhabra and Saif Khan. Before they began working in the stately Eisenhower Building, they had each published extensive reports for think tanks such as Brookings and CSET.

Washington is home to hundreds of these non-profit advisory institutions, which function as a source of information for the current administration and a talent pool for government employees. The highest officials of each department in the US are politically appointed, and both Republicans and Democrats have their own pools of specialists to draw from. Such networks tend to encourage a 'revolving door' style of politics, but the think-tankers prefer to characterize it as a symbiosis of policy and new insights. Whatever your angle, it is the engine that keeps DC running.

In 2019, Tarun Chhabra published the article 'The China Challenge, Democracy, and US Grand Strategy', in which he described how the 'democratic capitalism' of America and its allies was threatened by the 'authoritarian capitalism' of China. According to Chhabra, China's goal was simple: create economic dependencies, and then exploit them. China's alignment with Russia had created a hostile power bloc in Eurasia, which posed 'unacceptable risks' to the prosperity and security of the United States.

In March 2021, Saif Khan published a study on China's dependence on chip machines from Western countries. The report stated that China trailed far behind in the race but was attempting to take the inside lane: the country had allegedly been stealing technology, as well as using foreign investments and returning knowledge workers to accelerate the development of its own chip machines. Khan concluded that having access to ASML's advanced lithography systems was China's main bottleneck. But for the Chinese to truly feel the pressure, the Dutch government would need to play along. In fact, it would need a whole new playing field.

As mentioned, the Netherlands regulates export licenses based on the dual-use list of the Wassenaar Arrangement. The DUV machines were removed from that list in 2014 because a new technology had become available: extreme ultraviolet. In 2019 and 2020, the United States tried to use the Wassenaar Arrangement to again regulate DUV. The Netherlands, with both Belgium and Germany in tow, put their foot down. Veldhoven and The Hague agreed that, with the EUV restriction for China in place, ASML had already compromised enough.

But this was not enough to satisfy the Americans. If China could not be slowed via Wassenaar, then allies like the Netherlands and Japan would have to impose export restrictions on their own chip machine makers and their DUV scanners. Otherwise, the Americans would sort it out the American way – with unilateral measures.

Since Biden's inauguration in early 2021, the US had been in talks with each of these countries about what these restrictions could look like. The key question: who will do what, and when?

The trilaterals started as a slow diplomatic dance, as an American negotiator who conducted the initial talks on behalf of the Biden administration explained. 'We first had to demonstrate how committed the US were by imposing restrictions on our own industry.

Only then would we be able to open discussions with Japan and the Netherlands in good faith.'

ASML initially tried to prevent the Netherlands from taking part in the trilaterals. Veldhoven did not think it wise for a 'Mickey Mouse country' – as Peter Wennink described it – to get caught between the major powers. On the other hand, Wennink figured, it was better to have a seat at the table to avoid the Americans from enforcing their rules without consultation.

The Dutch government was open to imposing some restrictions on the export of immersion scanners to China from a national security perspective. However, it would do so only on the condition that all three relevant countries took the measures simultaneously, and that all steps would be taken to ensure the existing chip shortage would not worsen. Anything resembling a blockade or 'decoupling' was also considered too extreme. After all, China is the world's largest supplier of rare earth metals, which are indispensable for the energy transition and for the chip industry. And unlike America, a 'Mickey Mouse' country like the Netherlands does not have the natural resources to start mining its own.

The Dutch naïveté towards China has passed, albeit more recently than they'd care to admit. In 2018, Prime Minister Mark Rutte travelled to China with a large Dutch trade delegation and presented an award to Huawei as a token of appreciation for the company's large investments in the Netherlands. A year later, Rutte was bristling at the thought of the superpower becoming technologically dominant. The Netherlands was now on the same page as the US, and was edging increasingly closer towards Washington.

There was another strategic reason to be concerned about the rise of China. Should the country grow unchecked and further consolidate its capacity for chip production, it could become less dependent on Taiwanese factories like TSMC. This would then lower the threshold for claiming Taiwan, even before the Chinese People's Republic would celebrate its one hundredth anniversary. This scenario could cause the whole world to have a problem, but less so for China itself.

Blindly trusting the US was considered just as naïve as depending on China, however. As the Dutch Ministry of Economic Affairs warned, the Americans were also using national security to drive trade policy and protect the position of their own chip companies. To defend the interests of businesses and trade the ministry demanded a seat at the negotiating table. ASML is a key driver of the Dutch economy – they were not going to let the US limit that growth engine without a fight.

At the same time, the Ministry of Economic Affairs had also become more vigilant regarding China's ambitions, and the warnings from the security services led to increased government intervention in the business sector. For instance, the ministry was quick to take a stake in Eindhoven-based chip start-up Smart Photonics in 2020, which prevented a Chinese investment fund from gaining access to its high-tech knowledge. The Netherlands had finally realized that it needed to start protecting its open economy.

The line between the Binnenhof – the seat of government in The Hague – and the White House was short. Since the United Kingdom left the EU, the Netherlands became the closest transatlantic ally and best friend to the US. National security advisors Jake Sullivan and Geoffrey van Leeuwen updated each other every two months via an encrypted line, WhatsApp or Signal. ASML was often the topic of discussion, but with Russian aggression increasing and China seemingly transforming into a totalitarian state, it was not always at the top of their agenda. Both security advisors agreed that the technological superiority of the West needed to be maintained. But how?

The American proposed the first step: China should not be allowed to acquire the domestic capability to manufacture processors finer than 14 nanometers. For memory chips, a different set of standards would apply.

To estimate the consequences of these measures, the Dutch negotiators relied heavily on information provided to them by ASML. They trusted that the company with feelers across the entire global chip industry had the better overview. As a 'victim' of the export measures, ASML collaborated to prevent the situation from deteriorating any further. In Veldhoven, Peter Wennink personally provided Van Leeuwen with an intensive crash course on chip technology to help him get to grips with the subject. The chip industry had always been a perfectly optimized value chain, and it horrified Wennink to think of people pushing and pulling without understanding how it all worked.

Many of the technological discussions were held at the Ministry of Foreign Affairs, right next to the central train station in The Hague, or at the US embassy in Wassenaar, close to the castle where the Wassenaar Arrangement had been drafted. Experts from both countries would gather in a room on the second floor overlooking the embassy courtyard. The table, made of white frosted glass, had room for ten people, and others could join the conversations via a secure video connection on a large screen. The only decorations on the wall were a whiteboard, a clock and a map of the Netherlands – all the tools you need for slowing down China's semiconductor industry.

Sometimes there were dual sessions: one meeting at which state secrets could be discussed, and another including specialists from two Dutch tech companies. ASML was one of them, and alongside it was a familiar face: ASM International, the company that laid the foundation for ASML with Philips in 1984. Their advanced deposition machines granted them a seat at the table.

The Americans strived to not only halt, but even reverse the technological advancement of the Chinese chip industry. However, this message coincided with a severe shortage of all types of chips, including the less advanced or 'mature' processors that China produced en masse, and it was poorly received. This lack was partly due to the COVID-19 pandemic: in 2021, remote workers required a volume of computing power and cloud capacity that outweighed what the chip industry could supply.

The shortage had already forced French and German car manufacturers to pause their production lines, and they feared even more shortages would follow if the Chinese companies faced further restrictions. The Dutch delegation kept France and Germany in the know about the negotiations, but, much to the frustration of ASML, that was the extent of the European involvement. The company lobbied to turn the trilaterals into an EU-wide discussion, which would allow

Germany and France to also exert their influence. A unified European stance would be a stronghold against China and the US. But in the end, the Netherlands were on their own. In Veldhoven, they drew a different conclusion. It seemed the Dutch negotiators overestimated their clout compared to the Americans. The Dutch may be tall, but this time they had imagined themselves bigger than they actually were.

Over in Washington, the NSC exercised strict control over the Entity List of the Bureau of Industry and Security. Following that, dozens of Chinese companies with military connections were added to the list. Many license applications had been given the green light under Trump: in the eyes of the National Security Council, he was far too lenient towards the industry. The NSC wanted to keep a firm grip on export regulations with a 'top-down policy'.

The expansion of the Entity List led to significant tensions when ASML required an American license for a substantial order from the Chinese chip manufacturer SMIC. Some spare parts of the scanner were being produced in the US, such as the deep ultra-violet light sources made by the subsidiary Cymer in San Diego or the modules from the division in Connecticut. Even if they were sent to China via the Netherlands, they would still fall under American regulations. The long arm of Washington had a reach that even Veldhoven could not escape.

For CEO Peter Wennink, it was a reason to strengthen ties with the new administration in Washington. He reached out to Secretary of Commerce Gina Raimondo, whom he met in June of 2021 during the G7 summit in Brussels. Due to the pandemic, it was not until October of that year that he was able to visit Washington himself. In consultation with Dutch diplomats, Wennink squeezed twelve meetings into a handful of days, starting with a visit to the trade association of the American automative industry to discuss the chip shortage. The car lobby is powerful, and he figured it could help to convince politicians not to put the brakes on ASML too much.

In Washington, Wennink zoomed back and forth on the Capitol's subway linking the government buildings between discussions with politicians, meetings with representatives from the Bureau of Industry and Security and the Pentagon, and dinners with the National Security Council. Everyone cleared their agendas for 'that Dutch company'.

Once again, Wennink proved himself to be ASML's most important in-house ambassador. He felt like a fish in water among the dignitaries and gathered his staff in his hotel in Washington to practice conversations with the Americans. The team members would present the critical questions, and he would line up the arguments and build his case piece by piece, as if he were decorating a Christmas tree. Wennink adheres to the harmony model of resolving issues. Making connections is second nature to him: he knows the power of a quick nod, a look or a personal comment to put someone at ease.

The CEO tried to avoid ideological discussions, but that was not always possible. During a dinner with American diplomats, he was asked about the chip industry's role in relation to the Uyghurs in China. This Muslim minority is oppressed by the Chinese state and is being monitored with advanced electronics. 'As the chip industry, we're not responsible for that. We don't arrest people,' Wennink answered. When he bounced the ball back and asked about American school shootings and what responsibilities gun manufacturers might have, an awkward silence followed. Who was he to patronize the US?

Wennink prefers to throw in a lot of facts – an hour-long meeting usually consists of forty-five minutes listening to him detailing specifics. He is a natural teacher, especially when explains the mutual dependencies in the chip world. He repeatedly warned American politicians that putting the squeeze on China would have consequences for their cars and washing machines, and that it would take years for new chip factories to start production. He showed them the numbers: US firms receive the lion's share of chip industry profits, and any money they make in China could be invested into boosting their technological lead. 'Where's your self-confidence!' he would often say.

As one member of ASML's supervisory board pointed out, Peter was so well-versed in the subject, he would often present his solutions as if they were 'ready-to-use products', leaving little or nothing to argue about. Wennink tried to steer away from being rash and to suppress his own opinion – the storytelling had to be 'sophisticated' and weave a refined narrative.

But Wennink would not always hold back. He once interrupted a senator who had been discussing the threats posed by China for a solid ten minutes with a blunt 'You don't know all the facts.'

Those were the occasions when the CEO had been too direct, he later heard from Dutch diplomats. The Americans would easily get annoyed by his 'mark my words' attitude and the frequent sight of his index finger raised in warning. However, by the end of 2021, ASML had secured the necessary export license for SMIC.

Meanwhile, the Americans were growing impatient over the slow progress of the trilats. The Dutch negotiators were taking their time to shine a light on every detail of the US proposals. But in February 2022, it became clear that the Netherlands could be decisive if needed. When Russia invaded Ukraine, European countries immediately struck back with a heavy sanctions package. The EU showed that it was prepared to hit its own economy if necessary. National security became palpable – one look at their energy bills was enough for most Europeans to notice this.

The Americans were positively surprised by the decisiveness of the Dutch, which also extended to their supply of weapons to Ukraine. The start of a war on European soil had emphasized the strategic importance of technological superiority, and a new generation was exposed to the reality of what this meant. 'Everyday' Dutch chips ended up in the killer drones fired at Ukrainian cities, while advanced chips were used to help Ukraine's air defenses, data collection via satellites and the coordination of missile attacks far behind enemy lines. The stakes look different in the cold light of war.

It took another crisis for the negotiations between the US, the Netherlands and Japan to finally pick up speed. In August 2022, Taiwan was visited by the Speaker of the American House of Representatives Nancy Pelosi. The US feared that China had been inspired by the Russian invasion of Ukraine, and that it was preparing to invade Taiwan. In turn, the Chinese were furious that America was treating their 'renegade province' as a separate country by making these symbolic trips.

The Taiwanese population has been living at odds with the mainland for seventy years, and many are so accustomed to the Chinese military threat that it is simply part of daily life. In the eyes of some Taiwanese, Pelosi's visit disturbed the delicate cross-strait status quo. However, the majority still embrace US support: they don't want to be dragged closer to China, especially after witnessing Xi Jingping dismantle the democratic movement in Hong Kong with a strict security law.

The economic ties between China and Taiwan are strong. The democratic and free-spirited Taiwan – the first Asian country to legalize same-sex marriage – cannot function without trade from China. In 2022, it accounted for more than 40 percent of Taiwan's gross national product – that is more than three times higher than their trade with the US.

China responded to Pelosi's visit with large-scale military exercises that indicated a possible blockade of the island. Such an obstruction would be disastrous for the company and the global economy. For almost two years, the US had been trying to forge a joint techfront to take the wind out of China's sails. But with the Chinese warships circling Taiwan, they knew they needed to take the first step.

31

CODENAME MISSING

Gonzalo Suarez – or 'Gonzo' to friends – knows his place in history. He points to the ceiling of his office. During the Second World War, the headquarters of the Manhattan Project were housed right there, directly above on the fifth floor. From that very place, General Leslie Groves led the development of the first American atomic bomb in 1942.

The year is 2023, and this government building in Washington now houses the Department of Foreign Affairs. And it is home to a new frontline: the technology war with China. Here, Deputy Assistant Secretary Suarez of the Bureau of International Security and Nonproliferation carries out his mission to ensure that 'an industry with strategic security value' does not fall into the hands of the enemy. He learned the tricks of the trade at the Fletcher School of Law and Diplomacy. For instance, diplomats love to laugh, but when they want to convince you of something important, they will drop the volume of their voice until you can barely hear them.

Suarez was involved in all the discussions about export regulations that the US held with the Netherlands and Japan. But unlike Gonzo from the Muppet Show, the blue bird constantly trying to grab your attention with outlandish stunts, 'Gonzo' Suarez operated in the background. Since 2021, he has been overseeing the negotiating teams striving to clip China's wings. For example: if it were up to the US, Chinese factories would not be allowed to produce chips with 'finfet' transistors. These are fin-shaped switches that can be used in a processor at the smallest level. The first finfet technology came onto the market in 2011, and companies such as TSMC, Samsung and Intel subsequently developed better switches that changed a 'o' into a '1' even more efficiently. For these switches, advanced chip machines and design software are needed, something China would no longer receive if the US government had its way.

The US developed a plan to set China back by fifteen years, through choking China's access to advanced chip technology. To achieve this and to set limits for American suppliers, the departments of Commerce, State, Defense and Energy each sent a delegation of two or three specialists knowledgeable in the field of chip industry supply chains to form a team. From 2021 on, they would meet via secure video connections or at the NSC office in the Eisenhower Executive Office building. The NSC dominated these discussions, and largely left the diplomatic negotiations to Suarez and his team. For the technical details, they consulted the experts from the Pentagon or the American Ministry of Energy.

You cannot produce a good chip without high-quality etching machines, measuring equipment and devices to apply the wafer-thin layers. And for all this, you need a supplier such as Applied Materials, Lam Research and KLA – all billion-dollar enterprises, although their market value had dropped slightly below ASML's. American companies had been making huge sums of money from chip production in China – exactly as Peter Wennink said – and they risked losing a large portion of their revenue due to the export restrictions. It was something they continually complained about to the Biden administration. 'That criticism hasn't died down. But we're trying to proceed surgically to avoid causing major economic damage,' was Suarez's diplomatic response. Behind the scenes, this was accompanied by fierce discussions between the Department of Commerce on one side, and the Pentagon and the State Department on the other. And it led to endless changes in the overflowing shared Google document, edited by the Americans under the watchful eye of the NSC.

Meanwhile, China's technological advance marched on. In the summer of 2022, it became apparent that SMIC was capable of producing 7-nanometer chips using standard scanners from the Netherlands. The

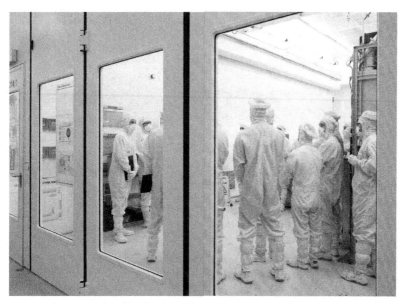

A maximum of ten dust particles ranging from one hundred to two hundred nanometers in size are allowed per cubic meter of cleanroom air at ASML. That is more than one thousand times cleaner than the operating room of a hospital is.

The High NA system is 14 meters long, weighs around 150 tons and costs about 400 million euros. It takes seven cargo planes to ship this system to customers.

ASML's campus in Veldhoven stretches from the tower (Building 8) almost to the horizon. In this photo from August 2021, the logistics center 5L can be seen next to the yellow crane in the distance.

In a small cabin in ASML's 'thrift shop' in Linkou, Taiwan, a PAS 5500 system is being repaired. These machines are over 25 years old and still operate.

The workplace in an EUV cleanroom cabin in Veldhoven.

ASML chief executive and co-president Peter Wennink (left) and Roger Dassen (right) during an investor call in 2019. Dassen previously worked at Deloitte, just like Wennink did.

Technical director Martin van den Brink took over leadership in 2013, together with co-president Peter Wennink. Here, Van den Brink is presenting ASML's strategy at an investor meeting in 2022.

In an enormous vacuum chamber, the German supplier Zeiss measures whether the mirrors of the EUV optics are smooth enough. The final imperfections are blasted away atom by atom.

A deep-ultraviolet-scanner's lens-system, hanging from the ceiling at the Zeiss Museum of Optics in Oberkochen.

The EUV machine's laser is developed by the German company Trumpf and consists of around 450,000 parts.

One of TSMC's chip factories in Taichung, on the west coast of Taiwan. TSMC produces 90 percent of all advanced processors.

'NanoCity' is the nickname given to the factories south of the South Korean capital Seoul, where Samsung manufactures memory chips. The colored panels on the buildings are an enlarged representation of chip patterns.

The inside of a TSMC factory. On the ceiling, small robots shuttle back and forth, transporting silicon wafers from one machine to another.

President Joe Biden at the TSMC factory under construction, just north of Phoenix, Arizona. To the left of Biden are Jensen Huang from Nvidia, Tim Cook from Apple, and US Secretary of Commerce Gina Raimondo, in red. To Biden's right are Peter Wennink and Mark Liu, chief executive of TSMC.

Intel's CEO, Pat Gelsinger. His company fell behind the Asian competition, and is now building modern factories in Europe and the US with the support of billions in subsidies.

On Intel's Ocotillo campus in Chandler, Arizona, two new factories are being built that will produce chips using ASML's EUV machines.

West may have taken away EUV, but that did not stop China's progress. And to improve their chips, Chinese factories were using equipment that mainly originated in the US. In technical terms: ASML's immersion scanners project lines to an accuracy of 38 nanometers. Anything below that is the responsibility of alternative chip machine suppliers. That stings in Veldhoven: they feel the US is shifting the economic damage to its industry onto the Dutch company.

But time was running out, and the Biden administration was no longer willing to wait to intervene. With the midterm elections looming in November 2022, Republican opponents were accusing the Democrats of being too soft on China. They demanded stricter measures.

And they got them. The first details were leaked in the summer of 2022, and on Friday October 7 the full plan was made public. The timing was a work of diplomatic precision: it was just before Xi Jingping was set to announce his third term in office, but not too close to the National Congress of the Chinese party that it would give Xi reason to adopt an even more aggressive stance towards the US. Despite this meticulous preparation, neither the NSC nor the State Department bothered to come up with a captivating codename like the iconic 'Manhattan Project'. Suarez had to laugh: 'We're a bunch of boring bureaucrats, so we just called it "the measures". We forgot to come up with a code name.'

The Bureau of Industry and Security presented the technical details in a 139-page document. Even Kevin Wolf, the world champion of export regulations, was left reeling. 'I've been doing this for thirty years and knew what to expect. But I had to read all 139 pages ten times over to make any sense of this jumble of rules.' In his eyes, the American export rules were simply too complicated for mere mortals to understand.

Throughout his time at BIS during the Obama era, Wolf designed the export regulations now at use in this tech war. He was the one who used the Entity List to bring the Chinese telecom company ZTE to its knees. Now, the legal expert guides tech companies through the treacherous forest of export regulations for the prestigious law firm

Akin Gump. The entrance to their office on K-Street, the heart of the Washington lobbying circuit, is large enough to park a few trucks side by side and not worry about denting their doors. After all, lobbying is big business in DC.

To maximize its technological advantage over China, the US built 'a high fence around a small yard,' in the words of National Security Advisor Jake Sullivan. But for chip companies and suppliers, it was difficult to gauge where exactly that fence stood. In short, they were no longer allowed to supply tools that would enable Chinese chipmakers to produce processors finer than 14 nanometers. Chip factories producing dynamic random-access memory (DRAM) were limited to 18 nanometers, and storage memory (NAND) could consist of at most 128 different layers.

The scope of the export regulations was expanded to cover all advanced commercial chips, which, according to Wolf, made things particularly complicated: 'During my time at BIS, I designed the rules for specific semiconductors that could serve military purposes, such as programmable processors and radiation-resistant chips. Now, the measures were aimed at an entire country.'

The rules were precisely tuned: in general, restrictions for China did not apply to companies as a whole, but were determined per factory, and sometimes even per production line. This kept the supply of less advanced chips from China intact. After all, the Americans still want to be able to buy their cars and washing machines.

However, panic swept through the chip industry in October after the announcement, prompting Kevin Wolf to work the longest hours of his career. Companies were particularly alarmed by the US Persons clause, which prohibits American citizens from working for Chinese chip companies. The stock prices of American chip machine manufacturers immediately plummeted, as chip designers like Nvidia and AMD suddenly found they were no longer able to supply their most advanced chips to China.

ASML erred on the side of caution, and American employees were required to temporarily suspend their activities in China until the exact legal implications were clarified. 'Our announcement was quite sloppy,' an NSC member later admitted. But at least that way, the 139-page document grabbed the attention of the worldwide industry all at once.

The measures also affected foreign companies operating chip factories in China, such as TSMC and the South Korean memory manufacturers Samsung and SK Hynix. BIS quickly came up with an amendment and granted these companies a one-year extension. But this was not very helpful. Typical investments in chip factories are counted in billions of dollars and take place over several years, not just over one year.

In November 2022, Dutch Prime Minister Mark Rutte embarked on a tour of Asia. Wherever he went, the topic was the same: ASML. First, he spoke with Chinese leader Xi Jinping at the G20 summit in Bali, where Xi warned of decoupling the economies of Europe and China. A few days later, Rutte met with South Korean president Yoon Suk-yeol in Seoul, where they joined a chat between ASML's Peter Wennink and the leaders of Samsung and SK Hynix. ASML had been expanding in South Korea, but the Korean president wanted to see the Dutch company make extra investments in his country to accommodate the 'reorganization' of the semiconductor industry. The conversation with Rutte and Wennink was widely publicized in the Korean press: it was as if two Dutch prime ministers had been visiting. Even though Martin van den Brink was also in Korea, he stayed out of the spotlight. He had technical discussions with clients to focus on.

The US had taken the first step on October 7. Now, Japan and the Netherlands needed to follow suit with their measures. From outside the White House, a Bloomberg reporter relayed from an anonymous source that the 'deal' was almost complete. The leak was a clear message to the Netherlands: let's get moving. But the responsible Dutch ministers, Liesje Schreinemacher of Foreign Trade and Micky Adriaansens of Economic Affairs, responded in interviews with NRC with their own message: the Netherlands needed more time to make a thorough and considered assessment, and in any case would certainly not copy the American export rules word for word.

On a Friday afternoon just before Christmas 2022, three Dutch ministers convened at the headquarters of ASML in Veldhoven to speak with Peter Wennink and Roger Dassen. Accompanying Adriaansens and Schreinemacher was Wopke Hoekstra, Minister of Foreign Affairs. The Ministry of Economic Affairs and ASML sought to rally as many allies as possible to defend the interests of the business community. Their stance was that the Netherlands had already made enough concessions with the export ban on EUV technology, and the ministry feared that even more drastic measures against ASML would impact other Dutch companies that also do business in China.

Convincing three ministers is one thing, but ultimately the decision is up to the boss. Prime Minister Mark Rutte had to make the call. In his eyes, national security trumped economic interests, especially at a time when the world seemed on the brink of exploding and China was moving in unpredictable ways. The Chinese threat was not imaginary, and neither was the scale of diplomatic pressure from the US government. The Netherlands was taking a similar stance to Washington, and it was dragging ASML along with it.

The trilateral cooperation was settled at the end of January 2023. Mark Rutte finally got his invitation to the White House, which had already hosted Japanese Prime Minister Fumio Kishida earlier that month. In front of the press, Rutte and Biden showered each other with compliments, and the warm relationship between the two countries was further kindled in front of the fireplace of the Oval Office. The name 'ASML' was never mentioned, but a slip of the tongue betrayed what was on the American president's mind: 'our companies...our countries collaborate closely to tackle the challenges posed by China.'

While Biden playfully let the Dutch prime minister sit behind his desk, security advisors Sullivan and Van Leeuwen went to meet each other in the Eisenhower Executive Office Building. As far as they were concerned, the trilats were over. But there were no signed documents, nor any pens exchanged. This was a mutual agreement between allies, and the start of a long-term partnership. Now came the hard part: figuring out the details.

When Minister Schreinemacher announced in early March that the Netherlands would implement export control measures in conjunction with Japan and the US, it was still unclear exactly how those would unfold. ASML immediately issued a press release in consultation with the Ministry of Economic Affairs. According to the company's assessment, only the sale of the newest generation immersion scanners would require a permit.

But that was far from set in stone. Although the 'deal' seemed finalized, negotiations about technical limitations were still ongoing. And if the Americans had their way, negotiations would never end. The NSC continued to insist on rolling back China's existing capacity, which would mean that some of the machines ASML already delivered would have to cease operations.

This was a best-case scenario for the Americans. To the Netherlands, it was unthinkable. ASML had over eight hundred lithography machines operating in Chinese chip factories. Without maintenance, repairs and spare parts, the most advanced versions would quickly grind to a halt. Veldhoven had obligations to prevent this from happening, and it wanted to fulfill them.

The US had the ability to force ASML to pull the plug, but they were reluctant to play that card too quickly. Even Trump never reached for it – such aggressive measures were considered unfitting for such a carefully crafted alliance. America preferred the softer option of using additional rules to 'plug any loopholes' in the agreements, which meant even more work for the already overloaded Bureau of Industry and Security. On the second floor of the US Department of Commerce in Washington, 350 people were frantically trying to keep a grip on the jumble of restrictions, sanctions and transactions in the chip sector.

But there was a catch.

The US export regulations made a distinction between Chinese chip factories and multinational companies that run factories in China. Additionally, the US created a third, extra-sensitive category of Chinese production lines. Dutch chip machines were completely barred from these, and even the maintenance of their existing machines was prohibited. These production lines totaled nine factories, six of which contained ASML's scanners. According to the Americans, those fabs made chips used for military applications. Because these Chinese companies often changed their names and addresses, the US wanted to be able to expand its blacklist immediately, without time-consuming consultation with their trilateral partners. The export controllers likened it to a game of whack-a-mole; you have to hit them quickly and you never know where the next one is going to pop up.

This distinction in its export rules meant the US would be able to directly influence Dutch export policy. For the Netherlands, that was not an option. Sovereignty mattered: without it, they could not ensure restrictions were only imposed for security reasons, not economic considerations.

The dispute was left unresolved, and the US and the Netherlands agreed to disagree. The deal remained open-ended, and the resulting uncertainty became a constant thorn in ASML's side. If at any point the Dutch government chose not to cooperate, the US could draw on the dreaded de minimis rule and force ASML to terminate contracts with its Chinese buyers. In Veldhoven's eyes, this gave the US license to curtail Chinese chip manufacturers for its own economic reasons. Unlike a game of chess that ends with a stalemate, ASML found itself locked in a seemingly never-ending struggle with no clear resolution in sight.

The Netherlands was opposed to a further decoupling of the Chinese and Western economies. The Americans insisted this was not the intention – hard to believe when listening to the Republican hawks in Congress. Loudly demanding more aggressive attitudes towards China was still their favorite pastime. But their constant calls were predominantly political grandstanding – an easy way to score points without having to follow through.

However, the NSC did want to be able to 'upgrade' the export regulations, just in case Xi Jingping extended his hand to Taiwan or decided to support Russia in the war in Ukraine. In case of emergency: break the Chinese chip factories. The only thing they needed was the hammer. The US has several tools at its fingertips that it could use to thwart China, such as denying the country access to commonly used American chip design software or to the British company ARM's ubiquitous chip designs. And with ASML, the Netherlands has an unprecedented economic weapon within its borders.

This is a large responsibility for a small country. To stand stronger among the great powers, the Netherlands continued to seek more multilateral support. In March of 2023, it proposed to add the export restrictions against DUV to the dual-use list of the Wassenaar Arrangement. It seemed an unusual move, as the Netherlands had previously obstructed an attempt from the Americans to do precisely that. And with 'Wassenaar' frozen due to the war in Ukraine, the Dutch diplomats were fully aware of their proposals' chances. But more than anything, the attempt was a gesture to show the outside world, especially China, the logic of the Dutch measures. If chip machines using extreme ultraviolet light require an export license from Wassenaar, the same had to apply to other techniques that could produce chips at the same level as EUV.

It sounds simple enough. But the geopolitical significance made it a burden The Hague did not want to bear alone. The Netherlands tried to rally other EU member states to add the export measures to a new European dual-use list, mainly to avoid being the only nation in the line of fire should China come up with countermeasures. But it was too little, too late.

The Chinese responded. Immediately. Mid-March, a Chinese delegation knocked on the door of the Ministry of Foreign Trade in The Hague to discuss the export restrictions. The Chinese had already filed a complaint with the World Trade Organization (WTO), describing the measures as industrial policy masquerading as matters of national security. According to China, America was a 'bully' that put its own interests above the rest of the world's. Vice Minister Ling Ji from the Chinese Ministry of Commerce had a clear message for Liesje Schreinemacher: be careful. The latter stressed that the Netherlands did not want to paralyze the Chinese chip industry, but it would take more than her words to convince them.

In early April, China urged the WTO for clarification on the new export restrictions. Shortly after, a Dutch delegation met with Chinese export specialists at the Jin Jiang hotel in the former French concession of Shanghai. The location was symbolic: it was the building where Richard Nixon and Henry Kissinger signed the first Sino-American agreement in 1972.

The Chinese view was that the pressure from the US made the Netherlands just as much a victim of American protectionism as it did Beijing. As a surprise, the entire leadership of the Chinese chip industry was flown in. Six top executives from companies like SMIC, YMTC and Fujian Jinhua sat across the table. Over the course of an hour, they each made a pitch to the Dutch delegation, each emphasizing how much their production lines depend on ASML.

In April of 2023, Peter Wennink flew to China to discuss with chip manufacturers and trade Minister of Commerce Wang Wentao the extent of ASML's wiggle room. All the Chinese customers were asking, 'When will it end?' but Wennink had no answer. The only certainty was that the Americans were not about to loosen their extraterritorial grip on the world, and the Dutch were going to be there to help them.

At the end of June, Schreinemacher announced the official measures. A licensing requirement for the export of DUV machines capable of producing chips with a resolution of 45 nanometers or better would be introduced, beginning in September of that year. Most importantly, ASML machines capable of aligning subsequent layers of a chip with less than one and a half nanometers of accuracy (or 'overlay'), would be subject to these restrictions, preventing the Chinese chip manufacturers from using multi-patterning techniques to make advanced chips. This was an attempt to slow down former TSMC employee Liang Mong Song, the chip wizard driving China's tech ambitions, who has been perfecting this technique at SMIC since 2017.

Schreinemacher estimated that twenty machines per year would no longer be allowed to be exported to China without a license. In practice, the restriction only took effect in January of 2024 – as per a silent agreement with Japan and the US – and made no mention of the maintenance of scanners that had already been delivered. China fiercely protested the 'unjust' measures via a public letter from the Chinese embassy. The criticism was sharp: the Dutch were allowing themselves to be used as pawns in America's game, and it was tarnishing their good name as a trading nation.

Of the more than eight hundred ASML machines in China, half are located at Chinese chip manufacturers. Most are at SMIC, and the remaining at branches of Samsung, SK Hynix and TSMC. By Peter Wennink's expectations, the export restrictions would have no effect on ASML's turnover. Foreign chip manufacturers would simply choose to expand elsewhere, and China was diving headfirst into older semiconductor technology anyway. ASML tried to keep the scanners coming, but found itself saddled with a mountain of bureaucratic red tape as tens of thousands of components of the 'forbidden' machines now required separate registration. Geopolitical barriers emerged everywhere at ASML San Diego and Wilton, since no American citizens were allowed to work on some of the products destined for China.

Meanwhile, Chinese customers were increasing their orders of chip machines. In the third quarter of 2023, almost half of ASML's revenue was coming from China. This was helped by the fact that other manufacturers like Intel and TSMC temporarily paused their orders due to a dip in the chip market, which automatically pushed the Chinese orders to the front of the line. In addition, the larger Chinese customers tried to stockpile spare parts to prolong the life expectancy of their machines. However, ASML was reluctant to play along – it wanted to keep to the spirit of the restrictions. Neither did they build a special machine for the Chinese market. ASML was never comfortable in the gray areas, and had no interest in challenging the Americans by pushing the limits of what was allowed. They practiced what they preached: yes meant yes, and no meant no.

China was forced to switch to 'more than Moore', and turned its focus to chips that were not necessarily reliant on the most sophisticated technology, but were needed on a large scale for purposes such as energy transition, electric vehicles, household items or industrial automation. At the same time, Chinese chipmakers were more careful and avoided boasting about their progress, for fear of being noticed by the US. To avoid restrictions, some factories renamed their existing 14 nanometer technology to '17'. No one wanted to catch the eye of the Americans.

Meanwhile, in 2023 Huawei launched a 5G phone with a 7 nanometer chip from SMIC – proof that China was lagging behind, but was still not at a standstill. The production method for this chip was so labor-intensive that it was uncertain SMIC would be able to make this chip in large volumes. Technically speaking, the 7 nanometer chip was nothing new, but that did not stop Huawei gloating about it when US Trade Secretary Raimondo travelled to China. That was asking for trouble, and fingers were immediately pointed at Veldhoven. The US pressed the Netherlands to slam the brakes before January 2024, and the cabinet duly revoked several approved export licenses for ASML machines destined for China. As it turned out, Washington actually pulled the reins because ASML was exporting far more DUV machines to China than had been expected. As the chip industry was pushing the pause button, China kept on hoarding. In Veldhoven, Peter Wennink was tasked with breaking the news to the Chinese customers, all via video. The machines were ready to be shipped, but the Americans insisted that ASML halt its shipment immediately. 'Close the gates, now!' Veldhoven was told. On top of that, the US had tightened its grip on ASML's exports to China by adjusting the 'de-minimis' rules.

To escape the American chokehold, the Chinese government encouraged its own chip industry to develop alternative machines. This seemed to work for Fujian Jinhua, a Chinese factory that had been added to the US Entity List in 2018. Fujian Jinhua converted to produce processors for Huawei. The Chinese chip manufacturers appeared to succeed in replacing Western technology with the help of local chip machine makers like Naura and Amec. Even though no American chip machines had gone to Fujian Jinhua in four years, wafers were still rolling off the production lines.

This is where the crucial input of knowledge workers comes into play. China learned vast amounts from US companies through former employees who brought their knowledge back home. Amec has progressed to the point where it supplies chip machines to TSMC, and even sued its American competitor Lam Research for patent infringement.

But lithography is a different story. ASML swept up the last remnants of American lithography technology from SVG in 2001, which meant there was no recent expertise in that field to collect from the US. This makes the Dutch scanners indispensable to China – for the time being.

China still has one competing manufacturer of lithography machines: SMEE, or Shanghai Micro Electronics Equipment. Founded in 2002, the company makes it no secret that it tries to copy the art of lithography from ASML. The Chinese even openly ordered one of Veldhoven's PAS 5500s in their early years in an attempt to unravel the machine's secrets. This did not lead to a sudden boost in the development of Chinese technology, as ASML's devices are far too complex to simply copy. SMEE had a slow start, as Frits van Hout and Martin van den Brink observed when they visited their competitor in 2018 and 2019. The visit came out of curiosity: they wanted to get a feel for what challenges the Chinese were facing. Despite financial assistance from the government, SMEE remains fifteen years behind compared to what ASML has to offer.

Now, this Chinese company mainly supplies machines for the back end, which involves the processing and packaging of existing chips. When it comes to the front end – the actual production of chips – it remains stuck at 90 nanometer technology. SMEE is working on better technology, such as 28 nanometer immersion systems, but those experiments prove to be difficult. Chinese chip factories prefer to use proven technology from ASML and Nikon, rather than take a chance on homegrown concoctions. So far, anyway. On occasion, you might see a SMEE system on display in Chinese factory lines. However, these machines are likely there for show, or to impress government officials, with the bulk of chip production done by foreign-made lithography systems operating elsewhere.

However, the export restrictions on China are offering SMEE a new perspective. If even more drastic measures are taken to block ASML and Nikon's scanners, it would back Chinese manufacturers into a corner. They would have no choice but to go for SMEE, automatically giving ASML's competitor more experience and the opportunity to work out the kinks in their own machines. SMEE would get more money, which in turn could be invested in the development of new technology, such as an immersion scanner of their own. As China is growing increasingly isolated, so too is the likelihood of a fully-fledged Chinese competitor emerging in the rear-view mirror capable of developing an independent chip production chain.

This is the exact opposite of what the Americans wanted to achieve. And this is what makes their strategy utterly incomprehensible to the ASML'ers.

China's reaction followed in July of 2023, shortly after the Netherlands published its measure that scaled back ASML exports. It imposed restrictions on the global export of gallium and germanium, two types of metal the chip industry relied on the Chinese for. The measure was far from drastic – China was still too dependent on ASML. Rather, China wanted to flex its powerful position as the world's largest supplier of rare metals, the raw materials the entire global industry needs for technological products and energy transition. It was a jab to let the West feel what could happen if China was further restricted.

The geopolitical fault lines were not only evident in the chip sector, but across the entire technology supply chain. Major electronics manufacturers that relied on China as a production hub started shifting part of their manufacturing process elsewhere. Apple began expanding operations in India, after being left reeling from protests in Zhengzhou, during which Foxconn employees shut down the largest Chinese iPhone factory. Samsung started to relocate its Chinese factories to Vietnam. Companies hoped that by reshoring – or 'friend-shoring' – they could diversify their risks and bypass the US import tariffs on goods from China. But completely disentangling from Chinese component suppliers and their massive electronics factories proved impossible. Where else in the world could you mobilize fifty thousand skilled workers at the push of a button to quickly assemble some extra phones?

The fluctuating internal regulations caused the economic climate in China to worsen. President Xi often intervened personally in the business sector, springing unforeseen and unclear new laws on the entrepreneurs. After the radical COVID lockdowns – which were lifted just as abruptly as they were implemented – the long hoped-for recovery struggled to gain momentum. The Chinese real estate market collapsed, unemployment rose, and foreign investments in China sharply declined.

Neither was Xi's flagship Made in China 2025 strategy going as planned. China continued to rely heavily on imported chips, and the share of Chinese factories in global chip production remained small. According to the SIA, in 2021 it was just under eight percent. Meanwhile, the US and Europe were adding fuel to their own chip fabs. Because if there is one thing the West does as well as China, it is showering the semiconductor industry with subsidies.

32

IT'S RAINING BILLIONS

Even though it is only February, the sun is beating down mercilessly on the roof of the Intel building in Chandler, Arizona. It is 2023, and this tall building on Old Price Road is the perfect place to watch the reconstruction of the American chip industry up close. Surrounded by a forest of cranes, workers assemble the steel frames for two enormous chip factories. The area once smelled of vast onion fields; now, the dust clouds from trucks and bulldozers mixed with the water vapor rising from the air treatment plants is giving off a new scent: progress.

In 2025, Fab 52 and Fab 62 will start churning out millions of processors. A staggering four floors high and four soccer fields wide, the production lines in these fabs will run Veldhoven's EUV machines and connect to the same distribution center that already supplies the existing cleanrooms with a continuous flow of gases and chemicals.

This is Ocotillo Campus, erected in Chandler by Intel in the early eighties. It became the main production site for the American chip giant and the breeding ground for a vibrant semiconductor industry – that is why ASML chose Arizona as the location of its first US operation.

Rainwater is scarce in the desert, which is why Intel recycles all cooling water from its factories. Still, in Chandler, subsidies are raining down by the billions. Intel's new chip factories are eligible for the US chips act, a support package totaling 52 billion dollars of which 39 billion is earmarked to stimulate chip manufacturing on American soil. Tens of thousands of jobs have been created, both to build the factories and to keep them running. The US is dependent on Asian factories for high-end chips, and has fallen from producing almost 40 percent of the world's chips in the early nineties to less than 12 percent by 2023. With the Chips Act in his arsenal, Joe Biden vows to turn the tide.

To qualify for government aid, companies had to agree not to build advanced chip factories in China or other 'countries of concern'. Nor were they allowed to expand their existing capacity in those countries. The Chips Act was effective on all fronts: more chips in the US, less in China.

Intel saw an opportunity and seized it with both hands. The chipmaker invested 20 billion dollars for the expansion in Arizona and claimed 8 billion in subsidies, while also relying on state support for its new factories in Ohio. The Chips Act was the spur the American chip giant needed; now, it had a chance to catch up with the Asian competition.

In February of 2021, Intel welcomed Pat Gelsinger as its new CEO. His appointment was intended to spell the end of a turbulent period, marked by a revolving door of CEOs and delayed products. Immediately after taking office, he reached out to ASML. The stars had aligned: he urgently needed EUV machines for the American expansion and wanted to capitalize on European subsidies for establishing their own semiconductor industry.

Meanwhile, politicians in the EU had recognized the strategic importance of having a resilient chip industry in their own regions. The COVID-19 pandemic had forced Europe to face some hard facts about the vulnerability of global production chains in times of crisis. European countries had panicked when confronted with sudden shortages of face masks and other medical supplies. In addition, a chip shortage had shocked the car industry, and everyone immediately understood the fragility of the supply line for semiconductors.

As of 2023, the EU accounted for just eight percent of global chip production. Complete self-sufficiency was never in the cards, but the EU Commissioner for Digital Affairs Thierry Breton hoped that by 2030, 20 percent of the world's chips would come from Europe. He certainly did not lack ambition.

To get Intel's European expansion plans off on the right foot, ASML gave Pat Gelsinger a helping hand with the initial discussions. When the Intel CEO visited The Hague in June of 2021 for a meeting with Mark Rutte, ASML provided the agenda for the prime minister. Given Rutte's technological ineptitude, this was not an unnecessary act. He still preferred to send text messages from his ancient Nokia, and to quickly delete them after that. To free up memory, so Rutte's explanation went.

After the meeting, Gelsinger travelled directly to Brussels to meet with European Commissioner Margrethe Vestager and to visit imec, the Leuven-based research institute and close collaborator of ASML. The lines of communication between Brussels and Brabant were short. For example, European Commissioner Breton called Peter Wennink after the summer of 2021 to ask whether ASML would set up a link with TSMC and Samsung. He wanted to approach the Asian chip manufacturers for expansion in Europe, but they seemed considerably less eager than Intel had been.

In November, Breton, along with Vestager and the President of the European Commission Ursula von der Leyen, paid a visit to ASML for a talk behind closed doors. They were joined by Peter Wennink, Mark Rutte and the Director General of Economic Affairs Focco Vijselaar for a tour of ASML's showroom, 'the experience center'. One day later, Von der Leyen issued a statement: 'ASML will play a significant role in making the European tech sector more competitive and independent.'

And she did not waste any time. Immediately after the visit, a request came in from Brussels. They wanted ASML to provide a position paper, a vision for the future of the European chip sector and the EU's Chips Act. This document needed to be done by the beginning of 2022, before the US and the EU continued discussions in the TTC, the Transatlantic Trade and Technology Council.

ASML set to work collaborating with chip companies to develop a long-term plan. It anticipated the demand for chips would double in the coming ten years, given the chips needed for data centers and the 'explosion' of artificial intelligence, self-driving cars and smart electricity networks. And if Europe wanted chip factories to produce the fastest processors on its own territory, it would need help from the major Asian or American chip giants. European chip manufacturers were too far behind to catch up in that race. Additionally, industries like the automotive sector were in need of more common chips, and European chip companies like NXP, Infineon, or STMicroelectronics also needed to expand.

As the key player in the industry, ASML seemed to be the one directing the formation of the European Chips Act. Peter Wennink found this a little over the top. He saw his company more as an 'influencer'. In the end, politicians have the final say, and economic logic is never the only thing they take into account.

But in this case, the playbooks of Brussels and Veldhoven were neatly synchronized. On February 8, 2022, the same day ASML published its position paper for the European chip industry, the EU announced a stimulus plan worth 43 billion euros.

As expected, Intel followed with an announcement one month later. The chipmaker would be investing 33 billion euros into European expansion projects, including 17 billion for a large factory near the German city of Magdeburg. This location ticked all the boxes: it was close to the German automotive industry, with a university around the corner and, unlike Arizona, there was not a cow in sight.

Intel continued to distribute its budget over Italy, Ireland, France, Poland and the Netherlands. In return, it expected substantial subsidies. 6.8 billion euros was requested for Magdeburg alone, accounting for 40 percent of the expected start-up costs. Meanwhile, France invested 2.9 billion euros in a chip factory operated by GlobalFoundries and the French company STMicroelectronics.

The EU Chips Act signaled a U-turn in European policy. Traditionally, state aid had been prohibited to prevent competition between member states, and countries were only allowed to use public funds to assist companies under strict conditions. The new law ran directly against these historic principles, but in light of the tensions between China and the US, the EU recognized its industrial policy needed to change if it were to become more resilient and independent.

Europe had already faced a painful punishment through its dependence on foreign powers. When the war in Ukraine broke out, it suddenly had to extricate itself from Russian oil and gas supplies, causing an unprecedented energy crisis. The bloc was desperate to avoid a similar situation around semiconductors. The chip shortage had been a wakeup call, and the nightmare scenario was front and center on everyone's mind: 'If China blocks Taiwan, we'll be without chips within two weeks,' Thierry Breton declared in September of 2022 during the opening of the academic year at Eindhoven University of Technology.

In reality, the 43 billion euros that made up the European stimulus package was a mixed bag of recovery funds, adjusted innovation programs and above all, large sums of money from the member states themselves. By the start of 2023, the proposal had made its way through the machinery of Brussels, only to coincide with a downturn in the chip industry. The sector might grow over the long term, but these peaks and valleys are dependable and unavoidable, just like the ebb and flow of the tide.

The dip caused Intel to slow its expansions in Germany. With the investment costs for the factory escalating from 17 to 30 billion euros, the chip giant surprised the Germans by upping its demand for state aid from 6.8 to 10 billion euros. Intel wanted to build more production lines in Magdeburg in response to the increase in TSMC's investment in its Arizona factory to 40 billion dollars. It was a tough pill to swallow, but the Germans agreed.

Pat Gelsinger was the shining star at the center of this downpour of subsidies, also in the US. He was present at the 2022 State of the Union address as Joe Biden attempted to push his Chips Act through Congress. This process took longer than expected: both parties agreed the American chip industry needed support, but their toxic disagreements on other issues destroyed any ability to make practical decisions.

This frustrated the Intel CEO to no end, and in June of 2022 he decided to halt construction on the Ohio project. His message: show us the stimulus money, then the bulldozers will keep digging. When the US Chips and Science Act was finally signed in the ceremonial garden of the White House in August, Gelsinger was smiling: threatening to hit the pause button had worked.

The factories Intel was building in the plains of Ohio – the 'fields of dreams' as Joe Biden called them – cost around 20 billion dollars, just like Fab 52 and Fab 62. They were exact replicas of the new construction in Chandler, down to the entrance and interior design. Even the restrooms were in the same place. Why spend money and time changing a design you know works?

Intel also applied this 'copy exactly' principle to its production lines. Every detail of the manufacturing process was meticulously examined to iron out any errors, and then replicated exactly in other factories. Chip specialists delved into research and re-research, before translating the methodology into elaborate procedures. Intel took it slow in this process. EUV machines had already been running tests for years in the cleanrooms of the development department in Hillsboro, Oregon. The company wanted to first eliminate all risks before taking one giant leap ahead of the competition. But such a leap is big, even for a giant chip company. After all, TSMC and Samsung had already begun high-volume EUV production five years earlier. The Asian competitors were less risk-averse, and had already set up production lines when the chip machines were still effectively held together by a threadbare wire. Scoring wafers and solving problems on the fly – that's what it was all about. Those who make mistakes fast innovate fast.

But Intel had a different approach. As an integrated device manufacturer, it designed and manufactured its own chips. Intel's so-called x86 architecture had long been dominant across the world, with these chips found in almost every Windows PC or server on the market since the 1980s. If you bought a new computer before 2006, chances are you would have peeled an 'Intel Inside' sticker off the front of it. The updated slogan 'Leap Ahead' didn't stick quite as well.

For decades, Intel dominated the chip industry with its solid sales market for PCs. But then the challenge from the East appeared, bringing with it a flexible foundry model and military-grade discipline. These Asian competitors responded better to the smartphone revolution, which had a much shorter innovation cycle than the PC market Intel had dictated. Intel's processors were also no match for the energy-efficient ARM chip designs that became the basis for the entire mobile industry.

By going fabless, chip designers such as Qualcomm, AMD and Nvidia had earlier access to more advanced technology through the Asian factories they used. To reflect the demand for wafers, they could adjust their orders with TSMC every quarter. Intel finally jumped on this 'fabless' trend, and upon assuming office Pat Gelsinger initiated a new business division, called Intel Foundry Services, to manufacture chips for other companies. It was no pure-play foundry like TSMC, but it was a necessity: without orders from others, the Americans would not have a large enough scale of operations to recoup their investments in the latest technology. For a company struggling with change, this was a radical cultural shift.

Gelsinger was betting the future of his company, but he had an ace up his sleeve. Intel was the only remaining transatlantic chip manufacturer with a chance to keep up with the Asian competition. Without Intel, shifting the power balance of the chip industry would be an impossible task. The epicenter would undoubtedly remain in Asia, since Samsung and TSMC preferred to keep the production of their most advanced chips in their own country.

The Asian chip companies were also benefiting from the shower of subsidies. Samsung began construction on a factory in Texas for 17 billion dollars, and considered opening up a factory in Europe. TSMC also expanded in Japan – another country that opened the subsidy floodgates with its 'Rapidus' project. Additionally, the Taiwanese also planned to build a factory in the German city of Dresden, along with European chip manufacturers Bosch, NXP and Infineon. This factory would receive five billion euros in subsidies.

These projects were modest in comparison to South Korea and Taiwan's plans for expansion on home turf. TSMC remained cautious about producing the most advanced chip technology in the US, as this could weaken the island's silicon shield by making the chip factories in Taiwan less indispensable. However, a solution was put on the table. In exchange for increasing advanced chip production in the US, Taiwan wanted additional guarantees of military support from the Americans. The US obliged. In September 2022, one month after Nancy Pelosi's controversial visit, the US approved a 1.1 billion–dollar weapons shipment to Taiwan. Three months later, TSMC increased its investment in Arizona from 12 to 40 billion dollars and included newer production technology. Chips for weapons, weapons for chips: that is the tech war in a nutshell.

Years before the first shovel ever hit the ground, ASML was well aware of TSMC's plans to build factories north of Phoenix, Arizona. The company needed time to train support staff: it takes two and a half years to learn how to maintain the complex EUV machines. ASML provided this training in the Taiwanese city of Tainan but decided to start a training center in Arizona capable of instructing 16,000 people per year. There was only one problem: you can build a school as big as you like, but can you get the students to fill it?

The lack of technical talent is the Achilles heel of the American chip strategy, with the level of education in the US falling far short of that in Asia. For Joe Biden, the Chips Act provided an opportunity to elevate the American education system. He asked Congress to allocate tens of billions of dollars to help prepare children for the technical jobs of the future. The whole country was in need of an upgrade, not just the chip industry.

In December of 2022, Biden welcomed the first chip machines into the TSMC factory in Arizona. To mark the occasion, a massive banner reading 'MADE IN AMERICA' was hung from the building, despite the factory belonging entirely to a Taiwanese company. The setting was quintessentially American: a desert plain dotted with cacti, with the Ben Avery Shooting Facility as the noisy neighbor. Everyone is welcome at this public shooting range: even a five-year-old child can shoot a pistol here – provided the firearm is carried in a lockable container.

Champagne corks were popping at TSMC, and after the opening ceremony Biden held a sit-down meeting with a select group. The leaders of AMD, Nvidia and Apple watched as TSMC's chairman Mark Liu presented an inscribed wafer to Biden. Such a glossy disc is a standard gift in the chip industry, but it still made Biden glow.

Peter Wennink was seated to the right of the American president. This time, they got his last name correct. When the presidential photographer snapped a picture for Twitter, Wennink stood right next to the American flag, his orange tie hanging neatly parallel to the stars and stripes.

The founder of TSMC and pioneer of chip technology Morris Chang was also present for the ceremony. He raised a toast to the new factory, but his speech took a somber turn. 'Globalization is almost dead, as is free trade,' he observed. Other than the political motivation, he thought it pointless to spread and duplicate chip production across the world. The entire supply chain would have to move along with it, and Chang had little esteem for the Western work ethic. No wonder that TSMC's American factory was slower to start up than planned. Despite the billions in subsidies, the costs of reshoring led to higher prices. And if manufacturers operated less efficiently, there was less money to invest in innovation. Moore's Law would also be dead, a victim of the tech war.

33

PANIC AT THE PENTAGON

Mona Keijzer doesn't like being the bearer of bad news, especially right before Christmas. But this time, she has no choice. The Dutch State Secretary for Economic Affairs steps out of her service car and rushes through the revolving door of ASML's headquarters in Veldhoven. On the twentieth floor, she tells the ASML board what she was unable to say over the phone: 'We have a problem with the Americans. It's about Mapper. The Pentagon... you need to help us!'

In December of 2018, the diplomatic lines between Washington, The Hague, and Veldhoven were bustling with activity. Even before the tech war between the US and China erupted in full force on the international frontpages, a completely different game was being played behind closed doors. It concerned Dutch chip technology at risk of falling into Chinese hands.

It was all down to Mapper, the company based in Delft that had been working on e-beam, or electron beam technology, since 2000. Electrons allow you to write intricate patterns on chips, and with its so-called multibeam technology, Mapper had a technical marvel on its hands. But it was difficult to sell. TSMC had tried out a Mapper machine in 2010 and concluded that ASML's lithography machines were better suited for the mass production of chips. No need for electrons: you could replicate a chip pattern all at once using photons – light, that is. TSMC opted for EUV and returned the machine to Delft.

Mapper had to switch lanes, fell into acute financial trouble and ultimately went bankrupt at the end of 2018. As a result, valuable knowledge came up for grabs. It may not have been a commercial success, but the technology from Delft was strategically important. And this made the Pentagon uneasy.

On January 28, 2019, one and half months after Mona Keijzer knocked on Veldhoven's door, ASML acquired the intellectual property of the bankrupt Mapper and snapped up all its highly qualified employees left out in the cold. What the press release failed to mention was how much ASML paid for the bankrupt estate, nor did it tell the unbelievable story that preceded it.

That story begins in America.

When GlobalFoundries pulled the plug on its EUV program in 2018, it confirmed the American defense specialists' fears that the US had lost its grip on the fastest chips. The Pentagon saw a problem looming. The US Department of Defense wanted the majority of modern chips to be made on American soil, under US supervision. The term for this principle is trusted foundry, and for the Americans, it was a strategic necessity. If the chips for F-35 fighter jets, advanced drones, or equipment for the secret services came from factories abroad, they would be far more vulnerable to sabotage or hacks.

The combination of GlobalFoundries' discontinuation and Intel failing to keep up with the Asian chip manufacturers had put the US at a disadvantage. For the Pentagon, that was unacceptable. In 2018, US defense specialists held discussions with TSMC and Samsung. These companies were willing to build more advanced chip factories in the US, but in return they requested three to eight billion dollars in state aid – far more than the Pentagon had available. But then, a high-tech gift from Delft popped up on the radar: Mapper.

Mapper was conceived at the Delft University of Technology, when Pieter Kruit, a professor in charged particle optics, asked his students to design a system for electron beams that could be applied in commercial lithography. Excited by the possibilities of this technology, two of his students, Bert Jan Kampherbeek and Marco Wieland, started their own company in 2000 after they graduated under Kruit. Wieland was the driving force behind the technology, while Kampherbeek was focused on the business end. As always, this meant needing to raise money to keep the business afloat.

Mapper was co-financed by Arthur del Prado, and once again the pioneer of the Dutch chip industry was at the forefront, helping to advance a technology with potential. Even though a lack of funds had forced him to withdraw from ASML in 1988, he never lost his eye for promising semiconductor technology.

With Mapper's approach, the expensive masks were no longer needed. The chip pattern, several terabytes in size, came from computer memory and was repeatedly written onto an electron-sensitive layer by an electron beam. This process would normally take hours, but with multibeam Mapper devised a way to use tiny lenses to split the electrons into over 13,000 different beams, each with 49 rays. Compare it to the way an old-fashioned convex TV creates its image by using an electron beam to draw a pattern on the screen using hundreds of scanlines.

Mapper's first concept was ready in 2007, and the company sold two prototypes: one to TSMC, and another to the French research institute CEA-Leti in Grenoble. The start-up believed it had a good alternative to the delayed EUV machines, provided it could increase the output to ten or twenty wafers per hour. If ten of these machines were put next to one another, it would still be cheaper than one of ASML's scanners. At least, that was the idea.

The reality proved far more unmanageable, and after TSMC returned their prototype, the Delft start-up changed its course. If the mass market had no need for e-beam, there still would be the low-volume market for advanced chips produced in much smaller quantities. The American defense industry was a prime target for this: for example, DARPA, the research arm of the Pentagon, had already invested money in an e-beam program in 2003.

The latest Mapper machine promised to be a step up, but an extra injection of capital was needed to produce it. In 2012, Rusnano – a Russian state fund that invests in nanotechnology – acquired a 14 percent stake for 40 million euros. Mapper gained a Russian board member, and subsequently built a factory in Technopolis, the cluster of high-tech operations in Moscow. The factory began producing microscopic electromechanical systems for the lenses. These so-called microsystems are a type of chip produced using a regular lithography machine. To do this, Mapper ordered a machine from their rivals over in Veldhoven. The internal newsletter ran a suitably ironic headline: 'Mapper buys ASML'. Del Prado also saw the funny side – during a visit to Moscow in 2013, he sat pretentiously on a discarded ASML crate, a mischievous look on his face as his rear end straddled the Veldhoven logo.

Despite the enthusiasm of the majority shareholder, technical set-backs kept Mapper's progress at bay. That is not to say the technology from Delft was unusable. To the contrary, the same electron beams were not only good for writing patterns, but could also be used to inspect chips for errors. This is what piqued ASML's interest in Mapper – they would serve as the perfect addition to HMI's inspection equipment, the Taiwanese company ASML had acquired in 2016. Around that time, Martin van den Brink and Jos Benschop paid repeated visits to Delft. They wanted to know if Wieland would be willing to work for ASML on electron sensors, but the founder refused to bite. He was determined to make his own company a success. ASML looked into whether they could acquire Mapper in its entirety, but a serious offer was never made.

In September of 2016, Arthur del Prado passed away at the age of 84. It came as a shock – he had been actively involved with Mapper until only a few months before his death, and with his passing the company also lost its most significant financial backer. Del Prado's family funds were unable to keep the tech company afloat for much longer, as he stipulated in his will that his capital should be put towards cancer research. It was a promise he made to his wife, who passed away from the disease at a young age.

By the beginning of 2018, Mapper was left with only six months to find another investor. No one seemed to believe Kampherbeek when he explained that the curtain was about to fall on the company – after all, more than 200 million euros had already been pumped into their machine, and it was nearing completion. Being partly owned by a

Russian state fund made it difficult, particularly given the sensitivity in the West after the annexation of Crimea in 2014 and the downing of passenger flight MH17 by a Russian surface-to-air missile, which resulted in the loss of 298 lives.

No stone was left unturned in the search for financiers. Kampherbeek flew around the world to speak with chip machine manufacturers in Japan, Singapore and America, but it was in vain. Briefly, Kampherbeek thought Applied Materials would bite, but the company backed out.

Mapper turned to China. Wieland traveled to Chengdu, the city known for breeding pandas, to interest investors and officials in developing a Chinese alternative to EUV. For his part, Kampherbeek flew to Beijing to meet with investors. There was serious interest, but Mapper was in a hurry: bankruptcy was imminent, and they needed to strike a deal. The Chinese were unable to immediately capitalize on this surprise offer from the Netherlands. In the meantime, Mapper reluctantly sold its Moscow factory to Rusnano to be able to keep paying the salaries in Delft a little longer. The 240 employees were already running on borrowed time.

In the summer of 2018, Mapper reached out to the US Department of Defense for help. They knew from earlier discussions that the Pentagon found the multibeam technology interesting; after all, it could also be used to 'write' unique chips for modern weapon systems or for equipment for its intelligence services. These agencies want to know for certain that their equipment cannot be hacked, and by giving each chip a unique number they could be sure who they are talking to and securely communicate without the enemy intercepting.

The Pentagon thought Mapper's technology could be used to produce advanced chips on a small scale in trusted foundries. But the presence of the Russian investor made the deal impossible. An employee from the Department of Defense tried to motivate American companies to take a stake in Mapper and get rid of the Russians. The major weapons manufacturers responded lukewarmly to the request. However, a call was also made to SecureFoundry in Fort Worth, Texas, a company founded by former marine and technical director of the US Cyber Command Lex Keen. He was still active in the field and specialized in semiconductors, spending his time acquiring patents from universities for advanced chips to be used in defense projects.

The Pentagon did not give SecureFoundry a direct order – that would lead to obligations – but dropped a clear hint: Mapper was in acute financial need, and it would be great if someone stepped in to rescue the Dutch technology to benefit the American defense industry. Keen rolled up his sleeves: this task had his name written all over it.

The former marine met with the team from Delft and invited Kampherbeek to Fort Worth for a few weeks to set up the deal. Kampherbeek was a guest at Keen's financial advisor's home. He was a local banker with Dutch roots, who gathered around the table with his deeply devoted family every morning at 6:00 a.m. for Bible study. Texan hospitality at its finest, accompanied by a large cupboard filled with rifles and pistols. 'It's a Hail Mary,' Kampherbeek thought while his hosts bowed in prayer. He would go to the trenches to save his company.

Keen and Kampherbeek devised a plan together with the National Security Agency. The American intelligence agency ordered two multibeam machines from Delft, for a total of 20 million dollars. If the Pentagon paid that amount on behalf of the NSA outright, SecureFoundry would receive the distribution rights to supply the machine to US government agencies and Mapper could move forward with new capital. The Pentagon was on board, but first, there were Russians to be dealt with.

Keen met with the Rusnano representatives in Amsterdam. Since 2012, the Russians had expanded their stake and now represented 27.5 percent of Mapper. But they had no interest in being bought out: the Russians would only get a fraction of their investment back and would be the laughingstock of their home country. Rusnano would prefer to see Mapper go bankrupt so they could blame higher powers. However, the Russians were willing to give up their seat on the board and transfer their stake to an external trust, if Mapper continued to purchase chips from Moscow for a few more years. Keen shook hands – it sounded like a deal to him.

SecureFoundry handled the whole episode in close coordination with the Dutch Ministry of Economic Affairs, as Mapper still had 32 million euros worth of outstanding loans from multiple innovation creditors. Keen received a signed declaration from the economic envoy at the Dutch embassy in Washington: he had permission to invest in Mapper, and the Ministry did not require the loan to be repaid immediately. Nothing seemed to stand in the way of the company's salvation.

In early December, Lex Keen addressed the gathered Mapper employees in Delft and told them the deal was done – there was light at the end of the tunnel. He was right about the last part, but for all the wrong reasons. When Keen flew back to the US the next day, he received an alarming phone call from one of his colleagues during his layover in Reykjavik. The Pentagon was no longer responding. It had gone into silent mode.

Mapper had fallen victim to internal Pentagon politics and scheming between the generals and the powerful defense industry. Although 20 million dollars had been earmarked for the two machines for the NSA, the person responsible for the deal was given another job and his successor channeled the funds to an Intel project for secure chips. The influential Intel was managing a GoCo, a 'Government-owned, Contractor-operated' factory, where processors were being made under military supervision. At the same time, a lobbying group from the American weapons industry had knocked on the Pentagon's door: they did not want a Dutch competitor on the scene.

Lex Keen watched his deal unravel in slow motion. By the end of 2018, the slow wheels of the Pentagon bureaucracy were dragging more than ever. The funeral of former President George Bush Senior brought Washington to a standstill for a few days, and when the Pentagon tried again to request funds for the Mapper deal, they faced another roadblock. On December 22, the US government shut down after Democrats blocked President Trump's plans to build a wall at the Mexican border. It lasted 35 days, making it the longest budget freeze in American history.

For Mapper, it took too long. The engineers in Delft had gone without pay for several months, and founder Wieland had calculated to the day when he would need to declare the company bankrupt in order to guarantee his employees would still be able to receive unemployment payments. On December 19, Mapper filed for suspension of payments, and on December 28 bankruptcy was declared. After eighteen years, the multibeam adventure was over.

When the Pentagon realized they had messed up the Mapper deal, panic set in. Suppose the Russians or the Chinese made off with the bankrupt estate – if the US military had recognized the potential of the invention from Delft, surely other powers also had their eyes on it. Their concern was well-founded: Mapper had already spoken to ASML's Chinese competitor SMEE in the past, and Chinese investors had expressed their interest in multibeam.

The Americans sounded the alarm in The Hague. In December, the Pentagon sent urgent letters to the Dutch Ministries of Defense and Economic Affairs. The message: your critical chip technology is at risk of falling into the hands of a hostile power, and you need to intervene. They personally reached out to Prime Minister Mark Rutte via the American embassy and pleaded with him to not allow this technology to vanish into China or Russia. He needed to make sure it remained in the Netherlands, even if it meant destroying it. The Pentagon figured that if Mapper went to ASML, the multibeam technology would hit a dead end. Anything was better than letting it fall into Chinese hands.

That is the reason why Mona Keijzer came bursting through Veldhoven's door on that winter's day in 2018 and told ASML, 'You have to buy Mapper.' There was nothing the Dutch government could do to stop the Chinese if they wanted to make their move: a law was being drafted specifically for this purpose, but it still needed approval. All hope was put on Veldhoven. ASML saw no upside to multibeam lithography – the technical possibilities were limited, and EUV was already operational in chip factories – but it was interested in the patents and technical knowledge in Delft. All it needed was for the Mapper engineers to agree to abandon their old dreams of producing chips: instead, they would need to inspect them.

'We'll definitely talk with them,' Peter Wennink said to a radio reporter from BNR the day after Mapper filed for suspension of payment. Like a skilled politician, he managed to dodge the follow-up questions, but it had been clear for some time that ASML saw the value of Mapper's knowledge. In June 2018, Marco Wieland had even received the 'Martin van den Brink Award' from the man himself.

In the meantime, the curator organized an auction of Mapper's remnants to repay the main creditors, the Del Prado fund and the Ministry of Economic Affairs. Sure enough, Lex Keen of SecureFoundry was there as one of the bidders. In January, the ex-marine had quickly assembled a team of Dutch investors to bid on the bankrupt estate together with former Mapper personnel. The curator had also reached out to the Chinese investment fund the engineers from Delft had previously approached. He was trying to drive up the price, but instead he was shooting the Americans in the foot. Mapper's technology had to stay out of China, and he had just invited them to the game.

For the politicians, there was only one way the auction could end: with Mapper's assets in Veldhoven's hands. ASML threw in a bid for 35 million euros, but Keen was still able to match that amount. When ASML dug a little deeper into their pockets and pulled out an offer of 75 million euros, the competition was flattened. Going once, going twice, and Mapper's legacy was sold.

Although ASML had to pay a high price, it was willing to work along with the plan. Mapper's expertise was highly valuable: where else could you find one hundred experts in chip technology, and all within 130 kilometers of Veldhoven? The directors also figured it wouldn't hurt to show some patriotism by retaining Mapper's knowledge. It was an easy way to score some points. Because ASML's relationship with the American and Dutch governments had started to sour, every bit of goodwill helped.

In January 2019, six weeks after Lex Keen had introduced himself to the Mapper employees as their knight in shining armor, a delegation from Veldhoven stood in front of a packed room in Delft. Just before they took to the improvised stage, one of the founders leaned over and whispered to the ASML'ers: 'You won.'

The 240 employees listened to the plan to preserve jobs and knowledge. Everyone could join ASML if they wanted to. Although the mechanics would have to work in Brabant, the engineers could stay in Delft to prevent the Mapper culture from immediately being stifled. Over one hundred technicians made the move and were added to the San Jose department, where HMI was located. Mapper founder Marco Wieland did not immediately make the switch, but after six months of consideration – and a lot of therapeutic gardening – he went on to accept ASML's offer. He was appointed as a fellow, in recognition of his groundbreaking technical work. Bert Jan Kampherbeek took a different path and chose to start a new company with some of his former colleagues building agricultural robots for tulip cultivation. Another fine Dutch export product.

Mapper's intellectual property fell into ASML's hands, which provided the necessary armor to fend off any patent claims – ASML had already faced enough battles in this area as it was. All remaining laptops and hard drives in Delft were carefully destroyed to prevent other parties from accessing sensitive software.

The Pentagon and the US Department of Energy tried to convince ASML to keep the multibeam machine alive for a trusted foundry in Massachusetts that would produce standard chips with unique codes. However, Veldhoven politely declined, and instead advised the Americans that they would be better off using different technology for this purpose. ASML had no interest in a Mapper 2.0 – that would only be a distraction to the talent at work in Delft.

In October 2019, the founders of Mapper and their stakeholders came together one last time. From across a round table at a fish restaurant in Delft, they reflected on eighteen years of multibeam history. They acknowledged that the deal with the Pentagon had been the final straw, even though they had been on a road to destruction for some time. There were no accusations or blame, only regret that they were unable to bring a machine to market during Del Prado's lifetime. If they could have given him one thing, that would have been it.

The Mapper case highlighted how little the Netherlands was aware of the strategic value of its own chip technology. The ease with which this sensitive knowledge could have fallen into Chinese hands served as a sharp wake-up call for the country. In 2023, the 'VIFO' Act was put in place, which screens investments, mergers and acquisitions on potential national security issues. This law oversees vital providers and 'businesses active in the field of sensitive technology,' such as the semiconductor industry, and was retroactively applied from September 2020 on. In addition, in 2023 the government set aside a sum of 100 million euros to be used for immediate intervention in cases where a strategic company was at risk of falling into undesirable hands. With this, The Hague hoped to prevent another Mapper-style panic.

There are still traces of the Mapper deal. 70 million euros are being held in the account of the Dutch auction curator, to be distributed among the creditors pending a lawsuit filed by a French trustee on an administrative issue. And if you want to take look at one of the multibeam machines up close, you only have to pay a visit to the physics building of the Delft University of Technology. Next to a coffee machine is a vacuum chamber with a window offering a view of the technical innards. This museum piece was unveiled in early 2023 by Bert Jan Kampherbeek and Professor Pieter Kruit, with whom the entire Mapper project began.

Kruit has since retired, starting a new career in 2021 leading the e-beam division of Applied Materials. This American chip equipment manufacturer is building an inspection machine that, just like ASML's, works with electrons. With his talented former protégé Marco Wieland in charge of the competition, it is now time to find out if the student has become the master.

For Lex Keen, the multibeam adventure is still not over. If there is one thing the former marine knows best, it is how to persevere – no matter how many setbacks he faces. Keen purchased the Mapper machine located at CEA-Leti in France, and had the device flown to the East Coast of the US in 25 crates, all while the world was gripped by the COVID-19 crisis. Since 2022, it has been standing in a clean-room at defense company Northrop Grumman in Maryland, waiting to start producing chips. As the holders of the Mapper patents, Keen is dependent on ASML's cooperation for the license. He is still unsure about who his customers will be, but he knows one thing for sure: if the Pentagon comes knocking, they will have to pay up front.

PART V

GROWING PAINS

'We can't hide our wealth any longer.' You can hear the regret in Martin van den Brink's voice. He looks out of his window over all the factories, offices and construction cranes stretching into the distance. The new buildings seem quite chic to him. Sure, the design could have been slightly different, but he can't meddle in everything.

Van den Brink's office on the twentieth floor is the perfect place to see how ASML is expanding. Or, better yet: exploding. An American-style campus surrounds the tower, complete with a lively restaurant, an auditorium with a rooftop garden, a private supermarket, a bright blue running track and 'recharge rooms' for reading, gaming or knitting. You could live your entire life and never have to leave the campus.

In 2023, ASML has over 42,000 employees and is ranked among the fifty most valuable companies in the world. This is a two-fold increase from six years earlier. Over 20,000 people work in Veldhoven, and this number is expected to double again over the next six years. Taking the suppliers into account, this means an additional 70,000 jobs for the Brabant region. This impossible growth is more concerning to ASML than the political turmoil captivating the outside world. In Veldhoven's eyes, they have better things to do than be sidetracked by geopolitics. The only way is up, and delays are not an option.

Over the course of forty years, ASML has undergone a remarkable transformation. What began as a start-up became a scale-up, emerged as a market leader and cemented its place as a monopolist. Even in the middle of the escalating tech war between the US and China, its expansion is unrelenting. The demand for chips exploded in the wake of the energy transition and AI revolution, which has left the world wanting one thing: more chip machines. Companies such as Nvidia are relying entirely on TSMC, and are struggling to produce enough processors to provide the computing power needed by ChatGPT and its derivative applications. Analysts predict that the global chip market will double in size and become a trillion-dollar industry by 2030. And this translates directly into ASML's order books.

These orders are the responsibility of sales director Sunny Stalnaker, a veteran when it comes to closing billion-dollar deals with chip manufacturers. But even someone as skilled as Sunny has found her craft pushed to the limit.

The year is 2017, and Martin van den Brink has just asked Stalnaker to make an agreement with Intel on the purchase of High NA EUV machines. The future of his EUV master plan rests on that single order. All Stalnaker has to do is find a way to bridge the half-a-billion-dollar difference in asking price.

It should have been an impossible task. At this point, the High NA machine only exists on paper, and ASML is still struggling to get its regular EUV machines to work properly. 'We didn't even know ourselves when things would finally start to work,' Stalnaker quips. Nevertheless, her powers of persuasion bring Intel on board, and the other chip manufacturers soon follow suit. Mission accomplished, future secured.

But as soon as EUV gains momentum, ASML's problems begin. Surprisingly, it is a sudden demand for deep ultraviolet machines that catches ASML off guard. For years, ASML has been producing around two hundred of these systems annually. It is expected that the demand for these immersion scanners will drop off once EUV hits the market, and ASML has already retrained its factory workers accordingly. But reality is taking a different turn. In 2020, Sunny Stalnaker watches the orders for DUV quadruple to almost two hundred per quarter. ASML is overwhelmed – it is simply far too many for them to make, although Martin van den Brink struggles to see the problem. 'What is so difficult about scaling up?' he sighs to a colleague. 'Just do the same thing as usual times two or three.'

One of the causes of the uptick in orders is the shift in strategy from the Chinese government. Under pressure due to the American export regulations, China has decided to embrace established chip technology, using DUV machines. With cars evolving into computers on wheels, these less advanced chips are in high demand. Meanwhile, the demand for EUV scanners keeps growing. Stalnaker's order book, already worth tens of billions of euros, is overflowing. And just to make things even more complicated: to produce EUV chips, you also need more DUV machines to expose the less critical layers in a chip. And so demand keeps going up.

It's a perfect storm, and it is hitting Veldhoven right in the middle of a pandemic.

The unprecedented success of the company has come around to bite itself in the tail. In 2021, ASML is only able to deliver two thirds of the machines ordered for that year. You can feel the pressure in the overcrowded factories, in the overworked logistics organization, and in the atmosphere around Veldhoven. The employees' workloads are increasing – despite hundreds of new colleagues joining every month – and construction cranes become a familiar sight at ASML's branches abroad and within their network of suppliers.

There is no longer any doubt about ASML's critical role in the manufacturing industry. A new economic wonder has risen from the ashes of Philips and become the foundation of the so-called 'Brainport' region, the high-tech area of the Netherlands. But the province of Brabant is beginning to groan under the weight of the prosperity, whether on the highways around Eindhoven, in the exploding labor market or at the overcrowded housing market.

When it comes to scaling down chips, there is nothing left for ASML to learn. But growing your organization at this scale without losing yourself – that's a different story.

34

ALL IN THE FAMILY

If you close your eyes, you can hardly tell which of them is talking. A Brabant accent, a little sonorous, not a word more than needed. One thing is clear though: they are a pair of no-nonsense entrepreneurs.

Wim and Willem van der Leegte are sitting side by side in the Eindhoven headquarters of the VDL group. The family of this father-son duo built the largest industrial conglomerate in the Netherlands. Their one hundred companies represent the entire spectrum of the manufacturing industry: whether you need mega-construction or nanometer precision, they've got you covered.

The VDL family tree spans three generations. The company was founded in 1953 by Pieter van der Leegte. His son Wim soon took the reins, and in 2018 his grandson Willem became CEO, supported by his sister and brother. The Van der Leegtes watched from the other side of the highway as ASML began to expand dramatically. And sure enough, they jumped on board for the ride.

'The circle is complete,' declared Wim van der Leegte when he bought the Enabling Technologies Group from Philips in 2006. He always had a feel for history. Back in the early 1950s, his own father used to work at ETG, during the time when its full name 'Philips Machine Factory' was still written in clear letters across the façade. Van der Leegte paid Philips 51 million euros for ETG. In hindsight, he realized this was an excellent deal. The family rode the waves of ASML's successes, which helped propel the business to more than 15,000 employees and nearly 6 billion euros in annual revenue. In 2015, Wim also acquired his brother

Gerard van der Leegte's company, GL Precision. Just to keep the family together, as you do in Brabant.

Together with Zeiss, VDL holds the title of ASML's most important partner. They supply Veldhoven with critical building blocks needed to assemble a functional scanner. The newer machines are comprised of more than three hundred thousand parts from around seven hundred suppliers, and this external network accounts for around 80 percent of the total manufacturing costs of a lithography machine.

One glance at the VDL ETG factories in Almelo tells the story of the transformation undergone by the Dutch manufacturing industry. You can still find moss-green Philips machines from the 1970s dotted between the state-of-the-art laser equipment, like relics from a bygone era. As long as they work, they aren't going anywhere.

In Almelo, the company produces the underside of ASML's lithography machines. What starts as a twenty-ton block of Italian aluminum ends up as a meticulously milled fifteen-hundred kilogram frame. Like filing down a city bus until you are left with a Mini Cooper.

The frame is filled with heavy magnets – if you get caught near it with anything metallic in or on your body, you will be stuck there forever. This force is needed to drive the electric motors that move the wafer tables back and forth in the machine, just like a magnetic levitation train.

The vacuum chambers for EUV machines are also produced in Almelo, as well as the modules that Zeiss mounts the EUV mirrors in. These components have to meet incredibly strict requirements, to the point that employees are only allowed into the cleanroom if they use the prescribed shampoo and deodorant. For Zeiss, any stray molecule from Almelo is one too many.

As a billion-dollar company, VDL has been able to handle the ups and downs in the chip industry. The industrial conglomerate has plenty of other customers in need of advanced technology, so VDL can recoup the investments that are required for ASML. 'Due to the high standards set by ASML, we have had to step up ourselves,' Willem van der Leegte explains. His company even took one additional step: VDL has full responsibility for one component of ASML's machine. The so-called "wafer handler" is a robotic arm that lays the silicon wafers precisely where they need to be on the wafer table, ready to be exposed to the world of nanometers. The design and maintenance is handled by VDL itself, and it ensures that other companies supply the necessary parts. This leaves ASML with one less issue to worry about. The machine is complicated enough – if someone else can do something better, it is gladly left to them.

Like all other suppliers, VDL must keep up with ASML's growth. This means recruiting new technicians and developers, investing in new buildings, and setting up emergency cleanrooms to expand capacity. However, not every party in the ASML chain can accelerate at the same pace, or even wants to. For smaller suppliers, ASML is a customer they both desire and fear. The demands this erratic buyer places on these companies are as daunting as the heights it can propel them to. Veldhoven has strict guidelines, and suppliers can only use products sourced from companies selected by ASML itself. There is no room for substituting the prescribed ingredients – anything that could lead to disruption in the chip factory needs to be eliminated.

The company continues to raise the bar. Each year, suppliers are required to work more precisely, more cleanly, and offer better value for money. Every fingerprint is one too many. Even the rubber anti-slip layer on the ear grips of your glasses could be a problem, as it can emit gases capable of damaging the delicate EUV mirrors.

ASML is not only demanding; it is unpredictable. In periods of growth, there is never enough speed and capacity in the supply chain. But as soon as orders decline, everything becomes too much, and suppliers are left with an abundance of capital-intensive goods. And it is never easy to stay afloat while carrying that much weight. Smaller companies also risk pricing themselves out of the market when investing in high-value production methods for ASML, as they might then become too expensive for other customers.

To limit the risks, ASML insists that its suppliers get a maximum of 40 percent of their revenue from Veldhoven. This guideline is intended to keep companies from collapsing during a downturn in the chip industry. However, when faced with the chip market's unrestrained growth and the floods of orders that come with it, keeping to that percentage is easier said than done. In these cases, ASML's response is usually the same: just figure it out.

The sourcing and procurement team keeps meticulous records of companies that are causing delays. If you land on ASML's 'Top 5 List', you have a serious problem. Whenever a supplier is becoming problematic, ASML sends in reinforcements to help smooth things over. And it does not hesitate to call the shots. For example, when a Dutch supplier was struggling with a capacity issue – a necessary production tool was not available in Europe – ASML immediately ensured that the equipment was flown over from the US. No ifs, ands or buts. Fronting tens of thousands of euros in transportation costs is worth every penny when it saves a few weeks of delivery time.

Every supplier has its own 'godfather' within ASML's organization. However, if there are serious problems, a higher power will intervene. In 2021, when a supplier failed to resolve a recurring issue with a critical mechatronics component, Peter Wennink insisted the company should change its management. And there was no room for discussion, according to the CEO: 'The investigation work had already been done by our team of experts. And I'm the judge that delivers the verdict.'

Sometimes ASML will help out its suppliers with an injection of capital, just like it did for Zeiss when it needed support for High NA. The last resort would be an acquisition, which happened with Cymer when that American company was unable to get the light source for the EUV machine to work. On a slightly smaller scale, in 2012 ASML acquired Wijdeven Motion, a company with ninety employees that supplies linear motors and was on the verge of bankruptcy.

The supplier Berliner Glas also failed to keep up with ASML's demands. This German family-owned company with 1600 employees makes the super-flat mirrors on which the wafers are placed. In 2020, ASML demanded that Berliner Glas make an investment of 70 million euros for the next generation of EUV. The Germans were not interested, so ASML bought the company to speed things up. If they needed to do it themselves, they would. You could see the effects at the Berlin location within a year. Berliner Glas was renamed ASML Berlin, surplus business units were sold off, new construction had already been completed, and leases for additional offices had been signed. And the cautiousness of the Germans had been thrown out the window.

'We don't *make* anything here,' claims Martin van den Brink. It's a slight exaggeration, but his point is clear: ASML only assembles the lithography machines, and the wide range of suppliers take care of providing the parts. This model has been essential to keeping everything moving. It granted ASML a remarkable ability to recover in the first decades of its existence, while its vertically integrated Japanese competitors were still stuck making most of the components themselves. Just like a lightweight boxer can bounce back to their feet faster than a heavyweight.

ASML avoids taking on more suppliers to maintain this flexibility. All suppliers have their own responsibilities, to encourage them to regain the high-tech investments they make for Veldhoven from other customers. This is also why the company turned down Wim van der Leegte's informal offer in 2006 to jointly acquire ETG fifty-fifty.

While the oversight and management for the lithography system as a whole lies with Veldhoven, ASML tries to spread these responsibilities further across the network. Because the most complex components of the machine are single-sourced – there's only one supplier for these crucial parts – a high level of trust is essential. This approach differs from conventional sourcing strategies, which typically pit suppliers against each other to drive down costs and mitigate risk. But ASML's model has an advantage. The suppliers effectively become co-developers of the machine, and their deep involvement in the material means they are also able to solve problems they are not the cause of themselves.

When Frédéric Schneider became chief operating officer in 2010, he was surprised that Veldhoven was so willing to tie its fate to the success of a handful of companies. Schneider wanted to seek out a backup supplier for all the sensitive parts of the machine, but the board of directors decided to stick to the principle of single sourcing and mutual dependency. Throughout the entire chip industry, the most reliable relationships are built with just one trusted partner. Frits van Hout has an analogy: 'Think how your spouse might react if you were to have an equally deep relationship with somebody else.'

Chip manufacturers also entrust their fate to a few crucial, highly specialized and non-interchangeable suppliers. ASML is the case in point: its monopoly over lithography machines makes it notoriously irreplaceable. The semiconductor sector is made up of deep but fragile connections, like an incredibly valuable yet brittle chain.

However, in December of 2018, the dangers of single sourcing become apparent. A fire breaks out at Prodrive, a tech company based in Son, a town close to Veldhoven. Prodrive is responsible for supplying the control system for the motors of lithography machines – in practice, this means software that runs on large data racks. And in one night, ASML's sole source of this component goes up in a cloud of smoke.

Prodrive's first call goes to the fire department, and the second straight to Veldhoven. The same day, ASML sends a crisis team to assess the damage. Their IT systems were no longer functioning, so ASML immediately provides fifty heavy-duty computers. Even before the insurance company has assessed the damage, employees have already salvaged usable equipment from the smoldering factory. Other suppliers also help out, although this is not entirely altruistic. If ASML is unable to deliver machines, everyone suffers.

This would not be the last time ASML played firefighter. When VDL falls victim to a cyberattack in October 2021, the IT experts from Veldhoven are immediately on the scene. There is little to be done, and VDL has no choice but to pull the plug on all the computers to smoke out the hackers. It takes a month to get all IT systems up and running again.

However, the biggest threat to the supply chain comes from ASML itself. The company completely underestimated the growth of the chip industry, which meant that the sudden escalation in demand during the pandemic also caught suppliers off guard. They were overwhelmed by the relentless stream of increases and changes from ASML, which were sometimes happening twenty or thirty times per week. In hindsight, ASML admits that their updates could have been better. This is a huge understatement about the demand the suppliers faced. In addition, the COVID-19 crisis disrupted their own supply chains, as the machines they needed to make components for new chip machines were in turn waiting for chips. It was a vicious circle of scarcity.

ASML became locked in a continuous battle to resolve these bottlenecks, like a traffic cop at a busy intersection full of honking cars. Which component is most urgent? Who has been stuck waiting the longest? Who gets priority?

To make things even more complicated, different departments in Veldhoven put pressure on the suppliers at the same time. The factory and the developers often get in each other's way, like two dogs fighting over the same bone. Technical drawings sometimes contradict each other, as different teams have been working on them at the same time to rush things through. Suppliers can also tell when they are dealing with ASML's new hires brought in to handle the rapid growth. Although well-versed in technical theory, many of the rookies lack practical expertise and struggle to navigate the maze of abbreviations.

VDL acknowledges the teams in Veldhoven are wrestling with the extreme expansion. 'When you hire such a large amount of people in a short time, it's difficult to preserve the culture of your company,' says Willem van der Leegte. He concludes VDL is in the same boat: 'Their problems affect us. That's part of our mutual dependence. It's win-win or lose-lose.'

From the outside, it seemed ASML was unable to handle the surging demand for chip machines because of their struggling suppliers. As a result, investors complained about ASML's shortcomings in its supply chain management. Little did they know that there was something else going on. Right in the middle of the most hectic year in the company's history, ASML had suffered an acute heart attack.

35

WELCOME TO FIVE-HELL

'...and thank you all for joining us today.'

As soon as the operator formally concludes the ASML investor call, Peter Wennink and CFO Roger Dassen start chatting in the Veldhoven boardroom. It is July 2021, and they have just finished presenting the second quarter results. Over the course of an hour, a team of seven financial experts watched as Dassen and Wennink took turns answering questions from analysts. They were there to field any unexpected questions, but none arose. Everything was about the chip shortage and the urgent need for extra lithography machines. As Dassen summarizes in the investor call, it was nothing more than 'twenty different ways to ask about capacity.'

The pair have known each other for a long time. Just like Wennink, Dassen worked for the accounting firm Deloitte, and together they make for a well-oiled machine.

'Roger, any changes in the stock price?' asks Wennink.

'Oh, just 595, and then back to 600,' comes Dassen's reply.

Wennink has been doing these investor calls for over twenty years. 'Every time is showtime. For one hour, you're at your most vulnerable.'

ASML is growing so fast it is virtually creaking – just like the tall headquarters in Veldhoven. When the wind blows, you can hear the steel structure groaning. 'That's how it is supposed to be,' says Wennink reassuringly, mimicking the noise.

A little further away, construction workers are putting the final touches on the logistics center at the Veldhoven campus. This 35-meter-tall state-of-the-art warehouse, nearly a kilometer in length and the size of ten footballs fields, rose from the ground in less than two years. On the top floor there are offices for three thousand people, while below there is space for thirty thousand pallets.

ASML previously spread its logistics center across different locations. Spare parts and components for new machines were kept in separate warehouses, and the assembled systems were packed for transportation in an entirely different hall. But this new building handles all the logistics processes at once. This is 5L, the new heart of ASML, with different 'flows' for both 'in and out'.

With its moving robots, automatic shelves and a spiral slide to distribute packages, the new logistics center is supposed to be a technical masterpiece. Everything is seamlessly connected to the aorta, the central corridor that leads to the cleanrooms in ASML's factories. On paper, it looks fantastic.

5L goes live at the end of July 2021. But as soon as the switch is flipped on ASML's new lifeline, it clogs up. Anything that can go wrong does go wrong. The software controlling the warehouse is not integrated with the software in the factory. Circuits blow, and there are no boxes or labels. Components always need to be carefully cleaned before going into ASML's factory, but this is no longer possible. Nothing goes in, and nothing goes out.

A long line of trucks from suppliers outside the warehouse tells the story of the congestion inside. Some drivers angrily take to Twitter – 'I've been sitting here twiddling my thumbs for one and a half hours' – while others turn around to make other deliveries, only to turn around again as ASML urgently needs the parts. 'The worst f#cking address in the Netherlands, ASML 5L,' tweets one trucker.

Sunny Stalnaker is on vacation when she receives a message from a Korean customer: 'Where is the lithography machine we ordered? It should already have been on a cargo plane.' As it turns out, the logistics center has been unable to find any packaging materials and the machine is still at ASML. Stalnaker hopes it is just a temporary congestion, and her email mentions 'a minor issue with the relocation of our warehouse.' But when she returns one week later, 5L has completely seized up. Right in the middle of an extreme growth spurt, while her customers are screaming for more machines.

For the first week, no one dares to inform top management that 5L has brought the factory to a standstill. When Peter Wennink takes the chairman of Intel Omar Ishrak on a tour of the ASML factory in early August, an unfamiliar scene greets them. In the cleanrooms there is barely a worker in sight. 'What happened?' he asks an employee. 'Where is everyone?'

'They all went home – we haven't received any materials in over a week,' is the response.

Wennink speaks Dutch to keep his guest from figuring out what is going on. The company that builds the most complicated machines on earth has failed to figure out how to move a warehouse. The second the door closes behind Ishrak, the polite smile vanishes from Wennink's face. Furious, he goes straight to his desk to hammer out an email: 'What the hell is going on?'

In the next quarterly report, Roger Dassen notes that ASML's logistics center experienced 'startup-issues'. Meanwhile, a crisis team has been assembled in Veldhoven. The issues at 5L kept replacement parts from being delivered to chip factories, and a mass shutdown of machines is the last thing the world needs during an acute chip shortage. ASML can feel the weight of the entire chip industry on its shoulders.

At the beginning of August, ASML sends out mobilization calls to thousands of workers, pleading with them to help 5L. A desperate tone permeates the emails: 'You can make the difference!' The floor soon fills with volunteers from all corners of the company, dashing back and forth with packing slips and bubble wrap. With no software to fall back on, there is no choice. It has to be done by hand, or not at all.

The volunteer teams wear yellow vests, the logistics staff wear blue. They already have a nickname for 5L – '5-Hell'. Employees in the factory have been warning for months that the move could lead to trouble, but their voices never reached the top of the tower.

Hundreds of millions of euros in revenue disappear because of the problems in 5L, and employees are hugely stressed. The works council is seriously concerned, as they write in their 2022 commentary on the board's remuneration policy. The bonuses for the top management do not take into account the chaos on the work floor. Absenteeism in the factories has increased, and the company's counselor is fully booked. With so much pressure to deliver machines, employees feel they are not allowed to say no, which leaves them stuck in an impossible position.

And the company never says no to a customer. ASML's orderbook may be overflowing, but the can-do mentality is set in stone and Veldhoven bends over backwards to increase output. They re-use parts to help expand capacity, and ASML starts its own speedy delivery service. Normally, machines are tested twice: once in Veldhoven, and once when they have been assembled in the chip factory. Performing some of the Veldhoven testing at the customer's site instead shaves three to four weeks off the delivery time. Chip manufacturers jump on the offer; they would rather have a machine that will probably work than one that arrives weeks later. After all, they have desperate car manufacturers and angry politicians breathing down their necks.

The serious delays 5L causes last for more than three months. The extensive investigation into what went wrong concludes it was a case of mismanagement. The risks were heavily underestimated, and what was assumed to be a small project for the factory turned out to be open-heart surgery for the entire company. Furthermore, there was never a plan B or backup in the event that things went south. Even Frédéric Schneider, ASML's chief operating officer, is caught by surprise.

Some managers are given new positions after the mistake, but nobody gets fired. Punishment was never part of ASML's culture. 'Accountability is one of our weaknesses,' Sunny Stalnaker bemoans. But Peter Wennink sees it differently. 'Of course, we were very angry. In other companies the person responsible would have been fired, but I felt just as responsible myself. In times like these, we all need to take a look in the mirror.'

The volunteer initiative in the logistics center was good for comradery, but it also brought ASML face-to-face with some harsh truths.

'We don't know how to grow,' explains Peter Ballière, head of human resources. 'We are so focused on customers and products that we've forgotten about ourselves.'

When Baillière started in 2018, he thought he would be entering a high-tech heaven where every process was tuned to perfection. The opposite was true. ASML was seriously lagging, and all the systems and processes that you would expect in a large company were simply not in place.

Baillière had worked in the automotive industry for years, where everything revolved around optimization – every penny counted. As he discovered, the laws in Veldhoven are different. Meeting customer deadlines is crucial, and profitability seems to be an afterthought.

ASML has reached a size where they recognize that processes needed to improve. 'But without turning into a bureaucracy,' Baillière adds. If there is one word that riles up an ASML'er, it's that B-word.

The company struggles with the organizational changes. The freedom demanded by the technical people conflicts with the supporting departments' procedures, leading to frequent clashes between the 'cowboys' and the 'bureaucrats'. Nowhere is this more evident than in the implementation of ONE, or Our New Enterprise.

ONE is a long-term project aimed at improving inventory management. With every scanner consisting of hundreds of thousands of parts, this is no task for the faint of heart. These components come from hundreds of different suppliers and are subject to continuous change – almost no chip machine is the same. The enterprise resource planning, or ERP, was based on software from the time of the Y2K bug. It was supposed to get a thorough update at a later date. Of course, this never happened.

This marked the birth of 'Frankenstein', as Peter Wennink calls the inventory system. It staggers its way through life at ASML, held together with nuts, bolts and confusing buttons.

If a chip machine goes down in a fab, spare parts either need to be within reach or rushed immediately to the site. When this happens, ASML pays a hefty premium to get priority on regular cargo flights. Other cargo is often hauled off to make space. However, ASML frequently struggles with the sending of packages – the content is incorrect, wrong items are sent, and even empty boxes find themselves on an express trip around the world. It is a nightmare, just like Frankenstein's monster.

After other improvement programs fail, Veldhoven turns to ONE. In 2019, the Wilton division becomes the first to test the system. However, the American employees find themselves running headfirst into a bureaucratic wall. Parts that are actually in the warehouse are unable to be shipped due to a faulty registration. The response is usually the same: computer says no.

Our New Enterprise clashes with the company's deeply ingrained habits and shortcuts. 'One half of the company is asking you to hurry up because a chip manufacturer urgently needs parts, while the other half wants you to follow all the rules,' one exasperated employee complains. She has the unfortunate task of explaining to Martin van den Brink that, just because of some administrative obstacle with the ONE system, he needs to wait a few weeks for material from Wilton. Van den Brink is fuming. 'Are you crazy?' he responds. 'You get in that car now and get that part out of the warehouse.'

Just like the machines the company produces, ASML's planning is full of uncertainties. New factories and offices often turn out to be too small, and even the logistics center is cramped from the get-go. It is a recurring pattern. In 2013, ASML built an EUV factory costing 600 million euros, but it turned out to need far more electricity and hydrogen then planned. New pipes had to be installed, and ASML flushed millions of euros down the drain fixing the mistake.

But guesswork seems an inescapable part of the process. Factories are built before it is certain how exactly the machines will work, or how many customers will order them. One thing ASML knows for certain: if you cover all the risks, you will never get a chip machine delivered on time. Every week counts when constructing a new cleanroom. If contractors in Veldhoven keep working during the nationwide three-week construction break in order to finish a factory, they receive a generous bonus.

ASML accepts that its organization does not always run optimally. Frits van Hout even has his own formula for this: 'Things you do a thousand times of course need to be standardized. But if eliminating an inefficiency takes up so much time that it stops you from doing other, more important things, then you should just tolerate that inefficiency. As a good Calvinist, you might ask, "Could we not have prevented it?" But we say, just let it go.'

It is the kind of luxury a company in good shape can afford. In 2021, for example, ASML made nearly six billion euros in profit – a 70 percent increase from the previous year.

But the accumulation of organizational problems that year forced ASML to face some hard truths. 'We have a blind spot for logistical blunders,' Peter Wennink explains. 'Because we can make EUV, we think we can do everything else too.' The high-flyers can see technical obstacles in lithography systems from a mile away. But they will not wake up to logistical problems until customers start calling to ask, 'Hey, where's my machine?'

This leads to the appointment of Wayne Allan as an extra board member in 2023. With his extensive operational background, Allan is given the job of improving procurement and managing the supply network. This move causes a shift in the balance between the 'cowboys' and the 'bureaucrats' in the boardroom. Van den Brink consistently positions himself as the champion of ASML's free technical culture, which he believes should never be allowed to get stuck by procedures and processes. The mere mention of KPIs, or key performance indicators, during a meeting is enough to send him storming out of the room. He finds it completely trivial – 'I'll be in the room next door talking about the actual content. Whoever wants to talk about KPIs can stay here.'

But ASML knows it needs to streamline its organization to save the whole operation from imploding again. After the trauma of 5L, Veldhoven initiated an 'improved' improvement program. BPI, or Business Performance Improvement, is a new abbreviation for an old problem: how to handle the logistical web of constantly changing products spread out over a network of hundreds of suppliers.

The plan is to approach inventory management the way ASML builds machines: with tight program management. Unsolvable problems can then be broken down into smaller parts with clear milestones. That is one way to tame the monster – at least in theory.

The BPI project starts with the fundamentals of machine design, and so falls under the wing of ASML's technical director Martin van den Brink. Ultimately, he would also like to bring order to the chaos – so long as a little chaos remains.

36

READ THE
FINE PRINT FIRST

It is a mess, and the host is loving it.

It's the summer of 2016, and ASML's annual barbeque for the top brass has become a mud bath. Martin van den Brink is hosting the event from his secluded house, located just off the side of an unpaved road. The guests are parked in an adjacent field, and after hours of torrential rain, it has turned into a swamp. More than fifty cars are totally stuck – even the tractor Martin borrowed from his neighbor has been swallowed by the sludge, and he has to arrange for a second tractor to come and pull the cars free.

Martin quickly changes into an old outfit and pulls on his favorite plaid shirt. This is going to be hilarious.

It is not about schadenfreude for Van den Brink, but about observing the social experiment unfolding in the Brabant mud right before his very eyes. The ASML leaders are vying for priority, falling all over their cars and bickering with their partners. When the pressure is on, the mask tends to slip – then you really get to know who your colleagues are.

Frédéric Schneider, one of the French board members, cannot get his Renault Espace out of the slop. Hans Meiling easily shoots past him in his four-wheel-drive Volvo. A smart choice of car, and an even smarter piece of advice: 'You should always back in, and make sure your escape route is clear. Even cavemen knew that.'

A few ASML'ers try another exit, but get stuck on some stray tree stumps. The software of one driver's Tesla is refusing to switch to off-road mode, leaving him stranded while his colleagues pore over the manual.

One Saab gets dragged even deeper into the ground by the tractor. Chief financial officer Wolfgang Nickl does not like the thought of anyone else coming near his car, let alone a tractor, so decides to handle it himself. His wife, wearing high heels and a white evening dress, pushes from the back while he sits behind the wheel. 'Einz, zwei...jetzt!' The car lurches forward, and so does his wife. Face-first into the mud. In the end, it takes more than four hours to free the last car.

For Martin van den Brink, ASML is one big social experiment. He loves to create some confusion and rub people the wrong way. Just to see how they function, or if they waver. He wants to gauge your reaction by toying with you, like a cat playing with a mouse. But as soon as a weakness or technical problem is found, Van den Brink encourages the others to step in: 'You see what he's struggling with? You need to help him.'

According to people that work with him, Martin has an uncanny ability to see right through you. He can smell when something is off, but he will never tell you what to do about it. You are there to spar, to defend your position. Not to agree with every word he says. Head of the research department Jos Benschop knows this all too well: 'The worst thing you can say to Martin is, "Oh, blessed Brink, what a brilliant plan!"'

In such chaotic and often noisy technical debates, the most creative solutions tend to arise. And it is the perfect way to bring problems to light. After all, there only needs to be one weak link in a lithography machine, one loose bolt, for the entire chip factory to come to a halt.

As a result, even the highest level of ASML leadership is clued in to the technical details. 'It can be extremely annoying,' Frits van Hout explains. 'It looks as if we think we always know better. That's not the case, but we need to know some details if we want to understand why something is going wrong. We have to dig to find out whether an error can occur once a year, or much more often.'

Van den Brink's approach laid the foundation for ASML's remarkable corporate culture. He created the environment that tried to preserve the feeling of a start-up in a global tech company. An impossible task, some might say, and it certainly had its battles.

Many managers at ASML try to emulate Van den Brink's style. There is even an acronym for this in the company: BIG, or Brink Imitation Behavior ('Brink Imitatie Gedrag' in Dutch). This confrontational approach is particularly popular in the technical teams. Colleagues openly challenge each other, and things get rough at the top, even by Dutch standards. 'You should have read the fine print in the patient insert before coming to work here,' Roger Dassen advises. The possible side effects include a hardened soul and thick skin.

Dassen's colleagues come down hard on him when he struggles to implement the ONE system in 2019. He knows it was nothing personal – after all, everyone knows that ONE is a tough task. Yet the intensity still affects him. He immediately notices upon his arrival that ASML'ers are constantly at each other's throats. 'In the beginning I thought, "Holy shit, what's going on here?" But when they would leave the room, they would slap each other on the back and go for a coffee or grab a beer.'

Finding mistakes is the number one pastime at ASML. And it is never just about technology. Peter Baillière notices colleagues even complain about the 'wrong' fonts being used in a PowerPoint presentation. He has his own baptism by fire when he takes over the HR department in 2018. During his first presentation to the board of directors about complex European privacy regulations, he is abruptly cut off. He doesn't fully understand the details of the legislation, and at this level, that is simply not good enough. 'Here at ASML, you always need to be able to go into depth,' he is told. This is the big league, not a tea party. The new director of HR walks out of the meeting, convinced he is about to be fired on the spot.

Many ASML'ers have stories of similar near-death experiences. You have to suffer through it, pick yourself up and go on to win a few of those battles. It is a way to see if you are cut from the right cloth: full of substance, and short on ego. At ASML, you are so often confronted with something that you have no idea about, that you never bother to brag about the things you do know about. 'ASML'ers can spot authenticity a mile away,' according to Peter Wennink. They value someone who puts the company first, not themselves.

The continuous focus on mistakes tends to either leave newcomers wrestling with the strict rules, or drive them away completely. ASML traditionally struggled to retain 'lateral incomers', especially in managerial positions. There used to be a nickname for such new colleagues: a *Horizontaal Instromende Stropdas*, or HIS (which translates to a 'Horizontally Inbound Necktie'). For the first thirty years, it was rare to bring people from outside into key positions. As a result, ASML remains more or less isolated from the outside world.

When Wennink and Van den Brink both become president in 2013, ASML'ers receive 'cultural awareness' training to learn how this confrontational style is perceived by colleagues from other countries. The first lesson: 'Put yourself in the other person's shoes before you say or do anything.' But for many ASML'ers, this empathy is a one-way street. They assume everyone should behave as Dutch as possible. Straightforward and direct – that's how it should be.

However, not everyone is raised on a diet of Dutch directness. ASML employs people from 144 different nationalities in locations all over the world, and the level of education is high across the board. Ninety percent of workers have university degrees or some form of higher education, and they range from physicists and mechanical engineers to software developers and computer scientists. They are all brought together by one thing: a passion for technology. But there are major cultural differences between the science students in Veldhoven and the foreign branches. In Asia, ASML's style is far looser than the strict hierarchies found in local companies there. You never openly criticize your boss there, even if they are a lousy manager. To reassure international employees, ASML started an anonymous reporting point called 'Speak Up' for complaints about managers or unethical behavior. It is a way to make your voice heard.

For employees in the US, home to more than seven thousand ASML'ers, the Dutch directness quickly crosses the line into bluntness.

'As Americans, we would never treat each other like that,' assert the employees from the San Diego division.

When SVG in Wilton is taken over in 2001, workers there initially experience their Dutch colleagues as tough and aggressive. And that is not the only cultural difference: American employees feel reluctant to just throw their problems on the table. It does not align with the Americans' winner mentality and their quest for perfection.

The Wilton staff is given training to overcome this hesitation, a course that ASML compares to the management of a Dutch polder. A polder needs to be protected from the water by dikes, and everyone needs to trust that the others have properly checked their part of the dike. The moral: don't hide your own shortcomings, but show your needs so others can help you. Don't try to save the world on your own – just like the famous Dutch fairytale by Hansje Brinker, if you try to plug the dike with only your own finger, everyone drowns.

Titles hold less weight in the Low Countries. You earn respect by contributing something – that's how the best ideas come to the surface.

That's the scientific ideal, believes Joost Frenken, who led the ARCNL research institute and worked closely with ASML for many years. 'No one tells the other what to do, and if you have a good plan or find a mistake, you speak up. Even a newcomer who has only been there for a week is expected to contribute to the discussion.' It is typical of the Dutch, he thinks. 'In other countries, hierarchies get in the way – the egos of people at the top suck all the power out of collective thinking.'

Rank may rarely play a role, but there are still laws in the Veldhoven jungle. Peter Wennink knows them well: dare to speak up, say what you think, and always make enormous PowerPoints to bombard your colleagues with data.

A day in the life at ASML is filled with competition: who can present the most numbers, and who can find the most mistakes in other people's slides? According to former head of the development department Herman Boom, 'there is always someone saying that what you are working on is not correct. It can take weeks for engineers to accept that they could actually be wrong. And forget about praising the colleague who pointed it out.'

The engineers work in teams on alternative solutions, competing to see which one of their brainchildren will end up in the machine. The end result is often a combination of ideas: rarely can any invention be traced back to a single 'progenitor'.

A great deal of attention is paid to mistakes, but compliments are rare. 'One colleague of mine created a separate folder in his mailbox. If he ever receives a compliment, he can save it in there,' one manager says. To encourage the Dutch to loosen up with their praise, ASML devised an app called the 'Recognition Tool'. Colleagues are now able to give each other a virtual pat on the back: accumulate enough points, and you receive a gift card for 50 or 250 euros to spend at an online shop.

Technical milestones are modestly celebrated, often with only a T-shirt or a photo. Veldhoven is about business, and there is always another deadline looming. When the light source achieves a new power record, the DUV machine produces one or two million wafers per year, or the two hundredth EUV machine is delivered, the reaction is the same: a solitary thumbs-up. But never celebrate a first, according to Frits van Hout. 'You never know if the first machine will keep working. It might as well melt down.'

Difficult issues also receive the most attention – 'easy problems' are not interesting enough to distinguish yourself as the smartest in the room. This phenomenon creates the perfect breeding ground for ASML's firefighting culture. Employees spring into action at the first sight of trouble, but there is less interest in avoiding problems altogether. As one manager puts it, 'ASML encourages heroes. If you jump on a plane to solve something urgent, then you're the man. If you just deliver on what you promised, you won't hear a thing.' However, this firefighting culture also risks cultivating arsonists – people who create a problem only to 'heroically' solve them as a way to put themselves in the spotlight.

ASML is a sprinter forced to run a marathon. The last serious down-turn was in 2009, and the company has been exponentially growing ever since. There is no time to pause and figure out how to improve the organization. When the chip industry temporarily slows down again in 2023 and orders are delayed, you can almost feel a sigh of relief in the air in Veldhoven. Almost.

At this point, Veldhoven has a flood of new recruits to soak up. In 2023, two-thirds of the employees had been with the company for less than five years, and a quarter for less than one year. Ten thousand new people joined in 2022, which is six thousand more than originally planned. Colleagues with more than two years of experience become coaches and buddies, enlisted to help the newcomers land gently on planet ASML. It seems to work. Ninety-five percent of the new hires were still employed after twelve months, a rate of retention unseen in the rest of the tech industry. But training these new employees takes time, and the workload for existing staff suffers as a result.

Yet the most important problem is the lack of empathy and people skills often displayed by the ASML managers. Even if you do not take the shouting or blunt behavior personally, it can still be hard to stomach. ASML'ers may be more accustomed to this style of management, but in other organizations, such harsh confrontations can easily be taken as crossing the line.

'ASML is longing for change,' says HR chief Peter Baillière in 2023. In his eyes, the company is a teenager that desperately needs to mature. That explains why more than fifteen hundred leadership training sessions are held each year, and the entire company's top management needs a workshop to prepare ASML for the future. With Baillière set to retire in 2024, ASML needs to grow up fast.

The upcoming generational shift is causing concern. Along with Peter Wennink and Martin van den Brink, a large group of engineers from the early days are nearing the end of their tenure at ASML. These veterans possess invaluable technical know-how that ASML will soon no longer be able to rely on. You cannot find their knowledge in any manual: they teach by word of mouth and in the cold light of the work floor. The old guard knows their way around the organization blindfolded: they know exactly who to call when needed, or who to chat with at the watercooler. With so many people coming in at once, this collective memory is fading, and the veterans are slowly disappearing with it. What once happened spontaneously now needs to be documented and formalized into rules, or risk being lost altogether.

But ASML'ers have never been fond of rules. They put their own spin on their work, which often leads to conflicts. One such conflict occurred between the employees in the factory and the development department when they each clashed over resources. Their respective managers had to resort to their schoolyard tactics, and decided to work out of the same office to set an example to the employees and demonstrate that they share a common goal.

This problem also lies at the heart of the issues with 5L. Peter Wennink had his own term for what ASML needs more of: 'horizontal loyalty'. 'When we hire new people, they immediately dive into their own specific task. It's almost a law of nature at this point. That might work for that particular task, but not for the overall picture.'

ASML needs leaders with more experience to help foster connections between hyper-specialists. It seeks to cultivate 'T-shaped' managers – individuals with expertise in one area and a sufficient grasp of the surrounding topics. To become a 'T', you need to have worked at the company for a longer time and have a few roles under your belt.

Wennink also thinks the ASML employees need to come out of their shells. As ever, the CEO leads by example and adjusts his morning routine to make himself more approachable. At 7:30 a.m., he always has a coffee, croissants and yogurt with muesli at Plaza, the restaurant on ASML's campus. The idea is simple: 'Anyone can come speak to me there if they want to.' When a young ASML'er from abroad dares to overcome the imaginary hurdle and tap him on the shoulder, it makes Wennink's day.

Meanwhile, diversity at ASML is increasing in all areas, whether it be gender, sexual orientation, nationality or neurodiversity. The baby boomers with sideburns and lab coats that started the venture in 1984 are now only a fraction of its population. The majority of employees belong to generations X and Y, with an average age of 39 years old.

Since women account for only 20 percent of the workforce, ASML makes an effort to increase the number of female employees. When a TV documentary about ASML aired featuring a large number of young female employees, Martin van den Brink quipped that his days are mostly filled with being around overweight white men. After all, the number of women at the top of the ladder is still limited, and only around 11 percent are in management roles.

But there is no systematic undervaluing of women's opinions in the company, at least according to Sunny Stalnaker. 'As a physics student, I was already used to working in an environment with few women. When it comes to the content of what I'm saying, they take me seriously at ASML. The fact I'm a woman doesn't come into play – and if it occasionally does, it doesn't bother me.' Once, when someone from another department turned to her male colleague and asked whether Stalnaker was correct about a technical issue, she quickly responded, 'Excuse me, but didn't I just tell you that's how it is?'

The estimated percentage of people with autism or ADHD at ASML far outnumbers the average. The highly specialized work, revolving around focusing on complex problems that require prolonged attention to the smallest details, makes it well-suited to some autistic traits. Van den Brink himself makes no secret about being dyslexic, and actively advocates for targeting this neurodiverse group. They are precisely the analytical and creative thinkers ASML needs, but also often the ones who find it difficult to put themselves in other people's shoes.

Integrating so many new faces and personalities into the well-oiled organization is a tough task. How do you maintain harmony in a workforce of more than forty thousand headstrong, highly educated people? ASML claims to provide a work environment where you can be free to play the nonconformist, but still have to take your colleagues into consideration. It is a contradiction summarized in 2020 by the introduction of ASML's three core values, otherwise known as the 'three C's': Challenge, Collaborate, and Care. Collaboration had been incorporated into the reward structure – those who focus solely on their own tasks instead of collaborating receive a lower bonus. Challenge has never been in short supply, but mutual care left something to be desired.

Just before the COVID-19 pandemic, all ASML'ers were given a card game to reinforce the three C's. It was like a game of Scattegories, but filled with dozens of personal questions, such as: 'What have you done for a teammate this week?' or 'When were you last asked for your opinion?' This helped to maintain a sense of comradery during the pandemic, but the intensity of the workload in the aftermath made playing cards a luxury no one had time for.

According to Peter Baillière, the three core values reflect Martin van den Brink's approach. 'People shouldn't copy his behavior, but rather his intentions and values. If you know Martin well, you know that he's a caring person. He's dominant, sure, but there's no ego or politics behind it.'

Van den Brink's style of leadership is not unique to the chip industry. One of the supervisory board members sees similarities in the media sector, in which companies are also often led by a visionary in the field who is fixated on the small details and demands absolute dedication from everybody. Even if that means shouting. The same combination of micromanagement and tight deadlines permeates the work at ASML. It became an organization ready to leap into action at a moment's notice: everything needed to be done yesterday, and would be outdated by tomorrow. Van den Brink describes his fiery meeting style as 'a fair fight based on arguments,' although his methodology matured over the course of his tenure. 'I don't shout at someone because I know that person is afraid of me and needs to become even more afraid. I shout because I want to set something in motion, to get something happening. That's why I put emotion into it. And I do it more for some people than for others – I know how far I can go.'

When the world switches to Teams calls and Zoom meetings during the pandemic, it becomes difficult to gauge the right amount of 'emotion' to administer. 'During video conferencing I miss 80 percent of my feedback loop,' he recalls. Martin needs to read body language, and it is difficult to do that when people are just a small square on a screen.

He even insists on sitting down with ASML's Asian customers in person. Despite the travel restrictions, in September 2021 Martin flies together with Peter Wennink to Taiwan to meet TSMC leadership at the Indigo Hsinchu Hotel. They arrive to find the hotel completely divided in two: one half for ASML, the other for the TSMC'ers.

Wennink and Van der Brink are supervised at all times. When they leave their rooms, they are taken via a predetermined route to a large meeting room in the center of the hotel. A demarcation line runs through the center of the room, and the attendees are made to sit four meters apart, separated by plexiglass. A guard is posted to ensure that everyone wears their face masks, even during dinner. The participants can barely understand each other and need to use microphones. 'Still, it was a fantastic meeting,' concluded Van den Brink afterwards. The plexiglass may have stopped any viruses from spreading, but it could not stop Martin from reading people.

37

NOT IN MY BACKYARD

Frits Philips would be proud. The band that is playing in the hall named after the famous industrialist at the Muziekgebouw in Eindhoven is knocking it out of the park. Sounds from other rooms float in, blending with their brand of Indonesian pop: a little Indian dance here, some South African rock there, a hint of Brazilian carnival music to finish things off. The artists have one thing in common: they all work at ASML, the high-tech company that has transformed the region around Eindhoven into a global city. A place where you encounter smart people from all corners of the world. This is 'ASML On Stage,' an annual music event where everyone, whether family, friend, or neighbor, is welcome.

It is March of 2023, and ASML has completely occupied center stage. Not that it has a choice – the company is too big to hide behind the other large Brabant enterprises. For a long time, the chip machine maker from Veldhoven was counted among the 'big five', the group of the most important manufacturing companies in the region, such as DAF Trucks, Philips, chip manufacturer NXP and VDL. But when the demand for lithography systems exploded in 2020, ASML was propelled head and shoulders above the rest. It is the fastest grower, the largest employer and the biggest investor in research and development, investing 4 billion euros in 2023. The southeast of Brabant has become home to the brain of the Dutch high-tech industry, which is why it is called the Brainport region.

ASML is located on a slice of land tucked between the A67 highway and a long road called the Kempenbaan. If you want to see how rapidly the company is growing, you can either take the Veldhoven-Zuid exit from the N2 highway, or jump on a bus from Eindhoven Central Station to the De Run industrial park.

The original headquarters from the 1980s, characterized by its distinctive white 'hat', was finally demolished in 2022. In no time at all, new office complexes designed to accommodate ten thousand employees were erected in its place. One piece of the old façade was preserved, just as a reminder of the early days. Another reminder came in the form of a visit by Frits Philips on a Friday in 1986. It was December 12, and Mr. Philips, well in his eighties, had insisted on driving over to the headquarters himself. However, he accidentally ended up at a different white building, owned by the manufacturer of office furniture Ahrend. Of course, they did not turn down the opportunity to give the esteemed industrialist a tour. As time went on, ASML management grew increasingly concerned. Following a few calls via the landline, they managed to track down the missing guest. He finally appeared in the correct white building later that day and was greatly impressed by what he saw. As he departed, he whispered some words of wisdom: 'Gentlemen, persevere.' And they did.

These days, ASML's headquarters is impossible to miss. The complex in the De Run industrial park is expanding, with the chip machine manufacturer absorbing all of the surrounding land, roads, businesses and houses as it grows. ASML has even bought an entire street, complete with thirteen houses and a nearby sports complex, to demolish at a later time. It is as if they are playing a game of Monopoly. But for the most part, the tech giant is tangled up in a game of Twister. It is bending over backwards to get its hands on any free spot of land, and is trying not to collapse in a heap in the process. They don't always manage. For example, in 2023 ASML is forced to demolish part of its own offices and research department. It is a waste of capital, but the factory urgently needs space to expand its cleanrooms. There's no time to hesitate – it just needs to go.

Nearby residents are constantly confused as their large neighbor continually shifts its boundaries and erects new buildings. In 2023, ASML spent over a billion euros on new construction projects across all of its locations.

When it comes to changing zoning plans, the municipality of Veldhoven consistently emphasizes the 'global, national and regional' economic significance of the chip machine manufacturer. In other words: it needs to be allowed to grow, even if that means vertically. The standard EUV systems are three to four meters high, while the new High NA systems reach up to five or six meters. Once you add in the additional meters required for hoisting components plus the entire floor needed for processing the air in the cleanroom, you end up with a factory twenty to thirty meters high. And no amount of green belts and sound barriers will stop a building like this from dominating its surroundings.

With an increasingly complex machine on its hands, ASML wants to keep the web of engineers closely knit. Instead of working remotely, the development department prefers to have the thousands of technicians physically together. It makes it easier to discuss interfaces, the connecting elements between the modules of the machine, and it helps to improve collaboration with the factory. ASML's employees are better able to 'read' one another when they sit face-to-face, just as Martin preached in his philosophy on feedback. This leads to less miscommunications, but also to more commuters.

It's a tough time to be a daily traveler in southeast Brabant. Most people go to work by car, which leads to everyday blockages on the access route across the Kempenbaan and the surrounding highways. And no matter how many parking garages ASML builds, it never seems to be enough.

In 2019, ASML contributed 12.5 million euros to help improve local roads, provide new shuttle buses and to implement biking alternatives. It even participated in a government-led experiment called Mobility as a Service, or MaaS, hoping this would encourage employees to get out of their cars. When congestion levels around Veldhoven return to their pre-pandemic levels, the government realizes that their magic cure has failed. The MaaS project is deemed 'too complicated', and the plug is pulled in 2023. As an alternative, the company offers employees free public transportation and it builds additional lockers to park their bikes. Now, about 40 percent of the Veldhoven employees commute by bike, which is more than the national average.

Attempts to make the campus more accessible also often run into democratic barriers. Residents in Eindhoven protest plans for a four-meter-wide high-speed bike lane between De Run and the High Tech campus. ASML's plans for mega-parking lots in the surrounding area receive similar treatment. No one wants a box with 2500 cars lumped in their backyard.

In reality, ASML rarely hears 'no' to its expansion plans. Occasionally a drawing might need to be adjusted, or some protesting residents need financial compensation, as happened when the 22-story headquarters was built without a permit. 'This is not Singapore,' said one project manager from the province. Even a global player must adhere to the rules in Veldhoven. Trying to fit all of ASML's expansion plans into this town is becoming increasingly complex, just like Moore's Law.

For years, the Brainport region has been scraping together money from all kinds of sources to improve the area's infrastructure. However, a bigger budget is needed to accommodate ASML's expected doubling in size. The metropolitan area of Eindhoven, made up of nine municipalities, will need to find around 62,000 extra homes and 72,000 jobs by 2040. For the 21 municipalities that make up the entire Brainport region, 100,000 additional homes will be needed. ASML is not entirely to blame for the scale of this increase, but they are certainly the main driver. By Brainport's estimates, every extra job at ASML creates one and a half additional jobs in the region. And even that is conservative, according to Veldhoven. The high-tech sector also generates work in construction, healthcare and education. Take this into account, and the number jumps to two or three jobs.

The Brainport foundation is the nerve center of the region, where local governments, businesses and educational institutions from the area all come together to collaborate. They form a united front that allows these groups to pressure the government for extra financial support. But no matter how much the mayors and companies hammer on the door in The Hague, the high-tech manufacturing industry in the south receives little structural help. This touches a historical nerve. Brabant lies outside of what is called the 'Randstad' – a collection of all the major cities and towns in the Netherlands that house half the population. Typically, the locus of power, cultural capital and state funding has been focused in these areas – to the detriment of those in the south. But as the Brainport Foundation points out, more investment in research is being made in Brabant than in the Randstad. In addition, due to ASML and its network of suppliers, the added value per resident in the surroundings of Eindhoven is higher than in Rotterdam or Amsterdam.

In The Hague, Brainport's pleas usually go in one ear and out the other. In the eyes of most policy makers, ASML makes incomprehensible equipment for an equally incomprehensible market – something to do with chips or computers, but they are not exactly sure. In 2018, the Rutte cabinet was more concerned with retaining large multinational companies in the Netherlands by scrapping the dividend tax. Their multibillion-dollar plan ended up a failure. Unilever left the country in 2020, and Shell relocated its headquarters to the United Kingdom in 2021, detaching itself and becoming entirely British in a sort of reverse Brexit. The Limburg-based food company DSM followed suit, making it the third multinational to jump ship. Philips remains in the Netherlands, but the company is a shell of its former self, and its market cap is dwarfed by ASML's.

It takes a catastrophic chip shortage and a dramatic escalation of geopolitical tensions for the penny to drop in The Hague. In addition to being the largest Dutch multinational, ASML is a major job creator, and it needs assistance to be able to progress and keep its surrounding area moving forward. But the responsible ministries are slow to jump into action. Along with other executives from the Brainport foundation, financial director Roger Dassen has been nagging the government for years to provide financial support. Coincidentally, Dassen is in the area when the decisive phone call comes through, albeit a few thousand feet in the air.

In June of 2022, ministers Micky Andriaansens and Schreinemacher are on a Dutch government plane on its way to a conference in Berlin. Roger Dassen is also present, as part of a delegation of tech companies sitting in the back of the aircraft. While in German airspace, Adriaansens calls Minister of Infrastructure and Water Management, Mark Harbers, to see if he wants to consider allocating money for the Brainport region. He agrees, and by the end of 2022, the Dutch government has reserved 1.6 billion euros for the improvement of Brainport's infrastructure and housing via a multiyear infrastructure and transport program. A third of the cost falls to local and provincial governments, and with the help of the business community, a high-quality public transport line will be created from Eindhoven Central Station to De Run. However, this is still not enough. New transport hubs need to be created around Veldhoven to ease congestion. And houses. Tremendous numbers of houses. By all projections, Eindhoven is set to grow from 230,000 to 300,000 residents in the next twenty years. Of course, many ASML'ers want to live in the city. But construction is slow, and new employees are forced to find housing in nearby towns and villages, which only causes further congestion.

New workers from abroad have an advantage in the housing market. They get a tax break during their first five years in the Netherlands, and pay no income tax on 30 percent of their salary. This gives them more flexibility when bidding on a house, but prices out people who are on a regular income. When Dutch politicians suggest axing the tax break, ASML and other technology companies are rubbed the wrong way. They argue it is crucial for attracting and retaining international talent, and thereby growing the Dutch economy. On the other hand, the severe housing crisis in the Netherlands is forcing many young adults with average incomes to live with their parents, with no end in sight.

In Brabant, they regularly reminisce about Philips' handling of the housing shortage. In the 1930s, the electronics company built Drents Dorp, an entire neighborhood complete with thousands of houses for migrant workers from the north of the country. In those days, the women and children went to work in the factories – their small hands were perfect for assembling devices – while the men were left to grow vegetables at home. As a result, many of the houses in Drents Dorp have remarkably long yards.

ASML has no intention of building its own village. But the company does invest millions of euros in a housing fund under the Brainport banner. The goal is to keep mid-range housing affordable for everyone, even people working outside of the technology sector. ASML does not want to be another Philips, but neither does Eindhoven want to become another San Francisco, where only a select few can afford housing and homelessness dominates the streets.

The foreign employees settling in Veldhoven and Eindhoven continue to enrich the region and add a whole new layer of character. The internationals seek each other out to play sports after work. Every weekend, Indian and Pakistani athletes take to the field to play cricket at the local soccer club, VV Gestel. Around two to three thousand people from India are now living and working around Eindhoven, with one street that is now known locally as 'Curry Lane' due to the thirteen South Indian families that live there. This is a slightly friendlier name than 'Wokhoven', the nickname for the international community that settled in Meerhoven, a new neighborhood between Eindhoven airport and Veldhoven. Subtlety has never been a strong point of the Dutch.

Yet the Brainport region needs even more technical brains. Available talent is in short supply, and ASML snaps up a large portion of the workforce. Even when the chip industry started slowing down in 2023, ASML continued to grow at a rate of 400 new employees per month.

The cramped labor market creates friction between ASML and other entrepreneurs in Brabant. Salaries are about 20 percent higher at ASML than at other Brainport companies, and it is nearly impossible to compete with Veldhoven's generous profit-sharing and bonus policy. This comes with its own risks: if companies in the supply chain are unable to bring in new workers, ASML will become stuck itself. At the same time, there's nothing it can do to stop employees from other companies wanting to apply for positions at ASML.

The chip machine maker prefers to fish outside this pool for new employees, turning instead to sources such as foreign universities. But like all manufacturing companies, ASML also needs skilled technicians to handle the assembly of chip machines. Craftsmen like these are scarce, which is why ASML makes a drive to attract car mechanics. But the campaign misses the mark, and the derogatory slogan, 'Swap the dirty garage for the cleanroom' is understandably unpopular in Brabant. It sits uneasily with Veldhoven's carefully curated image: they are supposed to be the friendly neighbor, with wholesome visiting days for the locals and a little memorial stone for 'Grandma Betsie', whose house had to be demolished to make way for the logistics center 5L.

ASML feels at home in Veldhoven. You often see the ever-approachable Peter Wennink shopping for his groceries in the local supermarket or waiting for his coupons – after all, he is a resident of the town himself. But ASML has not been 'just another neighbor' for a long time. It is the most valuable tech company in Europe, which means it is measured by standards that go far beyond the confines of this small village. It comes as no surprise then when the chip machine manufacturer tries to break free from the Metalektro collective labor agreement, much to the disdain of the unions. According to ASML, the collective financial arrangements for staff are no longer fitting of a high-tech multinational. And multinational it is – you can feel and see it when walking around the campus. With forty percent of their employees coming in from abroad, Veldhoven is becoming a global village.

For years, ASML's management was in survival mode. The only question on their mind was how they would survive the next week, or even day. But now that it has grown to such heights, the outside world is beginning to see the company in a different light. In turn, ASML needs to emerge from its bubble and have a more mature view on the world. With this in mind, the supervisory board urges the company to present itself differently in its annual reports. Don't just throw out some dry numbers, they say, but provide a compelling story – something for people to get behind. Traditionally, ASML's reports were just lists of numbers stapled together. Direct and to the point, in true ASML fashion. 'Just print it on toilet paper,' as former CEO Eric Meurice liked to joke.

ASML takes no half measures. The yearly report is now a massive publication, that recounts every detail of its commitments over the past year. The 2023 edition consists of more than three hundred pages, half of them dedicated to sustainability, diversity and the company's social responsibilities. ASML does not want to just make better chips – it wants to improve the entire world. It is a promise meant to inspire a new generation of high-tech talent, one that appreciates an employer who considers more than just the bottom line.

In 2023, the chip machine manufacturer starts a Society and Community Engagement initiative. The goal is to invest at least 100 million euros per year from 2025 in community projects that also serve ASML's interests, with the stimulation of technical education as a key focal point. For example, ASML has founded the Junior Academy to familiarize the sixty thousand elementary school students in southeast Brabant with technology. More hands and brains are urgently needed in the Brainport region to save the manufacturing industry, especially ASML, from falling into trouble. There are thousands of open positions in the tech sector, compounded by the growth of the sector and the aging Dutch workforce. But it will take more than a boost in primary education to fill the more than seventy thousand vacancies.

Higher education institutions such as TU Eindhoven, Fontys in Tilburg, and the Summa College lack the capacity to train the number of tech students that are required. The technical university wants to grow from 13,000 to 21,000 students by 2032, but finds itself turning away interested talent due to a lack of available housing. In addition, vocational education programs are seeing fewer young people who opt for technical studies, despite the high demand from companies.

And so, the limits of ASML's growth in Brabant are creeping into view. The company is projected to have eighty thousand employees by 2030, half of whom will be working in Veldhoven. The balance between the prosperity ASML brings and the well-being of everything around it is approaching a tipping point. A gigantic enterprise is growing, absorbing the technical talent in the region and dominating the supply chains. At the same time, it is the largest creator of jobs for the Dutch knowledge economy. That's not something you say no to.

The Eindhoven region knows the risks of placing all their bets on one large company. In the '90s, Philips' traumatic cuts decimated the city and the spirit of the workforce that populated it. The dismantling of Philips is still ongoing: in the summer of 2023, ASML suddenly hired one hundred Eindhoven-based experts from Philips that were in danger of being laid off.

Brainport wants to stay diverse, with enough room and talent for tech companies other than ASML to thrive. The foundation's goal is to have different companies in and around Eindhoven focusing on emerging key technologies, related to the medical field, energy transition, quantum chips or photonics, which are semiconductors capable of producing and guiding laser light. Once it becomes possible to scale up the industrial production of these new technologies, it can move into surrounding regions such as Flanders in Belgium or northern Limburg. It is a modern take on the old Philips approach, in which factories were built all over the country, but the NatLab, the heart of the innovation, was kept central.

Since Veldhoven is bursting at the seams, ASML now makes use of satellite offices, such as the High Tech Campus in Eindhoven, a 'home office' in Den Bosch and the old Mapper division in Delft. Part of the research lab has also moved to a location shared with the Eindhoven Technical University – one of the last free dots of land in this giant game of Twister. The investment costs hundreds of millions of euros, but ASML needs the space to breathe.

However, ASML is not only growing in Brabant. The foreign branches also need to keep up: the company made extra investments in the Korean province of Gyeonggi and in New Taipei City in Taiwan in 2022, with each expansion costing hundreds of millions of dollars and requiring thousands of new employees. The Wilton division in Connecticut also expanded considerably, transforming the town of 18,503 residents (according to the 2020 census) into a vibrant high-tech hub, complete with wide bike lanes for Dutch-style commuting. Billboards along Danbury Road try to attract new ASML employees: 'Be a part of the company that is part of everything'. The woods of New England have plenty of space to accommodate this growth – or at least, the local politicians are happy to offer it. ASML covers two percent of the municipal budget through paying property taxes, and more growth means more funds for Wilton's public services. We give you space to manufacture chip machines, you give us money for playgrounds and sports fields. For Wilton, it is not a bad deal.

If Veldhoven reaches its limit, the company would be able to assemble some of the standard machines abroad. Although this would bring them closer to the chip factories, ASML is trying to avoid this. The network of suppliers is not easily relocated, and the latest generation of scanners always needs to be produced in close proximity to the development department. That is the ASML way – short lines speed up learning, making it easier to identify and fix mistakes, which leads to faster progress.

ASML previously considered relocating part of its production far from Veldhoven. In 1997, there were serious plans to start an extra factory in Taiwan in collaboration with a joint-venture partner. TSMC was becoming a force of nature, and Veldhoven wanted to keep up. Their plan looked all set to go ahead: a location in Hsinchu was chosen, the engineers were selected and ready to move. But then the Asian financial crisis struck, and the plan was put on ice.

ASML's commitment to the maintenance of the oldest machines is also a frequent subject of discussion. The PAS 5500 generation, the machines developed by Martin van den Brink decades ago, are simply not breaking down. As of 2023, almost two thousand of these machines are still running worldwide, and chips made with this 'mature' technology are in high demand. One ASML division, affectionately called 'the thrift shop', refurbishes these machines at locations nearby Eindhoven airport and in Linkou, Taiwan. But with their unparalleled durability showing no signs of slowing, ASML faces the question: should they continue this maintenance indefinitely?

Although these machines may seem indestructible, they still require replacement parts. But ASML's suppliers have their hands full with orders for the newer scanners and charge high rates for manufacturing such outdated parts.

This is why, around 2018, ASML starts toying with the idea of licensing these machines to the Chinese competitor SMEE. If they take over the production of those machines and their parts, ASML can focus its resources on new, more complex technology. The deal will also limit SMEE to less advanced niche markets ASML has no interest in. But it never happens. Martin van den Brink cuts off the idea – he wants to maintain control of the 'installed base', the name for the more than five thousand ASML systems in operation all over the globe. The thrift shop is needed to keep the competition at bay.

This decision ages well. A couple of years later, having to explain a close collaboration with a Chinese competitor to Washington and The Hague would be the last thing ASML needed.

38

A PIECE OF THE PUZZLE

The chauffeur parks on the north side of the Pentagon. From here, you can gaze across the Potomac river and see the Washington Monument piercing the sky. On this side of the riverbank lies Arlington, Virgina, and the seat of the largest ministry in the US – the Department of Defense.

Peter Wennink strolls to the VIP entrance. ASML's chief is there for an appointment with Heidi Shyu, the Under Secretary of Defense for Research and Engineering.

It is the summer of 2022, and the negotiations over the export restrictions for China are in full swing. Wennink has thirty minutes to explain to the Americans the dangers of coming down too hard on the Chinese chip industry. But Shyu is curious about other risks – could the Chinese not simply take apart and copy the machines ASML supplies?

'Well, no, not really,' Wennink replies. They tried, but ASML's hardware only tells half the story. How to bring all those components together – that is where the real magic happens. Without the know-how of ASML's experts, the Chinese do not stand a chance of replicating the machines.

And Shyu wants to know something else. She was born in Taiwan, the country that is losing chip specialists to the lure of enormous salaries in China. Is ASML not afraid of corporate espionage from the Chinese employees who make off with their technical knowledge?

This time, the CEO could not say no.

The 2022 annual report tells the story. Earlier that year, a former employee in China absconds with trade secrets from Veldhoven. Although ASML does not confirm this publicly, the data is taken by someone who then goes to work for Huawei. Since the beginning of the tech war, the telecom giant has been focusing on the development of its own chip technology, and by the end of 2022, even receives a patent for something they called 'EUV lithography'. This does not prove Huawei can actually build such a machine, but it leaves no doubt about its ambitions.

The theft may have violated export rules, which means ASML needs to disclose the event. The timing is terrible. ASML is forced to stand and confess just how vulnerable it is, right at the height of the negotiations over the export regulations. But the debacle has no tangible consequences, as Peter Wennink assures the investors during a meeting in Veldhoven. The stolen information was 'only one piece of a huge jigsaw puzzle, that does not even have the box with its picture.' Useless, in other words.

But this is not the first time ASML falls victim to industrial espionage, and it will certainly not be the last. Geopolitical tensions throw Veldhoven into the international spotlight and turn ASML into a prominent target. The company recorded 2,800 cyber incidents in 2022 alone, ranging from ransomware attacks to attempts to steal intellectual property. Hackers are coming from inside and outside, and they all have their sights set on a piece of the Veldhoven puzzle.

ASML's knowledge is spread over a large number of different links, both internally and within the network of suppliers. The lithography machines are complex in every dimension – everything from design, production, and operation – which means there is no single blueprint for delivering a functioning machine. Not one single person knows everything there is to know about how these machines work. Not even Martin van den Brink, the commander-in-chief of lithography systems with forty years of experience under his belt.

Most engineers work on one small component and know everything there is to know about that piece of the puzzle. As Frits van Hout philosophically describes it: 'The people who know how it should be done don't know why it should be done. And the people who know why it should be done don't know how it should be done.'

Historically, ASML has invested minimal effort in protecting sensitive data. Drawings or other technical data used to be readily accessible, even if you were not working directly with them. You can still stumble upon scientific research online on how the EUV light source works. ASML practices a culture of open innovation, cultivating a large knowledge network where information can be freely exchanged, whether at conferences, or with clients, partner companies or research institutes. Expertise ASML lacks in-house is quickly hauled in. As the engineers see it, every dam created in this free flow of information only slows down progress. And in this environment, there is no room for distrust. 'I trust everyone who walks into my office out of principle,' says Martin. 'Otherwise, I can't do my job.'

It is a hopeful attitude. But to the supervisory board, it is naïve. They endlessly warn ASML that the company needs to build a higher fence around its intellectual property. But you never learn until you make the mistake. The hack in 2015 is the trigger for ASML to drastically professionalize its IT security. After 2015, what was once a security team of ten grows to more than three hundred experts.

Ever since, ASML's security specialists have had the tough task of convincing their colleagues to take better care of the sensitive information in their hands. Not because of some bureaucratic red tape, but out of dire necessity. Residents from countries such as Iran and Syria are no longer allowed to work on some of the technology due to sanctions, and ASML is required by law to shield certain information from them. Employees no longer have access to every part of the lithography machine – now, they can only request information about the parts closely connected to their piece of the puzzle. If you are an engineer working on wafer tables, you do not need to see what they are doing with tin droplets in San Diego, or with electron beams in Delft.

ASML also learns about internal data theft the hard way. In 2014, a group of Chinese employees from the Silicon Valley division jump ship with optimization software. The former employees launch the competing company Xtal, but are caught almost immediately.

By far the best way to prevent malicious employees from stealing data is to weed them out before they step foot in the door. This is why Peter Baillière is shocked to find that ASML is not conducting pre-employment screenings when he takes up the role of director of HR in 2018. Not a single background check is run on candidates who apply for positions with certain responsibilities. In 2021, ASML relents. People in critical positions are now required to provide a certificate of good conduct, and for some jobs ASML even wants security investigations to be conducted by the Dutch intelligence service, the AIVD. These investigations are similar to airport employees being screened in secure zones. But despite ASML's repeated requests for these extra-stringent control measures, the Dutch government is unmoved. AIVD just does not have the capacity to screen that many people.

ASML also tries to collaborate with foreign governments to screen new employees outside of the Netherlands. Since exploding onto the world stage, the number of applications to work at the tech company has increased to around three hundred thousand per year. 'If only we were still obscure,' sighs one ASML'er. 'Now we also attract a whole different type of person.'

The Dutch intelligence service has been warning for years about economic espionage targeting companies like ASML, and the AIVD has begun to advise people who travel to China with sensitive information to wipe clean or even destroy their equipment upon return. The managers at ASML find this to be a hassle, and they are far laxer with their devices. Sometimes too much so, as one of the managers admits. In their eyes, there is nothing shocking to find on their laptops, except for some plans to sell more devices or emails from clients about malfunctioning machines. The intelligence services think otherwise. The AIVD even occasionally uses traveling ASML'ers as bait, just to see if China is secretly installing spyware on pre-prepared phones. Nothing suspicious is found, but still, it does not mean espionage is not happening.

As the sole supplier of the most complex machine in the world, ASML assumes no other company is smart enough to bring together all the separate pieces of the puzzle. In the unlikely event that that would happen, ASML would likely wish you luck. The machine is far too complicated for an outsider to operate. It would be like letting a bad driver get behind the wheel of a Formula 1 car – you know they'll crash at the first turn.

This boundless confidence in their own abilities comes across as naïve or arrogant to some outsiders. Intellectual property theft seems to have little effect in the short term, but the consequences are noticeable in the long run. ASML takes a decidedly pragmatic approach to this. There is only one way to win the technological race – you have to run faster than your opponents. Do not gamble on the idea that your security will always be airtight, or that your patents will always be respected in China – that would be naïve. Industrial espionage comes with the territory, so count on everyone watching your every step. In the meantime, just try to make as much money as possible and invest that capital back into research to stay one step ahead. If you want to win against the competition, you have to 'out-innovate them'.

However, the economic logic of this strategy increasingly gets undermined by the tech war. The more China is backed into a corner and cut off from advanced chip manufacturing, the less reservations it has about obtaining the missing pieces of the puzzle by any means. In addition, the Chinese government has allocated a seemingly unlimited budget to develop an independent national chip industry. It is difficult to win when your opponent's pockets run that deep.

Chinese is the fourth most prevalent nationality at ASML, after Dutch, American and Taiwanese. Around 1,500 ASML'ers work in China, and around half of the employees in Silicon Valley are Chinese. Holding a Chinese passport precludes them from accessing all information or visiting some cleanrooms in Veldhoven, as this would violate the American export regulations. In turn, American employees are not allowed to work for Chinese chip companies.

These differentiating lines are also evident in the institutions ASML collaborates with, like the technical universities and TNO. The Dutch government is preparing a law which aims to prevent the leak via students of sensitive technological knowledge to countries such as China or Russia. Naturally, this includes research on semiconductors and chip machines.

Occasionaly, the Dutch universities seek the help of the AIVD to screen Chinese candidates wanting to conduct postdoctoral research. A blanket ban was instilled on students from the 'Seven Sons of National Defense', seven universities in China known to have ties to the Chinese military. Students from these institutions or their family members could be pressured to gather information for the Chinese government, and some have scholarships stipulating that they need to share the acquired knowledge. ASML is also scaling back its collaboration with these universities, but still offers tech talent from China access.

While Chinese talent is irreplaceable, and discrimination based on nationality goes against ASML's policies, the company cannot ignore geopolitical red lines. The ARCNL institute, founded in collaboration with the University of Amsterdam, has several Chinese PhD candidates who conduct research on nanolithography who are now prohibited from attending some meetings with ASML. Russia is a sensitive area: Veldhoven terminated its collaboration with the Russian scientific institute ISAN, which assisted research into the plasma source for the EUV machine. Located just south of Moscow, ISAN housed a miniature version of the EUV light source the Russian plasma physicists conducted experiments with. Their contribution was crucial in getting EUV up and running, as was the work of the Russian researchers who relocated to Veldhoven.

'We're inclusive, but no longer naïve,' says Peter Baillière. ASML also recognizes the danger within Veldhoven's walls, and begins monitoring the behavior of employees on the network. Advanced detection software is installed, which triggers an alarm if someone suspiciously begins copying documents or emailing files to a private address. This monitoring works, and people occasionally have been intercepted attempting to siphon off files. And if you get caught, rest assured the response will be harsh. Just to send a message, as Baillière explains.

The last thing he wants to create is a culture of fear at ASML. Employees need to be able to trust each other blindly: without trust, the vast majority of the work becomes impossible. Despite this, the security measures are becoming even stricter. ASML'ers in the factories and research labs now have to pass through a detection gate to prevent theft. The barriers have also been raised on the company network. You can no longer randomly download technical drawings from the inventory systems, and the Wikipedia-style site where engineers share practical tips has been moved to a stricter IT environment. ASML has also brought in heavy artillery to improve security in the chip factories, Sunny Stalnaker notes. 'They're overloading us with new rules we have to pay attention to. All incredibly important, but somehow we still need to find the time to get the work done.'

Employees also receive training to recognize phishing attempts. Random invitation to a job interview in your mailbox? Tread carefully – these situations are precisely the moments when people end up talking extensively about the company they work for. Some of these interviews are entirely fake, designed only to elicit information.

In-field expertise is particularly susceptible to such phishing attempts. Engineers perfecting the chip machines in the fabs have extensive practical experience, and frequently come into contact with sensitive data from clients such as Intel, Samsung and TSMC.

And this data is gold to the phishers, as the largest chip manufacturer, TSMC, is almost hermetically sealed off from the outside world. 'You can't trust anyone,' as the Taiwanese say. Their island is saturated with Chinese corporate spies, and there is a nationwide 'zero trust' cybersecurity policy. With good reason: between 2018 and 2020, a Chinese hacker group infiltrated more than seven chip companies in Hsinchu to steal chip designs.

It is the same hacker group that went unnoticed for two years in the computer network of chip manufacturer NXP, based just around the corner from ASML. The perpetrators targeted chip designs and stole mailboxes and other sources of sensitive information. When NXP discovered this in early 2020, it sent a warning to ASML. Fortunately, this time the systems in Veldhoven were not at risk.

TSMC's own computers are also not immune to breaches. In August 2018, several factories had to be shut down when an employee from one of TSMC's suppliers logged on with a laptop, only to accidentally spread a variant of the Wanna-Cry computer virus.

Audrey Tang, the Taiwanese Minister of Digital Affairs, brings this up at the Global Cybersecurity Summit in September of 2022, while the head of information security at TSMC, James Tu, is in the audience. The government and the tech industry in Taiwan are closely intertwined, and when it comes to protecting the chip factories, any resource that can help to shield them is sent to the frontline.

Then, a Dutch face appears on the screen. It is Aernout Reijmer, ASML's head of information security. Beaming in all the way from Veldhoven, he has woken up in the middle of the night to give a presentation on the 'Circle of Trust' – a collaboration between the security chiefs of the ten largest Dutch companies. Members of the group have permission to share real-time alerts about digital vulnerabilities and hacker groups with their suppliers, as well as share data from security services. The initiative serves as a bypass, as there is still no official mandate in place to help protect economic activity. In the Netherlands, policymakers tend to underestimate the strategic importance of the manufacturing industry.

The vulnerability of the suppliers had become apparent when a cyberattack shut down VDL in October of 2021. As a precaution, ASML had temporarily closed its corporate network to the outside world. One year later, VDL's Willem van der Leegte, accompanied by an AIVD representative, visited the ASML campus to share his experiences with nearly two hundred entrepreneurs from the Brainport region. VDL's point: if even the largest industrial company in the Netherlands can be struck down by a cyberattack, smaller suppliers to ASML need to act quickly and prioritize their own security. All it takes is one ransomware attack, one hitch, to affect the entire value chain.

Machine design is not the only sensitive matter ASML manages. Veldhoven also keeps an eye on almost all the major chip factories across the globe and receives real-time updates from the lithography systems of manufacturers who voluntarily share their production data. Most are happy to do so, which allows ASML to solve technical problems more quickly and keep track of the total production capacity. This way, chip manufacturers can better estimate how many machines they need to reorder. If they order too many machines, it creates overcapacity, and excess chips can cause the market to collapse. That is not what any manufacturer wants. You might think ASML wants to sell as many machines as possible annually, but it would much rather have a balanced market over the long run.

ASML introduces this approach after the major crisis in 2009. The connected manufacturers can only view their own current and forecasted share of global chip production. This means ASML has a unique and total overview over the entire chip production landscape. This highly sensitive data is so strictly guarded you can count the number of ASML employees with access to it on one hand. The system is audited by the customers and is even more tightly secured than ASML's own blueprints.

Veldhoven finally gets it: the dikes need to be reinforced to protect the trade secrets of Europe's most valuable tech company. But some things never change. At the beginning of 2023, no one is surprised when Martin van den Brink leaves his phone completely unattended for an hour in the back of a taxi in Taipei. Anyone could have taken it, but he is not bothered by the thought. He trusts it will find its way back – these things always do. The people around him realize that Martin's mind leaves little room for everyday matters. That's hard when you are thinking fifteen years ahead.

39

MARTIN'S LAW

If he wants to tell you something, he usually starts with an unrelated question.

'Thomas, when are you retiring again?' Martin asks.

'In about ten years, I think,' answers Thomas Stammler, the technical director at Zeiss. It is the summer of 2021, and the two are taking a moment to celebrate Zeiss and ASML's new commercial agreement. Beer is flowing, the food is excellent: the perfect time to look ahead.

'Let's make a plan for the future then, for five or ten years after you retire.'

During the last forty years, the lines printed by ASML's machines shrunk from a micron to a few nanometers. That is about a thousand times smaller – a journey that went from the invisible to the almost immeasurable. Each time it seems impossible that a machine could direct photons onto the light-sensitive layer of the silicon wafer even more accurately. So far, ASML has managed. But where does it end?

As the High NA machine draws closer to production, so too does Van den Brink's retirement. But Martin is determined not to let this be the final jewel in his ASML crown. 'You shouldn't stop after the last thing you made. I want to leave a legacy I won't see the end point of.' However, that point on the horizon already has a name: Hyper NA. Whether that machine will actually arrive is not certain. But what is ever certain at ASML?

After the conversation with Thomas Stammler in 2021, ASML asks Zeiss if it is possible to design an EUV optic with an even larger lens opening. If High NA has a lens opening of 0.55, Hyper NA would go beyond 0.7, a feat that would allow it to expose even finer chip structures. The lens is the best option, but if you increase the size of the mirrors, you will have to scale up the whole scanner. And the machine is enough of a beast as it is.

Designing the High NA machine had already been more complex than anticipated. The wide angle lenses were tricky, the wafers needed to move at even higher speeds, and mirrors needed to be accurate enough to hit a golf ball on the moon. But with these technological mountains conquered, Oberkochen has the mental capacity to take on a new challenge. From a technical standpoint, this new dot on the horizon seems reachable. Zeiss does not expect Hyper NA to need any radically new measurement technology, which will save valuable time. It is just not clear who will cough up the money to buy the machines.

As the monopolist in EUV, Veldhoven seems to call all the shots when it comes to introducing new lithography. But there is one wildcard Veldhoven cannot ignore: the economy.

Moore's Law has run its course. At the current pace, doubling the transistors every two years is simply not sustainable. According to ASML's director of research Jos Benschop, progress is limited by economics and not by physics. Unhindered, he figures it would still take another forty years before an atom would no longer be able to pass between the lines on a chip.

If you believe the marketing departments of semiconductor manufacturers, chip patterns are still rapidly shrinking. The latest craze is to describe their tech in ångströms – a tenth of a nanometer. However, this terminology hides the fact that the chip industry is fast approaching the point where the investments required to scale further down become too large to recoup – that's the real limit. And if chip manufacturers can no longer add value to Hyper NA machines, ASML stands to gain nothing by producing them. In layman's terms: it is getting too expensive.

There are only a handful of large chip manufacturers who can still afford the most advanced chip machines. If Intel fails to stay in the race against Samsung and TSMC, only those two front runners will remain. ASML is not concerned about how many chip manufacturers are left, as long as the underlying market continues to grow as predicted. And there is no reason for concern. Increasing amounts of computing power and storage are needed for data centers, for processing data deep within communication networks, for smarter industry and healthcare, for the energy transition, and for making artificial intelligence even more intelligent. The world is addicted to data, and it is proving to be an impossible habit to kick.

Manufacturers of these kinds of chips want what Hyper NA promises to offer: the chance to print even smaller details for complex structures at the nanoscale. The chance to gain more power. For example, a new and more efficient generation of transistors has replaced the old finfet technology, called 'gate-all-around' or nanosheets. Rather than fin-shaped, these switches are more like microscopic tubes that are pinched, and lose less energy while changing a 0 to a 1.

ASML is also trying to convince memory chip manufacturers to order Hyper NA machines. But for NAND chips, used for data storage, these smallest lines are no longer necessary. NAND chips consist of hundreds of layers stacked on top of each other, creating a 3D structure with relatively coarse details. And there is a possibility that DRAM chips, used for working memory, will also be stacked. If it all goes up, scaling down will slow down. But much to his own surprise, after discussions with manufacturers, Van den Brink believes Hyper NA to be compelling for the manufacturing of smaller memory cells. 'Yet once I've made a client excited about something, I start doubting myself the second I walk out the door. If we go for Hyper NA and have that thing ready in ten years, it could turn out completely different.'

He may have built ASML into a monopolist, but Van den Brink always emphasizes how dependent the company is on chip manufacturers. 'No matter how much money we make, we rely on our customers. If you lose sight of that, it will go wrong.'

But chip manufacturers are also entirely dependent on Veldhoven. With High NA, they pay 400 million euros for a machine that doesn't even work when it is shipped. All they have that guarantees any return on their investment is ASML's promise that they will make it happen. ASML's limited production capacity is also a weapon used in the competition between chip manufacturers. When Intel bought the very first High NA machines, they did so knowing that Samsung and TSMC would have to wait longer for their units as a result. This move is the first step in Intel's ambitious plan to beat the competition.

Some chip makers deliberately stick to ASML's older machines, as these systems still have Japanese alternatives. It gives them some bargaining power, and a stick to wield if they are unhappy with ASML.

Because of its dominant position, Veldhoven needs to constantly stay sharp. This is why Martin preaches humility on all fronts. His greatest fear is that ASML's enormous market power will open the door to arrogance or complacency – just like it did for Nikon in the 1990s. The Japanese dominated the market for lithography machines, but their failure to keep up with the demands of chip makers created the space for a new competitor to step in. If there were problems with the lithography machines, ASML took accountability and resolved them. Nikon was less flexible, and consequently, it watched the market slip out of its hands.

Colleagues who do not understand the 'stay humble' approach are 'taken by the hand' by Martin. ASML'ers should not only solve the pain of their customers – they should also feel it. When an engineer suggests that the problems with warped wafers a chip manufacturer is facing is of their own doing, Martin's eyebrows shoot up. 'Of course it's on them and not us,' he responds cynically. 'You know what, we'll just stop using wafers in the machine altogether. Problem solved.'

If a small gesture will smooth things over, you never have to think twice about making it, says one manager. 'You'll never get in trouble for giving away a lens worth a few million euros. But if that same customer calls Martin because you refused to cooperate, you get your butt kicked.'

Each day the company stays at the top, the harder it is to imagine a future where it would fail. It may feel part of the natural order of things, but as Van den Brink knows, the world does not work that way. He understands why this is hard for the younger generation to grasp: after all, they have yet to experience a severe chip crisis or mass lay-offs. 'Some think that everything will just happen automatically, that everything we come up with will work. If we succeeded twice, then of course the third time will work as well.'

He cherishes his paranoia. Danger lurks around every corner. Doubt courses through his veins, even when he consults with his engineers about the path they are embarking on. 'If we've made a decision to turn right, then I'll go home and lie awake that night, wondering: do we really need to turn right?'

Martin is no stranger to risk: after all, there is no other way to describe ASML's decision to invest billions into an impossible EUV program in the early '90s. At the same time, Van den Brink is afraid to take the wrong turn. In this, he sees no contradiction. 'I never gambled with the company for the sake of it. We always had another strategy on hand to keep making money.'

In the next ten to fifteen years, ASML is not only betting on linear scaling down – that is, increasing the number of transistors per square millimeter. In addition, improvement in the fabs will come from the optimization software and metrological inspection, soon to be enhanced with the technology from Mapper. With this, you can make sure the layers of the chips fit better together with minimal shifting. All these measurements feed into the lithography machine, which also makes the technology harder to replicate: an insurance for the distant future.

Now that EUV is somewhat reliable, developers have turned to upgrading their other scanners. The chips in demand for the automotive industry are made with less complicated DUV machines, and even older PAS systems – the 'vintage' models from the '80s. It's a rapidly growing market, and ASML is not about to let it slip through their fingers.

At the same time, engineers are trying to improve the yield and availability of existing EUV machines. The light source is still a limiting factor, and ASML ultimately wants to get the frequency of the droplets from fifty thousand to one hundred thousand times per second. As long as it doesn't all explode, says Van den Brink.

The droplet can also be fragmented more effectively. Currently, the laser hits the famous tin pancake in two strikes. However, it is not perfectly flat – think of it less as a crepe and more as a pizza with a thick crust. It means not all of the tin is fully utilized, but if you add an extra pulse to the laser, you can pulverize the droplet. As you might expect, this three-stage blast yields more power.

In the coming decade, everything will revolve around energy. The pace of scaling down may be slowing, but the energy consumption of chips continues to decrease. To achieve this reduction, chip manufacturers are experimenting with new materials and metals, the names of which would leave your high-school chemistry teacher speechless. Another trick is to stick together multiple specialized components of one chip, called chiplets, into one system which creates a more powerful processor. Combining these semiconductors into a single package is complex, yet TSMC plans to triple the energy-efficient performance (EEP) every two years. ASML's role is critical to providing the tools necessary to reach that goal. In 2021, Martin presented this EEP prediction as a guideline for the next ten years. Moore's Law may be slowing down, but Martin's Law soldiers on.

The efficiency of the EUV scanners remains a weak point. The laser consumes an extremely high amount of power, of which a great deal is wasted. The solution to this problem is to be found in Ditzingen, a town near the Southern German city of Stuttgart, where Trumpf builds the lasers that breathe life into the EUV machine.

Compared to ASML's austere buildings, the Trumpf factory looks like a modern museum. It boasts sleek lines, built in steel, wood and concrete. An underground network of corridors connects the immaculate production halls with the round Blautopf restaurant, which serves a warm midday meal as soon as the clock strikes noon. Lunchtime in the German state of Baden-Württemberg is always precise and on the dot, just like their lasers.

In a nearby test chamber, a Trumpf engineer puts the triple laser amplifier through its paces. The mixture of CO_2, helium and nitrogen produces a painfully sharp hissing sound plus a laser beam as powerful as a jet engine. Fifteen large computer racks surround it to control the power. The giant machine is so incredibly complex, so packed with delicate mirrors, pipes, filters and sensors, that it can take experts weeks to locate errors.

After the test, the 17-ton laser is dismantled, manually cleaned and shipped to the chip factory to be placed in the subfab. There, it is connected to the lithography machine via a periscope, where it can finally begin blasting droplets. Together with Cymer and ASML, it took Trumpf years to adapt the laser to the requirements of EUV. But the hard work is paying off: 1,500 people work in Ditzingen on the ASML lasers, and they generate 800 million euros in revenue each year. More than enough to transform the factory into a modern architectural masterpiece.

The EUV laser is more powerful than anyone could imagine. But why stop here? In the cleanrooms of Ditzingen, the Germans are working hard to crank out every last ounce of power. One way to better utilize the energy is to use a separate solid-state laser to trigger the first, gentle blow. This would no longer consume gas, leaving extra power for the hard hit.

Saving energy is a must. Trumpf did the math: in 2022, Ditzingen supplied over seventy lasers to ASML. When these run at full capacity, they consume as much energy in a year as all of Stuttgart's 630,000 residents combined.

That is not something to be proud of. According to an estimate by Greenpeace, the energy consumption of the global chip sector will increase to 237 terawatt-hours by 2030, double what it was in 2021. That's comparable to all of Australia's energy use. Greenpeace also estimates that the consumption of the world's largest chip manufacturer, TSMC, will triple in the same period. The forecast is troublesome for Taiwan, where the chip industry already heavily burdens the local infrastructure. TSMC consumes more than six percent of all the energy on the island, and in some regions uses ten percent of all available water for cooling.

But while an EUV machine drains vast amounts of power, the chips it produces are more energy efficient than their predecessors. Overall, this saves the world energy in the long run. However, as they know at Trumpf, you can make the generation of EUV light far more efficient by increasing the frequency of the droplets. The significant amount of heat generated by the laser system is also cooled with water, which could then be used to heat homes and neighborhoods in the area. Any means to convert residual heat into usable energy is welcomed by TSMC and Intel. They value reducing their impact on the environment, and what the customer wants, ASML needs to deliver.

Trumpf is on the case and is starting with a new design that cools the laser system at a temperature suitable for being reused in households. As a former specialist in district heating, it is a personal mission for Martin. A new goal has appeared on the horizon – utilizing the wasted heat from EUV light. Another part of his legacy to ASML.

40

AVOID THE RIGHT SIDE

Over the course of his forty-year career at ASML, Van den Brink created a larger-than-life version of his own character. A company so focused on the machine that everything outside of it seems to fade away. He is often compared to Apple founder Steve Jobs: they share the same combination of temperament and strategic insight, along with an eye for detail and clever marketing. And just like Steve Jobs, Van den Brink does not just give his customers what they ask for – he tells them what they need. And they trust him. You can recognize the traces of Apple's formula throughout ASML's strategy: the full integration of hardware, software and services, complete with a Genius Bar in Brabant.

'All nonsense,' grumbles Martin. 'This company doesn't stand or fall with one person.' In his eyes, his influence on ASML all came down to timing. He was lucky enough to build on the inventions of the pioneers at Philips: as far as Martin is concerned, ASML has existed for fifty years, not just forty. In addition, he is the last person in management who worked with the entire lithography machine. Naturally, this meant his number of roles expanded. Martin oversees research and development, intellectual property, engages in discussions with chip manufacturers, and, in his spare moments, comes up with new inventions. In 2022, Van den Brink registers a machine learning patent – his personal contribution to ASML's 'voodoo' software from Silicon Valley. The drive to understand the most complex technology has not left him, although with the breadth of ASML's technical prowess, it is a challenge to keep up.

After eight years of sharing the helm, Peter Wennink and Van den Brink renewed their contracts for two more years in 2022. The growth explosion, the coronavirus, the logistical nightmares and the geopolitical chaos all came together at once, and neither wanted to step down and leave ASML hanging while in the spotlight. 'It was like a freight train plowing towards you out of nowhere, smashing through everything in its way,' as Wennink describes it.

What will happen when the two close the door on this chapter of their lives? Who will step in and fill the void?

In the past few years, ASML has groomed a new generation of managers. Chief financial officer Dassen took over some tasks from Wennink, stepping in to represent the Brainport region and shake hands with politicians in The Hague. When the Dutch and Belgian kings paid a visit to the imec institute in Leuven, he was the one attending on behalf of ASML. And he is not just a friendly face: in 2021, Dassen led the commercial negotiations with Zeiss alongside Christophe Fouquet, the French board member responsible for the EUV product line. The latter joined ASML in 2008, after previously working at Applied Materials and KLA.

In addition to Wennink, Van den Brink now also takes other executives on a walk. It's his way to share knowledge and exchange ideas undisturbed. When it is Fouquet's turn, he trudges for two hours through the pouring rain at seven o'clock in the morning. The outside world is also getting to know the Frenchman: in June of 2023, Nikkei Asia and the *Financial Times* published an interview in which he explained his view on the 'impossible' decoupling of the worldwide chip industry.

But there will never be another like Martin. According to Herman Boom, ASML will need a group of people to take over his roles. Boom, who led the development department and later the DUV product line, is described as a 'mini-Martin' by his colleagues, and he is certainly a fan of Martin's leadership style. 'I never caught him telling you what to do. He just makes sure that you yourself feel you need to do it.'

Van den Brink's power of persuasion lies in his childlike enthusiasm, says Sunny Stalnaker. 'It works like some kind of reality distortion field. Martin can disrupt your perspective until you're convinced that you can make the impossible possible. He's the reason I've stuck around for thirty years.'

That enthusiasm also manifests itself physically, according to Stalnaker. You should never sit to Martin's right, and if you do, be prepared – something is bound to happen. Peter Wennink also knows this. He once joined a work meeting in Sunny's hotel room in Korea, and saw there was only one spare seat: on Martin's right. As Van den Brink launched into a fiery speech, he knocked a glass full of ice water all over Wennink's laptop and pants. Cursing under his breath, he flipped his laptop on its side to let the water drain out.

Martin is slightly clumsy, as Wennink later explains in his office. He imitates Van den Brink by walking around with a slight loll to his gait, his feet turned outwards. Those feet are asking for trouble. One Saturday morning, they ran into each other at the car dealership where they both buy their Porsches. They were standing around, having a cappuccino and admiring the sports cars, when one convertible caught Martin's eye. He walked over, caught his foot on a car tire and toppled over, spilling his full cup of coffee all over the leather upholstery. 'Shit,' he muttered to himself.

Every four years, Van den Brink exchanges his Porsche Cayenne at the dealer, full of dents and dings. 'Actually, it's too flashy a car, just like a lot of my colleagues have. We said it twenty years ago: it's not wise to drive a flashy car when things are not going so well for the company.'

Yet cars are the favorite toys of ASML's top management. Peter Wennink prefers to not flaunt his prized collection of Porsches, but Roger Dassen's love of Italian sports cars is well known. 'Mr. Dassen is more public about it,' says Van den Brink, pausing to consider how to finish the sentence. 'But that's just one aspect of someone's life. You should appreciate each other for your similarities, not judge the things you wouldn't do yourself.'

He doesn't want to preach, but he believes that ASML employees should be both modest and helpful. At moments like these, Van den Brink's upbringing still shines through. Although he is no longer religious, growing up in the Dutch Bible Belt leaves a lasting mark on you.

Reconciling his own wealth with this Calvinistic nature does not come easy. ASML's executives' compensation is aligned with that of international tech companies, and they earn millions per year. This is an enormous amount of money, as Van den Brink is well aware. And since 1995, his stock portfolio has only gone up. 'I've never found that an interesting parameter. It's a luxury to have this problem, I know.'

There is no shame in being rich, but it's bad-mannered to flaunt it. That is why Van den Brink is so unhappy to be photographed with his horse for the 2001 staff magazine. 'Horseback riding is expensive! How to explain to others that I live such a generous life? Other people will think I am completely full of myself, and that I am more concerned with making myself bigger than the company I work for.'

It would be easy for the financial success to go to the heads of the ASML'ers. Each year in March, during profit-sharing, the shops in Brabant notice that the ASML employees are suddenly tens of thousands of euros better off. And on top of this, there are also short- and long-term bonuses. These generous salaries are the reason why the people who work there call ASML 'a golden cage'. You cannot tell by looking at it: the plain straight and angular buildings scream functionality. Only the Plaza restaurant is playfully designed – it needs to feel inviting somewhere. The same artwork has been hanging in the offices of the presidents for years, but no one seems bothered.

As a traveling ASML'er, you continuously fly all over the world. You can guarantee a well-organized trip, but not much more than that. The engineers fly premium economy and receive a daily allowance of 60 to 100 euros when they stay abroad for a longer period. The VP's fly business class, while the other employees only get an upgrade if there are fewer than sixty days between their intercontinental trips. When you step off the plane, you get to work. And if you have to do one or two weeks of mandatory solitary confinement in a lonely quarantine hotel? Suck it up – that's just part of the deal. This also goes for the supervisory and executive boards. When they go on customer trips together to the US, they often stay in bang average hotels, with carpets from the eighties and drop-ceilings. The chip world revolves around yield, not around the jet set.

This Dutch frugality has long been the chip machine maker's trademark. Had you been a customer visiting Veldhoven twenty years ago, you would have been treated to a cheese sandwich and a glass of milk. They figured that manufacturers were there for the machines, not for the lunch. Nowadays, they are a little more extravagant – there are also croissants.

ASML was born south of the rivers that divide the country, but it grew up with the Calvinist spirit of the north. This fits the role it wants to play: not of an arrogant tech company striving for maximal returns, but of a steward for suppliers that add value to the chip industry.

The danger is that these norms and values will fade when the most characteristic carriers of the culture depart. Van den Brink will leave a gaping hole, and not just because of how many roles he combines. In this void, insights and motives that he specifically put an end to will now have room to grow, feeding ASML's greatest fear of letting more politics and ego creep into the organization. Van den Brink is less worried. According to him, from day one his company has attracted people who naturally put technology and the company above themselves, people who just want to be one piece of a big puzzle. He shares this notion with Peter Wennink. 'No one is important, there are only positions with a lot of responsibility,' the latter declares. Easy to say when you're the boss of a company that turns over 27 billion in revenue. When his wife asks if he realizes that people see him differently from twenty years ago, Wennink admits he finds it tough.

By talking to the technicians in the company, one might underestimate his role: after all, he lacks a technical background and is less outspoken than Van den Brink. However, Wennink's skills made sure that the 'cowboys' in the company had enough room to play and kept the most explosive characters on board. During one conversation, he walks over to a framed cartoon in his office – a gift from a consultant who assisted the ASML management. It's signed 'Petriduct' – for Peter, builder of bridges.

ASML'ers usually keep their work and private lives separate. That's what you get in a company where you are not supposed to take anything personally. However, Martin is one colleague Wennink will definitely continue to see after his departure. 'He's authentic and he's genuine. That's difficult in a world where not everything is pure and you often have to make compromises.'

That is what Peter does best – act as a buffer for the outside world. Martin regularly storms into Wennink's office when he is upset about something or with someone. Wennink lets the tirades wash over him. 'I just wait until the balloon is deflated. I want to know what got him so worked up – if there's something fundamental behind it, I need to help him.'

Van den Brink needs these buffers. In his early years, he was fortunate to have Steef Wittekoek as his guardian angel. 'He was my advisor. I often came in furious, spouting stuff like, "this is crap," and "that doesn't work", and then Steef would just let me sit for a while. I always calmed down, it was very soothing.'

But he never sits down for long. Every minute that can be spent working, Van den Brink is working. Even during meetings at ASML, where everyone has to pay attention to what is being presented, Van den Brink is always on his laptop. No one dares to question him. Presentations for investors or shareholder meetings? Great – a perfect moment to get some work done. Either that, or he will go and find a spot in the room nestled between the audience, where he can put his head down and work through technical drawings. His comments are always extensive. That is his secret to his continual mastery of complex materials: brute brain force.

After one such presentation, Wennink is approached by a retired investor. 'Does Mr. Van den Brink perhaps take the minutes?' he asks in an affected tone. Wennink bursts out laughing as he recalls the moment, tears in his eyes. Then his voice drops in volume. 'Martin is someone special to me,' he responds. 'There's a high level of affection.'

'They seem like a married couple,' laughs Sunny Stalnaker. She can see Peter rolling his eyes in meetings when Martin gets carried away or starts ranting. 'There he goes again,' sighs Peter, trying to calm him down. 'Martin, Martin, Martin...'

Acting on the world stage is exhausting.

'Are you at least taking it a little easy?' Van den Brink asks his fellow president.

It is spring of 2023. The two bump into each other on the twentieth floor in Veldhoven, when Wennink has just got back from China and Van den Brink has returned from the US. 'I notice you're busier than ever,' he adds.

Van den Brink knows that Wennink likes to be visible to the outside world. But he also sees that his colleague is tired after his two-year-long ordeal.

It is not clear whether his concern got through to Wennink. 'As soon as it's about himself, Peter won't be so quick to tell you that he's listening,' he says. In a soft voice, he adds, 'Peter finds it difficult to say no, so he quickly gets completely swallowed up by commitments.'

They haven't seen each other in four weeks. In recent years, that is unheard of. They normally drop in on each other far more often, especially now that ASML is growing so quickly and is preparing for new leadership. In such times, you have to see each other frequently. And calling is not an option. Conversations on the phone with Martin are always short – he wants to look you in the eye.

'We missed each other,' Wennink concludes. Time for a walk in the Kampina.

It is a Friday evening in May, and the tower in Veldhoven is nearly deserted. Wennink locks up behind him. The secretaries have already gone home, and the lights are off in the office across the hall. With his worn briefcase in hand, the ASML logo barely legible to the world, he walks to the elevator.

Since the IPO in 1995, there has been one large arc leading up to the success of EUV, the most complex machine on earth. It was a journey Van den Brink and Wennink largely took together. Like yin and yang in high-tech land.

Martin has one regret – about ten years ago, he said no to a documentary maker who wanted to follow the development of EUV. He didn't dare take that risk: 'Back then, I was afraid that everyone would laugh at me if EUV didn't work.'

But it did work. And with it, ASML wrote a new Dutch fairytale. Not about Hansje Brinker sticking his finger in a dike. But about Martin van den Brink, the man who spent forty years putting his finger on every sore spot he could find.

EPILOGUE

THE ASML WAY

Early photographs at ASML show workers kneeling and crouching around lithography systems. Some have their torsos swallowed up by the scanner as they disappear down into the machine, jamming themselves between the metal innards. ASML built a sealed dome, allowing people to fully concentrate with no distractions. They cherish this parallel universe in Veldhoven, even though it is also kind of isolated.

From day one, this continuous focus on one single product was the ace up ASML's sleeve. It allowed the Dutch to set a merciless pace that their Japanese competitors simply could not keep up with. After all, who in their right mind supplies lithography machines before they are completely finished? ASML's ability to identify and eliminate imperfections hinges on its close collaboration with chip manufacturers. This level of teamwork ensures the scanners are up and running right on time, churning out wafers.

Lithography machine makers in the US were stuck in the past, and it's easy to explain why. Market leader Intel followed a risk-averse strategy for high-end chip production. This strategy also impacted its American suppliers, who needed to ensure consistent results in Intel's factories with significant overcapacity. However, American lithography equipment manufacturers designed their machines with only their most important customer in mind. This meant they lost ground in Asia, where chip manufacturers had been investing in faster production technology. This trend played into ASML's hands. The fate of the

US suppliers was sealed, well before the first EUV machine had even started to run.

For a long time, ASML ignored anything that did not have an acute deadline. This includes the effect its confrontational workplace culture had on its employees, the thinly stretched logistics, and the vulnerability of sensitive data. When it came to restructuring its internal organization, ASML was haphazard at best. That approach fits a pattern: in Veldhoven, things needed to go terribly wrong before any changes were made. A strong firefighting culture is deeply ingrained into the company, as evidenced by Willem Maris's 1999 parting interview with Dutch paper *de Volkskrant*: 'Every day, something or other collapses around here.'

ASML's goal-oriented approach extended beyond its engineers. The company also set clear objectives for its strategic decisions, and was able to grow through a series of bold acquisitions, deep collaborations and investments based on ten- or fifteen-year forecasts. They bypassed the largest economic pitfalls by requiring customers to put down a deposit or agree to invest, and grew more resilient with every take-over attempt and patent attack they faced.

ASML represents the culmination of decades of experimentation and industrialization, built on the legacy of the Philips engineers. By relentlessly refining their designs, ASML engineers have ensured their lithography machines keep pace with Moore's Law, constantly pushing the boundaries of performance without reaching a breaking point. Like a rubber band stretched to its limit, but never snapping.

The company's ability to innovate branched out into its network of suppliers. And all this collective brain power was bonded together by Martin van den Brink. Everyone that enters the world of ASML is astonished by the confrontational culture he created. But as they often say in Veldhoven, there is 'no shine without friction'. Consequently, a self-selecting mechanism emerged: if you can't stand the heat, get out of the kitchen.

'Without Martin at the table, nothing is happening,' one ASML manager concluded. But that dependency on one charismatic jack-of-all-trades has its risks. ASML is growing fast, so the company needs a new style of leadership. In truth, Van den Brink never really led a big company. He guided it like a start-up, as if it were a defiant toddler in the body of a mature multinational. This could have been a recipe for disaster, if not for its unique dual leadership. And so entered Peter Wennink, the chartered accountant with the ability to judge when to take control, and when to step back. He built an organization that tempered Van den Brink's tantrums, without taming him.

A new season has begun at ASML, and it's up to the supervisory board to choose the leadership. In 2023, the Dane Nils Andersen took on the duties of chairman. The nomination was intended as a display of ASML's European credentials. In Europe, the Danish are about as close to the Dutch as you can get. And having previously been a supervisor at Unilever and AkzoNobel, Andersen is well-versed in the corporate culture in the Netherlands.

In late 2023, ASML selected Christophe Fouquet to succeed Wennink and Van den Brink, both of whom are retiring at the end of April 2024. Although the Frenchman Fouquet has lived and worked in the Netherlands for fifteen years, maintaining the company's independent and spirited culture under his leadership will be a challenge. Eric Meurice's experience as chief executive is still fresh in everyone's mind. As a self-proclaimed admirer of Napoleon, the lack of obedience in Veldhoven struck one too many nerves.

This comes with an additional risk. The Dutch leadership has always been attached to the region around Veldhoven, whereas a top executive from another country might not have an issue moving parts of ASML elsewhere should they no longer fit in Brabant. As ASML's growth explodes beyond all borders, this has become an urgent topic. In November of 2023, several ministries in The Hague form an interdepartmental group to accommodate ASML's national expansion. They did not forget to come up with a codename – 'Beethoven' – for a plan to invest an extra 2,5 billion euros to make the Netherlands a more attractive place for tech companies.

With Roger Dassen as the sole Dutch board member, the top leadership is more international than ever. ASML's culture is a global mix of talent, much like the powerful Bordeaux blends Peter Wennink is so fond of. If the connoisseur were to describe it, he would label it 40 percent European social capitalism, 40 percent Asian discipline, and 20 percent American free spirit. This unique character weaves together stakeholder values and a focus on innovation and freedom of thought, all home-grown in a country that embraces world trade, and imbued with more than a touch of Dutch directness.

In a way, ASML has an archaic Dutch style. At the same time, its size is not at all typical for the Dutch. White containers with blue logos are piling up in all corners of the world, while the management invests billions and rakes in orders that other big companies can only dream of, all without blinking an eye. These deals remain largely unknown outside the insular world of chip manufacturing, and rarely make headlines. This relative obscurity comes with the territory: the market leader in lithography only has a handful of customers, and does not sell products to consumers. ASML doesn't mind. It is fully convinced of its own potential, and any outside interference is noise it can do without.

Knowing all this, one could be surprised that ASML was willing to open its doors for the writing of this book. However, there was a reason for telling this story. For a long time, the company did not receive the political and social recognition for the unusual work it does. Chip technology was considered too difficult and too complicated. It never dawned on the politicians to ask whether the Netherlands, a country heavily reliant on trade and services, should perhaps be more interested in the well-being of its manufacturing industry. ASML often felt invisible to the national government in The Hague, yet it needed federal support to avoid outgrowing what it could handle, placing an unbearable burden on the local environment, or being squashed between rival superpowers. Even though a tech giant had emerged in the Dutch province of Brabant, these attitudes made them an underdog on the national stage.

Only when the world woke up to the importance of chips did it become clear how dependent the global economy is on ASML. Holding a dominant position in the semiconductor market bears a huge responsibility, which is why the quasi-monopolist imposed strict rules on itself: treat large and small chip manufacturers equally, and don't overcharge them.

Martin van den Brink was hell-bent on staying modest and humble. He knew that abusing the company's monopoly would be its downfall – which is why ASML's agreement to restrict sales to Chinese customers was so out of character. The Dutch chip machines are intended to serve a global market and enable technological advancement for the common good. Making a profit is a side effect, not a goal.

This perspective fits ASML's view on the world. Chips are defined as weapons in the tech war, but Veldhoven sees things differently. In their opinion, technology is non-political. It is a way to connect the world, to make it better, cleaner, healthier and more efficient. ASML presents itself as a neutral public utility company that supplies all chip manufacturers. It's not an odd comparison, according to Peter Wennink. 'But unfortunately, such public utilities are often strictly regulated. So who would regulate us? The Netherlands? Europe? The world?'

For now, America sets the rules. That is a bitter pill to swallow in Brabant. In retrospect, ASML's rise coincided with a period of favorable geopolitical conditions. After the Iron Curtain fell in 1989, Western capitalism seemed to be the sole viable economic system. Only economic logic and industrial ingenuity determined who could produce the best chips and the equipment to manufacture them. But when Xi Jinping's China challenged the established dominance of the United States, the geopolitical lines returned in full force. The Cold War had the Iron Curtain – now, the tech war has a 'Silicon Curtain'.

If Xi is to be believed, American democracy is in decline, while China offers the more viable alternative for the future. For their part, the Americans are approaching China's technological rise much like the proliferation of weapons of mass destruction: curbing China's chip development and production, and where possible, reversing it. The battle for technological supremacy is heating up, and ASML is stuck in the middle.

This continual threat is reconfiguring the global landscape. To mitigate the risk of export restrictions, American suppliers of advanced chipmaking equipment are diversifying their production and research to countries like Singapore. ASML is also considering duplicating part of its Wilton and San Diego production elsewhere, which would allow them to continue supplying all customers. It may not be an efficient move, but that's the way the world is headed.

While supply chains fall apart, new policies are emerging. The US and EU are increasing their scrutiny of foreign investments in sensitive Chinese technology, while the Netherlands plan on screening technology students from China. This hits ASML where it hurts the most: capital and know-how. It is forced to treat its workers differently based on their nationalities, while it desperately needs all the tech talent those 144 countries can offer to keep up the pace of innovation.

After the Dutch export measures against China were announced, Peter Wennink and Roger Dassen held a post-mortem to analyze the negotiations about the DUV machines. They found it hard to digest that there was no clear figure in government tasked with protecting the national high-tech industry. On paper, Mark Rutte – the prime minister whose fourth cabinet collapsed in July 2023 – was responsible. But Rutte shifted accountability to his ministers, who in turn leaned on their officials' liabilities. Responsibilities were spread between offices and passed around like a hot potato. At the end of it all, no one could be held accountable.

The rules of the game are diffuse. This is what makes politics elusive, especially in the eyes of a company used to handling matters with atomic precision.

ASML became a trump card for the Dutch government, allowing it to remain relevant and visible on the world stage when multinationals like Shell and Unilever had already left the country. Right before Rutte finally received his invitation from Joe Biden in January of 2023, the Dutch prime minister described the Netherlands as a 'world player in chip technology that could face the United States as an equal and with confidence'. In truth, that bordered on overconfidence. Having the whiz kids in Veldhoven in your back pocket makes you look like a superpower in the tech arena, but on the diplomatic stage, the Netherlands is dwarfed by the major players. You can count Rutte's own team of geopolitical advisers on one hand, while the Americans have dozens of hardened specialists working in their departments and the National Security Council. In addition, the US economy is about twenty times bigger than the Dutch economy. The Netherlands is too small to protect its own tech giant from the political forces at play, and it failed to bring together its European partners for additional support.

With that in mind, it should not have been a surprise to the negotiators in The Hague that America decided to strong-arm the Netherlands. On October 17, 2023, the US announced unilateral measures to 'close loopholes' and slow down the Chinese chip industry. These export rules are aimed at ASML machines that can align chip layers with an accuracy of 2.4 nanometers – while the Netherlands set the limit at 1.5 nanometers. These restrictions target advanced factories, hindering China's progress in chip technology by approximately five generations.

With each move, the US is taking back control of the lithography technology it willingly parted with twenty years ago. The lowering of the de minimis norm from 25 to 0 percent is the perfect leverage to bend companies to their will. As a result, ASML needs a stamp of approval from Washington to send those machines to China. And the Americans keep on pushing the Dutch government to stop ASML from servicing its equipment in Chinese fabs.

With Europe divided about the war between Israel and Hamas, diplomatic outrage about these measures has been restrained. While EU countries bicker, American aircraft carriers are cruising towards the coast of Israel. Again, the US is showcasing the importance of its military power, just as when they provided military aid after the Russian invasion in Ukraine. Executing control over ASML's exports to China seems to be a bargaining chip; an insurance fee the EU must pay to guarantee protection from the US.

Peter Wennink may have called ASML 'just an influencer', but it has undoubtedly become more than that. It is the spider to the Chips Act's web, a powerful industrial player that can shape a European answer to America's high-tech imperialism and China's drive to expand. Such a stance would need to be focused on the long term, as Wennink hastens to add. Just like how South Korea is aiming to take over Taiwan's position as most important chip center of the world. President Yoon even learned Veldhoven's product brochure by heart, much to Wennink's surprise. Despite this, the Netherlands still tends to underestimate the importance of its technology sector. The Dutch are 'fat, dumb and happy', as Wennink once sneered during a speech in Eindhoven.

During a state visit to the Netherlands in April of 2023, French president Emmanuel Macron insisted on a one-on-one with Wennink. He had just stepped off the plane from his visit to China, where he met with Xi Jinping. Afterwards, he told *Politico* that Europe needs to become a strong world player and should not get entangled in any conflict over Taiwan. It was a political hand grenade, not unlike the ones the French president had occasionally thrown before.

At the Science Park of the University of Amsterdam, Macron and Wennink discussed geopolitics and Taiwan for nearly 45 minutes. The French were astonished at how easily the Netherlands gave in to the pressure from the Americans to restrict ASML. They would never do such a thing – supposedly. For his part, Wennink found Macron and other French politicians to be serious about the need for a strong European high-tech industry, with ASML as its driving force. Finally, someone was listening.

The Netherlands proved to be a loyal transatlantic ally, but it could have positioned itself differently had it received diplomatic backup from more powerful EU countries. However, as long as export controls remain a matter of national concern, any EU member state will likely prioritize its own interests.

The French will not give up control over their own affairs. They sell too many weapons for that. Germany also avoids any economic damage from any export restrictions – as long as ASML keeps running at full speed. But it is also struggling with its own relationship with China, and these kinds of national blinders prevent the member states from acknowledging the overarching value of ASML. As a result, Europe is punching well below its weight in the technology war.

The image of the future that ASML projects is of a world that will forever need more chips, with increasingly smaller parts. This brings up an existential question: how much longer will the chip industry continue to lean on this one company's technical innovations? As long as the economic machine keeps humming, ASML's lead seems too big to beat. Just like a rocket that, after propelling itself at a speed of 40,000 km per hour to escape gravity, no longer experiences any resistance.

Veldhoven has feelers in all the big chip factories in the world. This network of thousands of 'learning' machines collects huge amounts of data to improve production. This make ASML's ecosystem indispensable to the entire industry. But for how long?

It is possible that a new technology or a more affordable competitor could arise. For example, Canon makes machines that pattern chip surfaces using nano-imprint lithography, the commercial value of which remains unproven. On the other hand, Chinese companies have achieved significant market share in solar panels, telecommunication networks, batteries and electric vehicles, and could also become major competitors in the chipmaking equipment market. ASML takes this seriously. Their go-to response: 'The laws of nature are the same anywhere.' What was achieved in Brabant, could be achieved in Bejing.

For now, ASML is Europe's killer app – a tool the whole world needs. This means the EU has a vested interest in protecting their home-grown champion from unfair trade practices and intellectual property theft, and sorting out the dire lack of talented engineers it needs for its future growth. Assuring the continuity of ASML is a shared responsibility, as it has been in the past. Without its partners in Germany, Belgium and France, and without the EU's stimulus projects, the high-tech fairytale in Veldhoven never would have happened.

PS

Now that his retirement is rapidly approaching, Peter Wennink is less diplomatic than usual. He publicly expresses his disappointment in Dutch politicians, who 'lack vision and leadership' and limit ASML's possibilities to grow in the Netherlands. This is a jab at Mark Rutte, the prime minister who is eyeing a leadership position at NATO. In December of 2023, when Rutte visited the local chip industry in Arizona together with a Dutch delegation, Wennink was absent. Instead, he chose to travel to Washington to meet with the National Security Council and the US Department of Commerce, where he tried to convince them to be less drastic with their measures. To him, these talks never felt like beating a dead horse: 'Things could have been way worse,' he says when looking back in February 2024.

After stepping down from ASML, Peter Wennink is looking forward to a new chapter. He will join the supervisory board of the Dutch brewing company Heineken and has invested in a French vineyard, indulging his passion for wine. The goodbye gifts are starting to pour in, and are piling up on his desk. An investor just sent Wennink a token of appreciation: a bright-orange Porsche 911 Lego kit. 'I have the real one myself,' the CEO chuckles.

Martin van den Brink is in a less celebratory mood. During his last presentation to ASML's top executives about the company's future, he was visibly emotional. Before giving the floor to Christophe Fouquet, he stayed silent for a long time, and then declared: 'It's your roadmap now.' His colleagues gathered around, their eyes locked in silence.

The ASML story has come full circle. Van den Brink is set to join the supervisory board of ASM, the same company created by Arthur del Prado in 1968 that co-founded ASML forty years ago, together with Philips. But, as he discloses in his office, Van den Brink will also remain a part-time advisor to Veldhoven.

Even so, letting go is painful.

'This is a tough one,' Martin says, wiping away his tears. He walks to the coffeemaker hidden behind his office. A cappuccino, like always, and a deep breath. 'For me this was never a job. It never felt like work.'

ACKNOWLEDGEMENTS

How do you paint a picture of the world of ASML – a company located in Veldhoven in the rural Dutch province of Brabant, a company that also makes the most complex machine on earth?

It started by doing tons of research. This book came to be through more than three hundred interviews and reports over the course of more than ten years. The past three years I was able to follow ASML behind the scenes. I travelled to Asia and the US, and had many talks with presidents Martin van den Brink and Peter Wennink and other ASML executives.

In addition, I met with ASML pioneers from the early days, visited the network of suppliers and customers, and talked with stakeholders in Washington, Brussels and The Hague, who helped me to reconstruct the geopolitical powerplay around the company from an insider's perspective. I am very grateful that they confided in me about this sensitive material.

To check the facts and to put all elements into perspective, I also conducted background conversations with people at different levels, who are at, or are closely connected to, ASML. The reconstructions of events have been verified by multiple independent sources. Some fragments of the book have been previously published by the Dutch paper NRC, and for ease of reading, only external sources are named in the running text.

This book has been an autonomous venture, made possible in part by the Dutch Fund for In-depth Journalism (FBJP). ASML did not financially contribute but did cooperate with an independent profile. After all, the company is proud of its success and not afraid of any type of confrontation. ASML inspired me to paint an honest picture of its internal operations, and of the unusual world in which it functions.

Team members helped me in setting up many company visits and interviews, but did not interfere with the content of talks, or the text. Although ASML assisted in checking the facts afterwards, I am responsible for any mistakes. Special thanks to Monique Mols, Ryan Young and former board member Frits van Hout, who took on the ASML archives and helped to explain complicated technology in simpler terms.

Thank you to my advance readers for your critical eye, and Roel Venderbosch for your infographics, Henk van Renssen, Igor Damen and Karin Kreuk at Balans Publishers, and to the editors at NRC who gave me the opportunity to immerse myself into the topic – to focus, one could say. Multiple colleagues helped me to sharpen my thoughts, and so thank you to Garrie van Pinxteren, Clara van de Wiel, and Maarten Schinkel, Michel Kerres and Stijn Bronzwaer.

For the English translation I would like to thank Mark Whittle and 'pink pen-ther' Dorien Muijzer. But I could have never completed this project without the unwavering support of my partner-in-crime, Lotte.

Utrecht, March 2024